The Simple Book

2nd edition

Prentice Hall Series in Innovative Technology

Dennis R. Allison, David J. Farber, and Bruce D. Shriver   *Series Advisors*

The Simple Book

An Introduction to Internet Management

2$\underline{^{nd}}$ edition

Marshall T. Rose

P T R Prentice Hall
Englewood Cliffs, New Jersey 07632

Library of Congress Cataloging in Publication Data
Rose, Marshall T.
    The simple book : an introduction to internet management /
    Marshall T. Rose -- 2nd ed.
        p.   cm.
    Includes bibliographical references (p.   ) and index.
    ISBN 0-13-177254-6
    1. Computer networks--Management .   2. Computer network protocols-
-Standards .   3. Data transmission systems .   I. Title .
    I. Title.
TK5105.5.R68   1994   93-25019
    004.6'7--dc20   C

Editorial/Production Supervision: *Mary Rottino*
Buyer: *Mary Elizabeth McCartney*
Acquisitions Editor: *Mike Hays*
Cover Designer: *Tom Nery*
Cover photo: *The Stock Market / Ron Lowery*

©1994, 1991 by P T R Prentice-Hall, Inc.
A Simon & Schuster Company
Englewood Cliffs, New Jersey 07632

The publisher offers discounts on this book when ordered in bulk quantities.
For more information, contact:: Corporate Sales Department, P T R Prentice Hall, 113 Sylvan Ave.,
 Englewood Cliffs, NJ 07632 Phone (201) 592-2863   FAX (201) 592-2249

INTEROP®is a registered trademark of Interop Company. Ethernet is a trademark of the Xerox Corp.
NFS is a trademark of Sun Microsystems., Inc. The X Window System is a trademark of the
Massachusetts Institute of Technology. UNIX® is a registered trademark of Unix System Laboratories.
AppleTalk® is a registered trademark of Apple Computer, Inc. NetWare® is a registered trademark of
Novell, Inc. MS-DOS is a trademark of Microsoft Corp.

Printed in the United States of America
10 9 8 7 6 5 4 3 2 1

ISBN 0-13-177254-6

Prentice-Hall International (UK) Limited, *London*
Prentice-Hall of Australia Pty. Limited, *Sydney*
Prentice-Hall Canada Inc., *Toronto*
Prentice-Hall Hispanoamericana, S.A., *Mexico*
Prentice-Hall of India Private Limited, *New Delhi*
Prentice-Hall of Japan, Inc., *Tokyo*
Simon & Schuster Asia Pte. Ltd., *Singapore*
Editora Prentice-Hall do Brasil, Ltda., *Rio de Janeiro*

for Rough Consensus and Running Code

Contents

List of Tables

List of Figures

Foreword

I am very pleased to have the first word in the second edition of *The Simple Book*. This book is Marshall's most recent work in a series of fundamental contributions to the development of the global Internet and, in it, he continues his series of contributions to internet management.

Marshall has been a key contributor to the design, specification, implementation, and documentation of internet management technology, and as such, is extraordinarily qualified to write this book. Marshall was one of the four designers of SNMPv2, and, as a result, co-authored nine of the 12 documents which define the SNMPv2 specification. He also served as the editor of all 12 documents. His experience includes producing one of the four reference implementations of this new technology, and, as we say down on the farm,

"Experience is the father of wisdom."

This book will be an important addition to the documentation of SNMPv2. One of the things that made the initial version of SNMP so popular and successful was that it was easy to implement and easy to learn. The 1st edition of *The Simple Book* contributed to that success by providing documentation in a readable reference.

It is timely that this new, improved, and updated 2nd edition of *The Simple Book* is finished just after completion of version 2 of the SNMP specification. It is expected that this text will be an easy-to-read introduction and handy reference for both implementers and network administrators, just as the 1st edition was.

This is Marshall's 5th book, which is truly impressive to those of us who are in real trouble when we try to write anything more ambitious than a grocery list. Marshall may not wear boots or eat possum, but he can sure crank out text. All who are interested in open, interoperable, and tractable network management technology will do well to read and understand this book.

Jeffrey D. Case
"Dr. SNMP"
Knoxville, Tennessee
April, 1993

Foreword to the First Edition

It is a pleasure to say a good word about *The Simple Book* and its remarkable author, Marshall Rose.

The book provides a clear, readable, and sometimes entertaining description of perhaps the most important topic in internetworking today, network management and the Simple Network Management Protocol (SNMP).

The author embodies in a single large and brilliant individual probably the two most important philosophies of the Internet community pertaining to standards development: the importance of implementation experience, and the importance of lean design with an absence of extraneous features and mis-features. His role in internet management has been to *marshal* the resources necessary to allow others to produce a workable solution to practical problems of internet management. This text is as simple, elegant, concise and unambiguous as the technology and "oral history" that it describes.

As regards the minimalist approach, Marshall expresses it in specific terms related to network management of internets:

> *The impact of adding network management to managed nodes must be minimal, reflecting a lowest common denominator.*

This philosophy focused Marshall's chairmanship of the SNMP Working Group, which gave the Internet-standard Network Management Framework the fundamental "simple and implementable" flavor that guaranteed its widespread adoption and deployment.

Marshall's colorful writing style makes for an interesting and fun read. He skewers both OSI and Internet camps (and even himself on occasion) whenever due. I don't agree with all of his opinions (which he clearly labels) — I dare say no reader could possibly agree with all of them! — but I do recognize the perspicuity of observation which led to those opinions. As an implementor of both OSI and Internet protocols, he is well-versed in both technologies and (rightfully) has a unique perspective on the strengths and weaknesses of both.

Although he is critical of OSI's efforts in network management, it should be noted that OSI recognized the importance of both global "electropolitics" and "infinite" scalability in the global network architecture. This foreword is not the place to write a treatise on these OSI "philosophies," nor to describe how they should complement — not compete with — the Internet philosophies. This foreword *is* the place to say that Marshall Rose is among the small handful of senior Internet people — and he surely is the youngest in the handful! — who understand the philosophical strengths of both the Internet and OSI protocol suites, and who see the networking "big picture." This picture, which is coming to everyone's neighborhood in the next ten years, describes how the OSI, Internet, and proprietary architectures fit together in the future global-Internet that is now coming about due to the efforts of many good standards people and fine engineers in the global networking community. This book — in fact, Marshall's work as a whole — is a fundamental contribution to the development of that global-Internet.

Dick desJardins
Past Chair, ISO Subcommittee 21 on OSI
Interop Company
Mountain View, California
May, 1990

Preface

Welcome to the 2$\underline{\text{nd}}$ edition of *The Simple Book*. This edition has been updated to reflect developments in the world of network management since 1990. Since that time, the field has seen a maelstrom of activity. It would be foolhardy to attempt a tome that spans the whole of the field. Instead, *The Simple Book* focuses on the center of the activity, the *Simple Network Management Protocol* (SNMP), and the newly standardized version 2 of the protocol, SNMPv2.

This book is about the technology used to manage large communications infrastructures, termed *internets*. These are composed of wide and local area networks and consist of *end-systems*, such as hosts, terminal servers, and printers; *intermediate-systems*, such as routers; and, *media devices*, such as bridges, hubs, and multiplexors. In the last few years, the rapid growth of the number and size of internets has made management of these internets difficult:

- equipment additions and changes often lead to configuration errors;

- increased scale makes earlier, *ad hoc* tools impractical;

- increased heterogeneity makes proprietary tools unusable; and,

- wider range of staff expertise requires more sophisticated tools which are easier to use.

In addition to the need to keep today's networks running, there is also a need for traffic and utilization data, so as to design, plan, and justify new extensions.

Throughout *The Simple Book* the emphasis is on managing internets built using the Internet suite of protocols (commonly known as

"TCP/IP"), the first success of the Open Systems philosophy. As such, it shouldn't be surprising that these internets are, by their very nature, heterogeneous, multi-vendor environments. Even so, the perspective presented is meant to be generic towards any kind of internetworking technology. Indeed, for better or worse, many of today's internets carry traffic from more than one protocol suite.

History of Internet Management

At the very end of the 80's, the *network management protocol wars* drew to a close.[1] The solution of choice was based on something called the *Internet-standard Network Management Framework*. This was a modest set of three documents defining:

- a set of rules for describing management information;

- an initial set of managed objects; and,

- a protocol used to exchange management information.

This framework, at under 150 pages, was sufficient to provide a base for vendors to develop products that users could deploy. In fact, the document defining the protocol, the Simple Network Management Protocol (SNMP), was a mere 36 pages in length.

In order to promote stability, and yet allow for incremental evolution, the group that oversees the development of the Internet suite, made an important policy decision: the framework could be extended by defining new managed objects, but changes to either the description rules or the protocol weren't allowed. Today, with literally hundreds of SNMP-capable products, and thousands of managed object definitions, it is easy to appreciate what a wise decision this was. Because the protocol remained stable, vendors could incorporate SNMP early into a product line's lifecycle, and have interoperability across the wire. Then, as managed objects were defined for the particular kinds of products, only those specific products were affected.

---

[1]This "ancient history" was discussed at length in the 1st edition of *The Simple Book*; in the interest of brevity, the narrative has been removed from this edition.

Unfortunately, the initial three documents weren't entirely complete. Some details were inadvertently absent. Other details, learned through implementation experience, were also missing. Of course, as more people started implementing SNMP-based products, they occasionally would interpret parts of the document differently than the writers had intended.

These problems partially motivated the 1st edition of *The Simple Book*, which attempted to capture a great deal of the missing "oral tradition". Hopefully, the first edition was a success in this regard.[2] More importantly, *The Simple Book* tried to present the material in a more readable fashion.

A Digression

Before continuing, it is time to introduce a typographical convention used in this book. The author strives to present a balanced set of perspectives. When discussing technical matters, this is usually straightforward. Unfortunately, a lot of the issues involved are inherently non-technical in nature. From time to time, this book will express non-technical perspectives, but will label them as such, namely as *soapboxes*. Look for text bracketed between the symbols `soap...` and `...soap`, which appear in the margin.

At this point, it is customary to berate "the opposition". In this case, I am referring to people who think that the OSI-based approach to network management (as encompassed by CMIP, the GDMO, etc.) is a good thing. After all, we are in soapbox territory! To understand the technical reasons why the OSI-based solution is fatally flawed, consult Appendix C. For now, I will merely observe that market has made its choice: people interested in real solutions to real problems go out and buy SNMP-based products, whilst people interested in politically-correct networking and marketing posturing favor talking about how wonderful the OSI approach will eventually be. As might be expected, the burdens of reality very rarely enter into these weighty marketing discussions of OSI-based network management, despite the fact that the market requires solutions, not apple juice and cookies.

`soap...`

`...soap`

---

[2]There was, however, a rather embarrassing error in the protocol definition (`readOnly`) which also found its way into the first edition!

Where We are Now

Since the three documents were originally issued in 1988, two independent trends have demonstrated the desirability of an evolution to SNMP.

First, the work on SNMP security was completed in early 1992. These security features introduce rigorous authentication, authorization, and privacy features. Unfortunately, they also require a change to the envelopes used to carry SNMP traffic.

Second, considerable implementation experience led to a greater understanding of how SNMP could be improved to be more effective, in terms of both efficiency and power. In mid-1992, a proposal termed the *Simple Management Protocol (SMP) and Framework* was suggested as the basis for the second version of SNMP.

Although both efforts were considerably motivated to minimize the number of incompatible changes, some were necessary. As such, the community decided that it would be best to merge the two efforts and have a single (long-lived) transition. (The alternative, two transitions, was unthinkable!)

So, a working group was formed to develop a new version of the Internet-standard Network Management Framework (simply called SNMPv2), and to coordinate their efforts with the SNMP security working group. The working groups completed their efforts in early 1993. And this has led to the publication of the 2$^{\underline{nd}}$ edition of *The Simple Book*. The good news is that the "oral tradition" is already written down in the documents. The bad news is that there are now twelve documents instead of three. That's progress for you!

Acknowledgements

First, everyone who helped out on the 1st edition of *The Simple Book* deserves my thanks once more: Geoffrey Baehr, Jeffrey D. Case, David H. Crocker, Adrianne K. Glappa, Geoffrey S. Goodfellow, Ole J. Jacobsen, Keith McCloghrie, Craig Partridge, Dave Perkins, Jon B. Postel, Joyce K. Reynolds, Martin L. Schoffstall, Einar A. Stefferud, and, Joseph Touch.

Of course, the 2nd edition has also had several reviewers who have provided many useful comments: James M. Galvin, Frank J. Kastenholz, Deirdre C. Kostick, Keith McCloghrie, Donna McMaster, David T. Perkins, Samuel M. Roberts, Robert L. Stewart, and, Steven L. Waldbusser.

The 4BSD/ISODE SNMPv2 package described in *The Simple Book*, was derived from the original package that was a part of ISODE. Work on the original package was partially supported by the US Defense Advanced Research Projects Agency and the Rome Air Development Center of the US Air Force Systems Command under contract number F30602–88–C–0016. David L. Partain of the Department of Computer and Information Science at Linköping University, Sweden, added most of the administrative framework facilities as a part of his Masters work at the University of Tennessee. Dr. Jeffrey D. Case of SNMP Research supervised his work, and Keith McCloghrie of Hughes LAN Systems provided implementation guidance. The MD5 implementation used in this package is taken from RFC-1321, and is hereby identified as "derived from the RSA Data Security, Inc. MD5 Message-Digest Algorithm".

Ole J. Jacobsen, editor and publisher of *ConneXions—The Interoperability Report* was kind enough to perform the copy-editing on *The Simple Book*. His efforts brought this work to print in time for the Fall INTEROP® conference and trade show of 1993.

Finally, my cat, Cheetah, did not tirelessly wake me each morning at 5:00 am during the writing of this book (as he has with previous projects), he was nonetheless as obtrusive and attention-demanding as ever!

/mtr

Mountain View, California
May, 1993

Chapter 1

Introduction

In earliest days of computer-communications, it was quite a chore to reliably move bits from a mainframe to an applications terminal. As technology advanced into the late-70's, terminal networks evolved into host networks: hosts were attached to a single "packet-switched" network when they were supposed to communicate. In the mid-80's, various economic and technological factors made *internetworking* feasible.

In an *internet*, several networks are connected together through the use of routers and an *internetworking protocol*. The routers (sometimes called gateways), using the protocol, hide the underlying details of the actual networks, in order to provide a uniform service across networks.

For example, a site-level network might consist of a local area network based on **Ethernet** technology. This network, along with several other nearby site-level networks, might be attached to a regional network, consisting of several routers and point-to-point connections. In turn, this regional network, along with several other regional networks, might be attached to a national backbone, consisting of another set of routers. Finally, this national network, might be connected to several other backbone networks, and have international connections.

Going in the other direction, although a site-level network might appear as a single logical network to its regional network, the site-level network might actually be composed internally of several media segments, each connected together with either repeaters, bridges, or other routers! Although the use of repeaters at the physical layer, and bridges at the data-link layer, make multiple segments appear as a single "wire", it may still be desirable to divide the site-level network into several internal networks for traffic isolation. (In fact, some sites might be so large as to make infeasible the use of physical or data-link connections.)

Although each "network" might consist of an entirely different underlying technology (Ethernet, proprietary point-to-point, X.25, and so on), each having its own specific rules for transmission, all hosts attached to those networks have a common view of "the network". This is the power of the *internetworking abstraction.* By use of a common protocol and algorithms, even the most byzantine network topology consisting of myriad technologies can be made to look like a simple point-to-point connection over a homogeneous physical network!

The premiere internetworking technology is the *Internet suite of protocols*, commonly referred to as TCP/IP (after the two core protocols in the suite). Initial work on the Internet suite of protocols was principally funded by the *Defense Advanced Research Projects Agency* (DARPA). The work on the Internet suite of protocols has paid off so handsomely that the premiere global network, the *Internet*, uses this technology. As a consequence, the term *internet* (lower case-I) is used when making a generic reference to a network built using internetworking technology, whilst the term *Internet* (capital-I) is used when specifically referring to this network.

1.1 The Need for Network Management

Of course, the internetworking abstraction doesn't come without its price. There are several problems, of which only two will be illustrated in modest detail.

1.1.1 Different Devices

Because internetworking allows several different kinds of devices to participate in the internet, these components (the hosts, routers, and media devices) will usually be multi-vendor and heterogeneous in nature, as has long been the case with the Internet.

As of this writing, there are devices from hundreds of vendors and several models from each vendor's product line, which implement TCP/IP. It should be clear that a network management technology specific to a particular vendor is unusable in such environments. Thus, just as using an "open" (non-proprietary) internetworking technology has made multi-vendor internets a reality, an "open" network management technology must be used to manage these internets.

1.1.2 Different Administrations

Because internetworking allows several networks of different size and purpose to be interconnected, these networks will almost certainly be under different administrations, as is now the case with the Internet!

As of this writing, in the United States alone, there are at least four national backbones, along with a dozen or so regional (sometimes termed "mid-level") networks, and, according to one source, at least 8000 connected networks with perhaps as many as five to ten million daily users.[1] Each of these national, regional, and site-level networks is owned and operated by a different organization. Further, these organizations receive funding (and direction) from different sources, and only a small number of them are under common coordination. To further complicate matters, there is interest in

---

[1]Note that it is clearly impractical to even consider determining the number of connected hosts or users. The scale of the Internet is such that this problem is easily shown to be unsolvable!

"policy-based" usage of portions of the Internet, e.g., so that traffic is routed differently, depending on the administrative entities associated with the source and destination. And, to achieve an even higher level of unmanageability, there are now at least six commercial vendors offering commercial internet service, with connections to the Internet.

To appreciate the full breadth of networking available on an international scale, the reader might consult *The Matrix* [1]. Although this work isn't specific to internetworking technology, it does provide excellent coverage of many internets.

1.2   Roadmap

A *comprehensive* discussion of network management should cover all aspects of managing a multi-protocol internet, from both the technical and organizational perspectives. However, *The Simple Book* doesn't attempt this level of discussion. To begin, this book is about technology, not procedures. Further, although the technology discussed throughout is meant to be applicable to a wide range of areas, two limiting assumptions are made:

- first, management is done in the context of the Internet suite of protocols; and,

- second, management is focused on managing the end-to-end portions of those internets, rather than the application or media-specific portions.

Even so, the reader should appreciate that other aspects of the technical perspective are also beyond the scope of *The Simple Book*. In particular, the following topics are quite intentionally **not** covered:

name-to-address resolution: this is handled by the *Domain Name System* (DNS) [2,3]; and,

software loading and distribution: this is handled by protocols such as BOOTP [4,5].

(For a discussion of the former, you might want to to consult Section 2.2 of *The Internet Message* [6].[2])

---

[2]Since the author of both *The Simple Book* and *The Internet Message* is indeed the same person, critics might (justifiably) find this selection suspicious. The author agrees.

To find out more about the general problem of network management, there are two good sources of information:

- *Network Management: A Practical Perspective* [7], a book which discusses how technology (and in particular SNMP technology) can be used within an organization to provide effective management.[3]

- *The Simple Times*, an openly-available bi-monthly newsletter of SNMP Technology, Comment, and Events. Section B.1 starting on page 396 contains additional contact and subscription information.

With these qualifying statements out of the way, what does *The Simple Book* cover? The next chapter discusses the Internet suite of protocols. Since this is a book about managing TCP/IP-based internets, many of the management details can make sense only in the presence of a discussion of the protocols and systems being managed. The text tries to present a "detailed introduction". That is, the level of information must be deep enough so that management issues can be explored later on, but not too detailed so as to dwell on the nuances of each protocol.

The second part of the book, Chapters 3 through 6, details the new management framework for the Internet community. After introducing the basic concepts, we'll look at how managed objects are defined, the administrative model for management entities, and protocol operations. With each, we'll consider coexistence issues between the original SNMP and SNMPv2.

The third part of the book, Chapter 7, gives an overview of an actual implementation, the *4BSD/ISODE SNMPv2* package. The example isn't presented as the ideal means for implementing this technology, but rather to help the reader visualize the technology described by *The Simple Book*.

---

[3]It is worth noting that the 1st edition of *The Simple Book* contained a brief chapter on these issues. After reflection, the author decided that the readership would be better served if the chapter were removed from 2nd edition and a citation to [7] was given instead. Although this reference is hardly definitive, it provides a much better start towards discussing how the technology can be used within an organization.

Finally, as the book concludes, open issues and future trends are identified in Chapter 8. In the appendices, the book contains chapters on how to find more information, and where to find openly-available software. *The Simple Book* concludes with an amusing technical analysis of the OSI approach to network management.

> **NOTE:** Although *The Simple Book* has been carefully produced to provide accurate information about internet technology, it isn't the "official" definition. Appendix A contains a list of the relevant documents, as of this writing, which are germane to the topics covered in *The Simple Book*.

Chapter 2

The Internet Suite

The need for standardized networking technology has long been recognized. Computers must adhere to a common set of rules for defining their interactions, i.e., how they talk to one another. How computers talk to one another is termed a *protocol*. Protocols defined in terms of a common framework and administered by a common body form a *protocol suite*.

Conventional theory holds that a single, non-proprietary suite of protocols is required to achieve information mobility. To ensure that all computers within an enterprise can communicate with each other (regardless of their manufacturer), there has to be exactly *one* protocol suite. The protocol suite has to be *open* so that no one vendor can have an unfair competitive advantage in the market. Free market forces are critically important.

At present, the market has chosen the Internet suite of protocols $\boxed{\text{soap...}}$ as the *standard* for open systems. In the past, the author used to employ the terms *de jure* and *de facto* when referring to standards. For example, he would note that, although the Internet suite of protocols is the *de facto* standard for open systems, some people hope that the OSI suite of protocols, as promulgated by the international standards community, will become the *de jure* standard for open systems. In retrospect, the author, a well-known OSI cynic, was being far too kind. In [8], Tony Rutkowski observes that none of the international organizations which standardize computer-communications technology produces documents with the force of law. Further, we all ob-

serve that it is only the marketplace which is truly empowered to
set standards — despite the various attempts to set industrial policy
for computer-communications through the use of Government OSI
Profile (GOSIP) mandates in the US, UK, and elsewhere. So, the
author apologizes for helping further this false dichotomy — there is
only one kind of standard, one that's accepted by the market; other
`...soap` labels lack the burden of reality!

For the purposes of *The Simple Book*, it is unnecessary to consider
a full treatment of the Internet suite here. Instead, we begin with a
brief synopsis of the factors which led to development of the Internet
suite. Following this, we'll look at the architectural model for the
Internet suite of protocols, and then examine how Internet technology
is developed and standardized.

The Internet suite of protocols grew out of early research into
packet-switched networking sponsored by the US Defense Advanced
Research Projects Agency (DARPA). In the beginning, there was only
one network, called the ARPANET, which connected a few dozen
computer systems around the country. With the advent of different
networking technologies, such as **Ethernet**, packet radio, and satellite,
a method was needed for reliable transmission of information over
media that don't guarantee reliable, error-free delivery. (Information
transmitted using these technologies can be lost or corrupted as the
result of problems such as radio propagation or packet collision.)
Thus, the Internet suite of protocols was born.

Although the Internet suite might be thought of as the property
of the US military, this is an entirely pedantic view. The protocol
suite is administered not by the US military, but by an international
community of researchers, engineers, and users. All computer users,
regardless of nationality or profession, have benefited tremendously
from the Internet suite.

The best term to use when describing the Internet suite of protocols is *focused*. There was a problem to solve, that of allowing a
collection of heterogeneous computers and networks to communicate.
Closing the internetworking communications gap required a good deal
of cutting edge research. The Internet researchers made open systems
a reality by limiting the problem, gauging the technology, and, by and
large, making a set of well-thought-out engineering decisions.

2.1 Architectural Model

The architectural model for the Internet suite of protocols is espoused
in [9]. For our purposes, it is useful to view the Internet suite of
protocols as having four layers:

- the *interface* layer, which describes physical and data-link technologies used to realize transmission at the hardware (media)
  level;

- the *internet* layer, which describes the internetworking technologies used to realize the internetworking abstraction;

- the *transport* layer, which describes the end-to-end technologies
  used to realize reliable communications between hosts; and,

- the *application* layer, which describes the technologies used to
  provide end-user services.

The major emphasis of the Internet suite is on the connection
of diverse network technologies. As such, the current generation of
protocols is *primarily* based on:

- a connection-oriented transport service, provided by the
  Transmission Control Protocol (TCP) [10]; and,

- a connectionless-mode (inter)network service, provided by the
  Internet Protocol (IP) [11].

There are several application protocols available for production
use in the Internet suite:

- the Simple Mail Transfer Protocol (SMTP) [12,13], which
  provides store-and-forward service for textual electronic mail
  messages, and RFC 822 [14], which defines the format of those
  messages;

- the File Transfer Protocol (FTP) [15], which provides file
  transfer services;

- TELNET [16], which provides virtual terminal services;

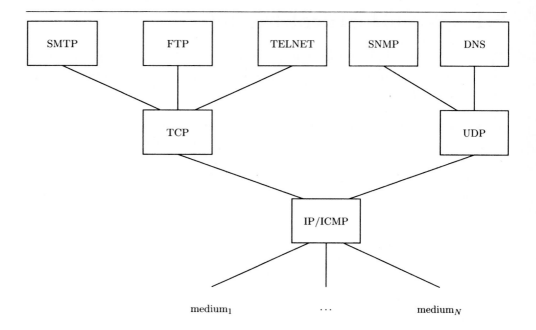

Figure 2.1: Brief Overview of Internet Protocols

- the Domain Name System (DNS) [2,3], which primarily provides mappings between host names and network addresses; and,

- the Simple Network Management Protocol (SNMP) [17,18], which is the focus of *The Simple Book.*

The relationship between the application protocols and the end-to-end services is shown in Figure 2.1. This figure, which emphasizes simplicity over detail, also shows a protocol called the User Datagram Protocol (UDP), which is a connectionless-mode transport protocol that's little more than a simple pass-through to IP, and a protocol called the Internet Control Message Protocol (ICMP), which is used to report on the "health" of the internet layer.

There are actually many more services, supporting everything from cross-network debugging, to remote file access, to voice protocols, and so on. As of this writing, perhaps the two with the most impact have been:

- **NFS** [19], a distributed filesystem developed by Sun Microsystems; and,

- the **X Window System** [20] developed by Project Athena at the Massachusetts Institute of Technology.

It should be noted that both of these application protocols were designed to be independent of the actual end-to-end services used for data transfer. Nonetheless, they have seen the most widespread deployment on the Internet suite of protocols, for both technical and economic reasons.

2.2   Development and Standardization

The technical body that oversees the development of the Internet suite of protocols is termed the *Internet Architecture Board* (IAB). There are two subsidiary bodies of the IAB: the *Internet Engineering Task Force* (IETF), which is responsible for short-term engineering and standards-setting; and, the *Internet Research Task Force* (IRTF), which is responsible for longer-term research.   Each task force is managed by steering groups, namely the Internet Engineering Steering Group (IESG), and the Internet Research Steering Group (IRSG), respectively.   The IAB and IESG, per se, produce very few documents.   Any person or group can design, document, implement, and test a protocol for use in the Internet suite.   The IAB requires that protocols be documented in the *Request for Comments* (RFC) series, a convenient place for the dissemination of ideas.   Protocol authors are encouraged to use the RFC mechanism regardless of whether they expect their protocol to become an Internet-standard.

Each RFC is assigned a number by the *RFC Editor* (a member of the IAB). If the text of the RFC is revised, a new number is assigned. In order to prevent confusion, if an RFC supersedes or updates any previous RFCs, this is clearly stated on the cover of the newer RFC (and the RFC index file is annotated accordingly).   In addition to the RFC Editor, there is an *Internet Assigned Numbers Authority* (IANA), that's responsible for keeping the authoritative list of values used in the Internet suite of protocols (e.g., protocol numbers).

In addition to RFCs, there is a second set of documents, the *Internet Draft* series.   These documents are produced by working groups in the IETF, and have no standardization status whatsoever, being viewed only as work in progress. At some point, if an Internet Draft matures (usually after some revision), it may be considered for standardization. In fact, Internet Drafts are not archival documents. They are available for a relatively short period of time, and are then usually removed. Finally, it should be noted that vendor product and user procurement literature should cite only RFCs and *not* Internet Drafts. In particular, note that the phrase "adherence to an Internet Draft" is oxymoronic.

It is difficult to list or even categorize all of the RFCs which have been published. However, Appendix A starting on page 379 lists the RFCs relevant to the topics discussed in *The Simple Book*. This appendix also discusses how RFCs and Internet Drafts may be obtained.

2.2.1 Internet Standards

The IESG assigns to each RFC a "standardization state". The vast majority of RFCs are termed *informational* — they enjoy no level of standardization status at all. That is, the majority of RFCs are research notes intended for discussion. In order to reduce confusion, the RFC Editor has introduced a second document series, the standard (STD) series [21]. This series is composed of RFCs which are full standards in the Internet community.

Although somewhat dated, [22] describes, in detail, the Internet standardization process. For our purposes, only the highlights are of interest: If an RFC is placed on the *standards track*, it must progress through three states: from a *proposed* standard, to a *draft* standard, and finally to a (full) *Internet-standard*. At each stage, the RFC is reviewed along with implementation and deployment experience. In between each step, proponents of the document are given up to two years to demonstrate implementability and usefulness. To transit from proposed to draft standard, there must be significant experience with implementation, and two independent implementations (with preferably at least one openly-available reference implementation). Similarly, to progress to full standard, there must be several independent implementations, along with extensive deployment, and considerable interoperability experience. During the course of each review, changes may be made to the documents. Depending on the severity of the changes, the document is either re-issued at its current state, or is reduced back to a *proposed* standard, and the appropriate deadline is set once again.

It is critical to observe that implementation, deployment, and interoperability are all important criteria that are considered as a document progresses through the Internet standardization process. Further, note that an openly-available reference implementation is also required in order to foster understanding and availability.

It shouldn't be surprising, therefore, that the entire standardization process is based on "rough consensus and running code". As eloquently spoken by Dr. David D. Clark, the first chair of the Internet Architecture Board, in a presentation at the July 1992 meeting of the IETF:

> *"We reject kings, presidents, and voting;*
> *we believe in rough consensus and running code."*

Indeed, lock-stepping implementation into the standardization loop has proven an invaluable philosophy in standardizing technology that actually works.

In addition to assigning each RFC a standardization state, a *"protocol" status* is also assigned. This states the level of applicability for the technology documented in the RFC:

required: a system must implement this protocol.

recommended: a system should implement this protocol.

elective: a system may, or may not, implement this protocol. In a given technology area (e.g., routing) there are usually multiple elective protocols. A system usually implements at most one of the elective protocols in the area.

limited use: a system may implement this protocol only in limited circumstances, because the protocol has a specialized nature, usually of limited functionality.

not recommended: a system shouldn't implement this protocol.

Note that when an RFC is superseded, it is usually termed **historic**.

2.2.2   Official Standards and Assigned Numbers

The *Official Protocol Standards* document summarizes the positions of all protocols on the standards track. This RFC is issued quarterly with a strong warning to retrieve the next version when the current document reaches its expiration date. As of this writing, the latest version was [23]. As of this reading, that version is obsolete.

In addition, the *Assigned Numbers* document is a registry of assigned values used for various purposes in the Internet suite of protocols [24]. Both documents are periodically updated. As with the rest of the RFC series, the most recent document always takes precedence.

2.2.3 Host and Router Requirements

There has been an ongoing effort to provide technical explanation and expertise in the form of *Internet Router Requirements* and *Internet Host Requirements* documents. Presently, the two documents detailing Internet Host Requirements are stable, and the document detailing Internet Router Requirements has just undergone revision with a new publication due out soon, probably by the time you are reading this book.[1] In addition, there is increasing interest in developing requirements for specific application domains, such as electronic mail gatewaying. As of early-1993, this work has not yet begun.

[25] provides a brief overview to the Internet Host Requirements. There are two Internet Host Requirements documents:

- one dealing with applications issues [26]; and,

- one dealing with communications issues [27].

Further, the original "Internet Gateway Requirements" document [28] is often referenced. Among other things, this document provides guidance on link-layer issues along with generic IP issues. (Note that the Internet community now uses the term "router" in place of "gateway".)

Although there were many motivations for writing the Internet Requirements documents, the author finds it useful to focus on one key observation:

> *During normal operations, it is difficult to distinguish between mediocre and optimal implementations — it is only when the network comes under stress that quality becomes important.*

---

[1]The author made this prediction, in print, a year ago and was proven wrong!

This means that proper realization of the Internet suite of protocols requires that an implementor be familiar with the Internet Requirements documents. These documents contain much implementation and fielding experience which can be leveraged into high quality, commercial-grade products. The goal is to maximize the robustness of the Internet in the face of stress.

Having described the process by which Internet standards are produced, we now turn to examine some of the key protocols. This is necessary in order to understand how management of these protocols is accomplished. Although the remainder of this chapter isn't a thorough exposition of the Internet suite protocols, the author hopes that it is suitably detailed so as to provide the reader with the knowledge necessary to appreciate the management techniques in the chapters that follow.

It should be noted that other descriptions of the Internet suite of protocols use similar (or slightly different) terminology to describe the architecture. The author feels that this organization strikes a useful balance between historical perspective (from the original Internet research) and "modern" terminology (from the OSI Reference Model).

To briefly remind the reader about layering, when referring to a particular layer, one usually refers to the *entities* residing at that layer. For example, at the internet layer, one refers to the IP entity. This entity provides the internet service to the entities at the layer above. Similarly, the entity uses the interface service provided by the entities at the layer below.

Each of the four layers is now examined in turn.

2.3   Interface Layer

The interface layer is responsible for the transmission on a single physical network, termed a medium. Examples include Ethernet, token ring, X.25, and so on. Thus, the interface layer corresponds to the two lowest layers of the OSI model, the physical and data-link layers. The purist will observe that this also covers part of OSI's network layer, but that distinction is ignored in this text. The technologies that implement these layers vary too widely and change too quickly to be considered here. Instead, consult [29] for an excellent exploration of these topics.

Note that an internet usually consists of several different kinds of media. Thus, the interface layer is really composed of several different parts, each responsible for providing a uniform service to the layer above.

For our purposes, there is only one topic of interest:

> *How is data from the Internet suite of protocols sent over a particular medium?*

In order to answer this question, we have to jump ahead a bit to look at part of the layer above and, in particular, the internetworking protocol used, IP.

IP is termed a connectionless-mode (CL-mode) network protocol. This means that it is *datagram-oriented*. The basic unit of commerce in IP is the datagram. Each datagram consists of one or more octets (simply termed "bytes") of *user-data*. Associated with each datagram is an address indicating where the datagram should be delivered. This address consists of an *IP address*, and an *upper-layer protocol* (ULP) number. The syntax and semantics of IP addresses are considered later on. For now, simply think of IP as delivering datagrams to arbitrary addresses.

Of course, the first thing to be observed is that IP has no "wires" associated with it. Instead, IP must rely on the services of the interface layer below in order to deliver the datagram. So, IP takes the user-data and encapsulates it in an IP datagram, which should contain all the information necessary to deliver the datagram to the IP entity at the destination. The remote IP entity will examine the

IP datagrams it receives, and then strip out the data and pass it up to the appropriate upper-layer protocol.

The second thing to be observed is that because IP is independent of the "wires", it must therefore use addresses which are independent of any physical hardware addressing. That is, although an IP address might indicate where a network device resides in an internet, the IP address needn't (and preferably shouldn't) have any relationship to the corresponding media address of the wire where the device is physically attached. This indirection is important for two reasons:

- media addresses are often assigned administratively by the manufacturer, so there can be no correlation between network attachment and media address; and,

- media addresses can change when interface hardware changes (e.g., to replace a broken board); this shouldn't result in a change in the IP address.

2.3.1   Transmission of IP Datagrams

Given this rather simplistic, yet particularly elegant design, it appears that the interface layer must provide two services:

- mapping from IP addresses to interface-specific addresses; and,

- encapsulation of IP datagrams for transmission over a specific medium.

For each medium which can be used to transmit IP datagrams, there is a document which specifies how these services are provided.

On page 386, a list of defined mappings is presented. In general, the mechanisms used by these documents fall into one of two categories:

- if the underlying technology is connectionless-mode, then the mechanism is straightforward: IP datagrams are encapsulated in media frames; otherwise,

- if the underlying technology is connection-oriented, then the interface layer must perform connection management in order to find an underlying connection over which to send the IP datagram. In this case, it is usually advantageous to manage multiple connections simultaneously, both to support multiple IP destinations (downwards-multiplexing) and to increase throughput to a single IP destination (upwards-multiplexing).

In either case, address translation occurs through one of three mechanisms:

- *algorithmically*, if there is a deterministic method for achieving a one-to-one mapping between IP addresses and media addresses;

- *statically*, if a table is built during system configuration; or,

- *dynamically*, if a protocol is used to determine the mappings.

Of the three approaches, the dynamic mechanism is clearly the best as it determines the address mappings in a decentralized fashion.

IP datagrams over Ethernet

To conclude this section on the interface layer, we now examine how IP packets are encapsulated on Ethernet networks [30].

IP datagrams over Ethernet – Frame Format

Each IP datagram is encapsulated in the data field of an Ethernet packet. Since the maximum size of this data field is 1500 octets, if the IP datagram is larger, the IP datagram must be fragmented prior to transmission. (This topic is discussed in greater detail in Section 2.4.6 starting on page 37.)

Since the minimum size of the data field is 46 octets, if the IP datagram is smaller, then the sending process adds padding after the IP datagram to bring the data field to the minimum length. Note that this padding is transparent to IP. When the data field is extracted on the remote system, the IP entity will consult a count in the IP datagram indicating how long the datagram actually is. Thus, the octets used for padding will be ignored. The frame format is shown in Figure 2.2, and is used for all Ethernet packets, regardless of whether they carry IP or something else.

Some implementations optionally use a different encapsulation technique to improve network performance on a particular hardware architecture. This is commonly termed "trailer encapsulation" or just "trailers". This format, the use of which is entirely elective, is described in [31].

IP datagrams over Ethernet – Address Mappings

Because IP addresses are 32 bits in length and Ethernet addresses are 48 bits in length, an algorithmic mechanism cannot achieve a one-to-one mapping between them. This leaves either a static approach or the use of a protocol to achieve a dynamic mapping.

In the case of Ethernet, the *Address Resolution Protocol* (ARP), defined in [32], is the dynamic mechanism used in virtually all implementations. ARP makes use of the *broadcasting* facilities of Ethernet technology. When the local IP determines that it must send a packet to a device on an attached Ethernet, the interface layer consults its

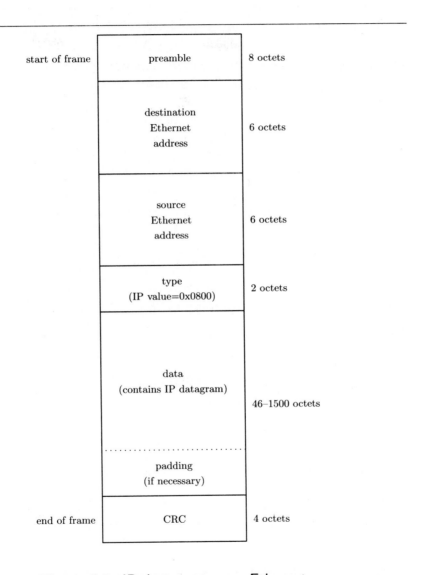

Figure 2.2: IP datagrams over Ethernet

ARP cache to see if the address mapping from the remote IP address to an **Ethernet** address is already known. If so, the IP datagram can be sent in an **Ethernet** packet to the corresponding media address.

If not, the interface layer constructs an ARP request packet. The format of an ARP packet is shown in Figure 2.3. Note that the format of ARP packets is actually media-independent.[2] The "media type" field indicates what kind of hardware is being used. The value 1 is used for **Ethernet**. Similarly, the "network type" field indicates, in the context of the specified media, which networking protocol is being translated. Since IP datagrams are transmitted using the value 0x0800 over **Ethernet**, this value is used. As can be seen from the packet format, ARP assumes that both media and network addresses are of the same length for both source and destination.

An ARP request uses a value of 1 for the operation code. All fields in the packet, except for the target media address (obviously) are filled in by the sender. The ARP packet is placed in the data field of an **Ethernet** packet (**Ethernet** type 0x806 is used), and is then sent to the **Ethernet** *broadcast* address.[3] (Since the length of an ARP packet for **Ethernet**/IP mapping is 28 octets, and this is less than the minimum size for the data field of an **Ethernet** packet, the remainder of the **Ethernet** data field will be padded accordingly.)

Upon receiving an ARP packet, the interface layer verifies that it supports the media type and protocol type described. If not, the packet is discarded. Otherwise:

1. A check is first made to see if the sender's protocol address is already in the local ARP cache and, if so, the corresponding media address is updated.

2. A check is then made to see if the target's protocol address corresponds to the local IP address. If not, the packet is discarded.

---

[2]The ARP specification uses the term "hardware address" when referring to media addresses. In striving for consistency with the previous discussion, the author has chosen to use the term "media" instead.

[3]In the days back when ARP was invented, implementations of multicasting were few and far between. If there is a successor to ARP, it will most certainly be multicast-based.

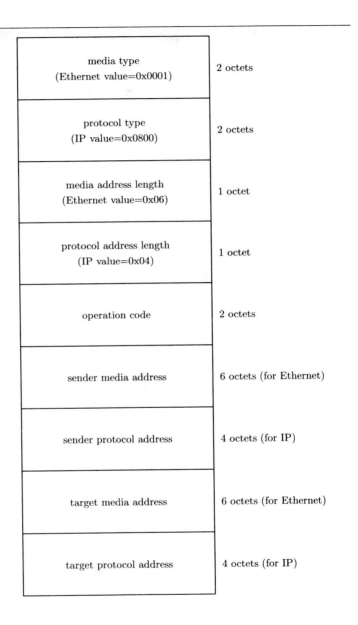

Figure 2.3: Format of ARP packets

   3. Otherwise:

      (a) If the sender's protocol address was not already in the local
          ARP cache (the first check), then a media/protocol address
          mapping for the sender is now added to the cache.

      (b) If the operation code of the ARP packet indicated "ARP
          request", then an "ARP response" packet is formed (usu-
          ally by reusing the incoming ARP packet), with all of the
          fields filled in. This response packet is then sent on the
          same physical interface as the original request packet to the
          Ethernet address of the original sender (i.e., not broadcast).

Note that one of the very last things checked for in the algorithm is
whether the ARP packet is a request or a reply. The rationale for this
is quite clever: when the local interface layer consults its ARP cache
and doesn't find the desired information, in addition to generating and
sending an ARP request, it could simply discard the IP datagram it
was going to send. As will be discussed in the next section, inherent
to the internet layer is the notion of unreliability. Thus, if the IP
datagram is gratuitously discarded, a protocol somewhere above IP is
responsible for retransmitting it as necessary at a later time. Usually,
this will be TCP at the transport layer, but this needn't be the case
(e.g., if the application uses UDP at the transport layer, then the
application protocol is responsible for retransmission). Regardless of
whether or not the IP datagram was discarded, when an ARP packet
containing the desired mapping arrives, the ARP cache is updated.
Thus, when the next IP datagram (e.g., a retransmission) is to be
sent to that remote device, the ARP cache should have the desired
information. Since holding onto the IP datagram while waiting for
an ARP reply has resource implications (i.e., buffering), the ARP
algorithm allows for a simpler, buffer-free implementation.

    Although this behavior is permitted, the *Host Requirements* doc-
uments [26,27] strongly discourage its use.

2.4   Internet Layer

The internet layer is responsible for providing transparency over both the topology of the Internet and the transmission media used in each physical network comprising the Internet. To achieve this, the internetwork service must provide:

- a common level of *delivery service* which is independent of the capabilities of the underlying media;

- a global *addressing* mechanism; and,

- a *routing* scheme to transfer data through the concatenation of physical networks.

All of these issues are fundamental if the internetworking abstraction is to be realized. This allows network devices to view an internet as homogeneous in nature.

2.4.1   Delivery Service

At the internet layer, the delivery service is connectionless in nature. User-data is sent as packets containing an integral number of octets termed *datagrams*. Further, from the perspective of the internet layer, there is no explicit relationship between the datagrams. That is, the internet layer is inherently *stateless*. As a consequence, the service is said to be unreliable, because the internet layer doesn't keep track of the datagrams it has previously sent. It is up to the upper-layer protocols to implement the desired level of reliability.

It should be observed that all media technologies can easily support such a delivery paradigm. Clearly, it is easy to map a CL-mode service at the internet layer onto a CL-mode service at the interface layer. Further, given modest connection management algorithms, it is also straightforward to map a CL-mode internet service onto a CO-mode interface service. Of course, the inverse mapping (constructing a CO-mode internet service over a media which is inherently CL-mode) can be quite complicated. (But it has been done; there are research groups in Europe running X.25 over Ethernet!)

Naturally, a stateless model implies that datagrams may be lost, re-ordered, excessively delayed, or (even) duplicated. Further, data contained within a datagram might be corrupted. It is the responsibility of other portions of the protocol suite (at some higher layer) to deal with these conditions.

It is important to appreciate that the extremely modest demands made by the internet layer is one of the primary strengths of the protocol suite. By minimizing expectations of the interface layer, the largest number of different media may be easily accommodated. Further, by placing reliability concerns at a layer above, these functions may be centralized at one layer for both efficiency and robustness. However, this argument, usually termed the *end-to-end* argument [33], must be qualified: there are several kinds of reliability. One is data integrity; the other is recovery from lost, duplicated, or mis-ordered datagrams. The philosophy of the Internet suite of protocols is that data integrity is best performed at the interface layer where there are usually powerful checksum algorithms implemented in hardware. In contrast, reliability above the packet level is best achieved at the transport or application layer. (Of course, both the internet and transport layers include a modest checksum, efficiently implementable in software, to provide a simple "sanity check" against potential misbehavior at the layers below.)

2.4.2   Addressing

As foreshadowed above, an IP address is a 32–bit quantity, divided into two fields: a *network-identifier*, and a *host-identifier*. The network-identifier refers to a particular physical network in an internet, and the host-identifier refers to a particular device attached to that physical network. Because of this, an IP address precisely identifies where a network device is attached to an internet. Thus, a network device with multiple attachments will have multiple IP addresses associated with it (usually one IP address per attachment). Such a device is termed a *multi-homed* device. Finally, note that unlike a media address, an IP address is said to be a *logical* artifact. It bears no relation to hardware, media, or any other physical artifact.

The choice of 32 bits was both lucky and *problematic*. The lucky part is that it allows for extremely efficient implementation of software at the internet layer. The problematic part is that a 32–bit address space, whilst sufficient for the needs of the 80's, may find itself too small for all the devices attached to the Internet by the end of the 90's.[4]

The problem is made harder by the fact that the 32 bits must be divided between network- and host-identifiers. Fortunately, the designers of the IP address developed a flexible scheme for allocating the 32 bits: IP addresses are divided into five *classes*, of which only three are germane to the topic at hand:

	bits for identifying	
class	network	host
A	7	24
B	14	16
C	21	8

Thus, there are potentially 128 class A networks, each containing up to $2^{24} - 2$ hosts; potentially 16384 class B networks, each containing up to 65534 hosts; and, potentially 2^{21} class C networks, each containing up to 254 hosts. As one might expect, due to the small amount of class A network numbers possible, it is quite difficult to successfully petition the IANA for such a number — even class B network petitions receive extensive scrutiny!

In each address class, there are two special values for the host-identifier. If all the bits are zero, then the resulting 32–bit quantity refers precisely to the network identified in the IP address, and not to any host attached to the network. Similarly, if all the bits in the host-identifier are one, then the resulting IP address refers to *all* hosts attached to the network (the IP broadcast address for that network).[5]

---

[4]In late 1991, a group was formed to examine the situation. Although the group produced a short-term solution as of this writing, there are at least three different approaches being considered for the long-term.

[5]Some early versions of Internet software used all zeroes for the broadcast address. As long as all the devices on an IP network honor the same convention, few problems ensue. If different values are used on the same network, disastrous anomalies, termed *broadcast storms*, occur. However, because of the multi-vendor, heterogeneous nature of IP networks, a single convention (all ones) was chosen.

Finally, by convention, an IP address with all bits set to one refers to all hosts on the local network (another form of the IP broadcast address).

Address Encodings

As one might expect, choice of a fixed length address, allows for an efficient encoding:

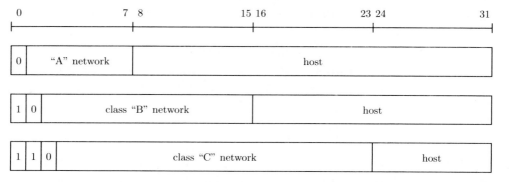

These 32–bit quantities appear in many packets: it is crucial that the ordering of the octets is consistent among implementations. In the Internet suite of protocols, the term *network byte order* is used to refer to the octet ordering which is used by *all* implementations. When an IP address is transmitted, a "big endian" scheme is used. The most significant byte (the one with bit 0 in the figure above) is sent first, then the next significant byte, and so on.

The implications of this should be well-understood: if a network device treats IP addresses as unsigned, 32–bit integer quantities, and if it represents integers in a different format, then, prior to transmission it must perform the appropriate conversion when stuffing IP addresses into packets. Similarly, upon receipt of a packet, the device must perform the appropriate conversion from the network byte order to the local format, prior to performing any manipulations.

Finally, when describing addresses as printable strings (e.g., for use by humans), the *dotted quad* (or *dotted decimal*) notation is used: each octet is expressed as a decimal number, separated by a dot, e.g.,

    192.33.4.21

At the application layer, when referring to a host whose name is unknown, a similar notation, the *domain literal* notation is used, e.g.,

    [192.33.4.21]

2.4.3   Routing

Given that IP addresses allow globally unique addresses to be assigned to each network device in an internet, the next question is, how is data transferred between two devices? That is, how is routing accomplished?

To begin, the local IP entity must decide the "next hop". If the destination is on the same IP network (determined by comparing the network-identifier portion of the relevant IP addresses), then choosing the next hop is simple: it is the destination IP address. This is termed *direct* routing.

Otherwise, the next hop must be to a *router* (usually termed an *intermediate-system* in OSI parlance), on the same IP network as the local device, which is somehow "closer" to the destination device. This is termed *indirect* routing.

In the interest of clarity, the discussion will use the term *host* when referring to either the source or destination device, and the term *router* when referring to an intermediary device. The term *network device* will continue to refer to any device attached to the network.

First, note that the routing responsibilities of hosts and routers differ considerably: a host typically has only one interface and needs routing information only to make a simple determination of the next hop on that interface. The routers need much more routing information, as they don't originate traffic, since they have multiple interfaces and need to choose a next interface and a next hop for the datagrams they *forward*.

Each network device maintains a *routing table* containing, among other things, a list of addresses reachable via routers on an attached IP network. It is often convenient to think of the routing table as being an associative array keyed by destination IP network numbers.[6]

---

[6]By routing based on IP network numbers, rather than IP addresses, the size of the routing table is dramatically reduced.

The other columns in a row in the array contain the IP address of the router and various routing metrics.

Given this terse discussion, two questions present themselves:

- How does a host find out about the routers on its IP network?

- How do routers find out about one another?

Usually both hosts and routers start with some initial configuration information on stable storage (e.g., a local disk). Then, they dynamically learn about the network topology through protocol interactions. In addition, there is also the notion of a *default route*, which can be used to reach a destination if its IP network isn't in the routing table.

It is beyond the scope of *The Simple Book* to discuss routing protocols, other than to note that routing has been the subject of intense investigation for over a decade, with each new advance leading to a re-occurrence of the "horizon effect" (i.e., every time one problem is solved, another more complicated one arises).

Two-level internets

In the mid-8o's, when the Internet was beginning to enter a period of fantastic growth, it was based on a two-level connection scheme:

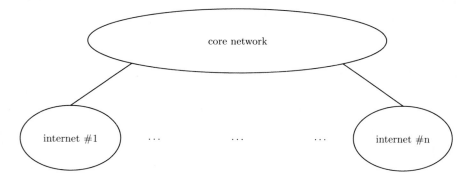

In this scheme, internets are connected to the Internet through a collection of *core routers*, and the core network is used for *all* traffic between these internets (i.e., the resulting topology is an acyclic graph). As a consequence, the core routers are required to have routing information on all networks available in the entire topology.

Each internet connected to the core is termed an *Autonomous System*, which underscores the notion that each is under a single administrative control and uses the same routing procedures.

In such a scheme, the routers in each Autonomous System need different kinds of information about a network. If the network is inside the same Autonomous System, then routing information is needed. Otherwise, if the network lies outside the Autonomous System, then only *reachability* information is needed (since the only way to route traffic is through the core).

To exchange reachability information between Autonomous Systems and the core, a special protocol, the *Exterior Gateway Protocol* (EGP) [34] was developed. Although the needs of the Internet have long outgrown the capabilities of EGP, it provided a much-needed service for several years. The successor to EGP is the *Border Gateway Protocol* (BGP) [35].

2.4.4 Addressing Revisited: Subnetting

Although the two-level addressing hierarchy seems reasonable at first glance, in practice many sites have found a need to have multiple physical networks. Earlier we noted that the network-identifier corresponds to precisely one physical network. A logical conclusion (no pun intended) is that if a site was running several physical networks, then it would need several IP network-identifiers, one for each physical network.

Unfortunately, this solution isn't scalable since it increases the size of the routing tables with semantically redundant information. A better solution is to introduce a three-level addressing hierarchy which allows each site to partition the host-identifier portion of its IP network address. A network so sub-partitioned is termed a *subnet*, and the mechanisms used to achieve subnetting are described in [36], which is now an Internet-standard.[7]

The idea behind subnetting is simple: outside of a site using subnets, the IP address appears to have two components, the network-

---

[7]This name chosen (*subnet*) for this concept is unfortunate. In OSI parlance, the term *subnetwork* is used to denote a physical network. Needless to say, the similarity of these terms causes endless confusion and consternation.

and host-identifiers. Inside the site, the host-identifier is further divided into two parts: a *subnet-number*, and a *host-number*. The subnet-number refers to a particular physical network within the site's IP network, and the host-number refers to a particular device on that subnet:

network-identifier	host-identifier	
network-identifier	subnet-number	host-number

As with "ordinary" addresses, the question arises as to how the bits in the host-identifier should be divided between the subnet- and host-numbers. To provide maximum flexibility, a *subnet-mask* is used. This is a 32–bit quantity which is logical-ANDed with an IP address in order to derive the actual physical network being identified:

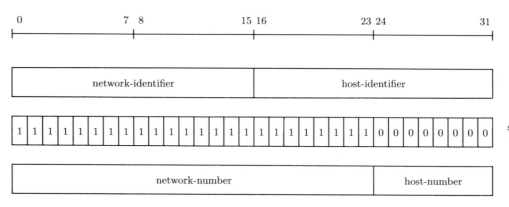

So, a new column is added to the routing table, the subnet-mask. As a default condition, if the network device doesn't know if an IP network is subnetted, the subnet-mask consists of a 32–bit quantity in which all of the bits corresponding to the network-portion of the IP address are set to one.

In such an architecture, the routing table is no longer considered as an associative array. Rather, when the next hop for an address, say *A*, must be determined, the device scans its routing table: for each entry, it logically-ANDs *A* with the subnet-mask associated with that entry. It then checks to see if the resulting quantity is equal to the destination address in the entry. If so, then it forwards the packet to the corresponding IP router.[8]

Note that this approach generalizes quite nicely with the addressing architecture: if the network device is connected to a non-subnetted network, the mask is set to extract just the network-identifier, and this algorithm is equivalent to scanning the routing table sequentially, comparing A to the destination address in each entry. Of course, it is slightly slower since an additional 32-bit logical operation is performed for each entry.

Finally, one might wonder how information about subnet-masks is determined. The same mechanisms are used as with the routing table: usually there is some initial configuration from stable storage; following this, there is usually some dynamic learning through protocol interactions.

---

[8]As one might imagine, the default route in such a scheme consists of an entry with both the destination address and subnet-mask set to all zeros.

2.4.5   Devices Revisited: Routers or Hosts

Earlier it was noted that all routers and some hosts have multiple network attachments and as such have multiple IP addresses. This leads to the obvious question as to how one distinguishes between a router and multi-homed host.

At the highest level, the distinction is simple: routers forward packets, whilst hosts don't. Therefore, routers have additional requirements placed on their internet layer. Of course, a network device might function in both capacities, and the distinction can be made only from context of usage.

Although one might view participation in a routing protocol as the only requirement, the difference is much more fundamental:

> *If a device isn't configured to act as a router, then it should never forward datagrams.*

Thus, if a host receives a datagram for a remote IP address, it should discard the datagram.[9] This behavior is critical in determining problems at the internet layer. If the failure was due to transient causes, a protocol above the IP will cause a retransmission and communications will resume. Otherwise, the failure will become visible and network management tools can be used to determine the cause of the problem.

In order to heal transient problems, routers use both ICMP (a protocol discussed in Section 2.4.7) and routing protocols to synchronize their view of the internet. A host doesn't employ these mechanisms, and therefore can only *contribute* to the problem by forwarding the IP datagram. In particular, it is difficult to see how any good can result when a host, with only a single network attachment, decides to forward some of the IP datagrams it receives.

---

[9]There is one exception. An IP datagram can contain an option for source-routing indicating the path that a datagram should take through an internet. So, if an IP datagram with such an option is received, it should be forwarded according to the source route, regardless of whether the IP entity is functioning as a host or router.

2.4.6 The Internet Protocol

We finally come to the actual protocol used in the internet layer, the *Internet Protocol* (IP) [11]. For our purposes, little need be said. Each IP datagram contains a header containing addressing and other information, followed by user-data:

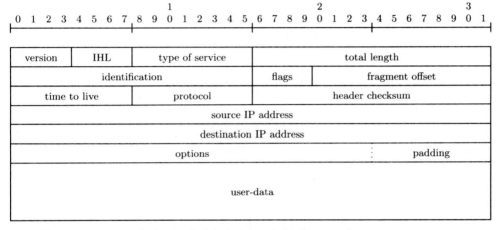

The meaning of these fields is straightforward:

version: identifies the format used. The current number is 4.

IHL: the length of IP header in 32–bit words (the minimum allowed value is 5).

type of service: indicates the quality of service (precedence, delay, throughput, and reliability) desired for the datagram.

total length: the length of the datagram (both header and user-data), measured in octets. As noted earlier, this is necessary since some media (e.g., Ethernet) require padding if a small amount of data is transferred.

identification: a 16–bit value assigned by the originator of this datagram. It is used during reassembly (discussed below).

flags: control bits determining if this datagram may be fragmented, and if so, whether other later fragments exist.

fragment offset: a 13–bit value indicating the position of this fragment, in units of 8 octets, in the original datagram.

time to live: the upper bound (in seconds) that the datagram may be processed within the internet. Each time the datagram passes through the internet layer on any network device, the IP entity must decrement this field by at least one. If the field reaches zero at a router, the datagram is discarded. In practice, this field is actually a hop-count, and not a timer.

protocol: identifies the upper-layer protocol using IP.

header checksum: a one's-complement arithmetic sum, computed over the header of the IP datagram. This value is re-calculated each time the datagram is sent (originated or forwarded) by the IP entity on any network device.

source IP address: the IP address of the initial sender.

destination IP address: the IP address of the final recipient.

options: a collection of zero or more options.

padding: zero to three octets used to pad the datagram header to a 32–bit boundary.

user-data: zero or more octets of data from the upper-layer protocol. (Note that it is an artifact of the convention used in producing the figure above that this field appears to be a multiple of 4 octets in length. No such requirement is made by IP.)

As noted earlier in the discussion of the interface layer, each medium has a maximum size for the data field used to encapsulate an IP datagram. This is termed the *Maximum Transmission Unit* (MTU). The interface layer communicates this information to the internet layer using a local mechanism.

When the local IP entity (either a host or a router) wishes to send a datagram larger than the interface's MTU, it must *fragment* the datagram prior to transmission.

Here's how fragmentation works: Each datagram generated by an IP entity is assigned an identification number, which is carried in the IP header. When an IP entity attempts to send the datagram, it checks the MTU of the associated interface. If the MTU is greater than or equal to the size of the datagram, then no further processing is required. Otherwise, the IP entity checks to see if the **flags** field in the datagram permits fragmentation. If not, the datagram is discarded, and an ICMP message is sent to the originator. Otherwise, the IP entity generates two or more fragments. Each fragment contains a portion of the user-data from the original datagram: the user-data portion in each fragment, except the last, is a multiple of 8 octets. The **fragment offset** field contains a number corresponding to the position of the user-data, in 8–octet increments, in the original datagram. Then, for each fragment, except for the last in the sequence, the *more fragments* bit is set in the **flags** field.

IP fragments are treated just like IP datagrams when they are in transit. When they arrive at the destination IP address, the IP entity must buffer the fragments until it has received all of them.[10] At that point it can reassemble the original datagram. Of course, since fragments may be routed over different paths, the fragments may arrive out of order. Further, some of the fragments may be lost or corrupted. In this case, the datagram cannot be reassembled and the fragments which did arrive intact are discarded. Because IP fragmentation has no concept of selective retransmission of fragments (this would be contrary to the stateless behavior described earlier), it is up to the protocols above to retransmit the original datagram.

Although necessary to provide the internetworking abstraction, fragmentation has its drawbacks. Because a richly-connected internet may have several paths between two devices, there is (as yet) no deterministic mechanism to determine what value the IP entity should use as the optimal MTU for the entire path.[11] Hence, if an IP datagram is to be routed indirectly, the IP entity might "guess" that a lower MTU will be encountered along the path taken by the datagram. If the guess is too high, fragmentation will still result.

---

[10]Routers don't reassemble fragments as they may be sent over different paths.

[11]ICMP provides a mechanism to estimate the optimal MTU, but this estimation isn't deterministic in some topologies.

If the guess is too low, additional overhead will be generated by excessive fragmentation. The current "rule of thumb" is to assume an intervening MTU size of 576 octets if the first hop is to a router. But even then, this may be unrealistic. For example, if IP is being run over X.25, a packet size of 128 octets might be optimal for that portion of the path.

Further, note that if repeated fragmentation occurs and if the network experiences only modest congestion, the likelihood that a single fragment will be lost is alarmingly high. Because of this, the entire datagram will be discarded, presumably causing retransmission by the protocols above. Of course, only one small part of the datagram was lost, so this is a rather inefficient use of resources.

2.4.7   The Internet Control Message Protocol

Associated with IP is another protocol providing low-level feedback about how the internet layer is operating. This protocol is termed the *Internet Control Message Protocol* (ICMP) [37]. ICMP provides very simple advice as to how the internet layer might tailor its behavior. The end of this chapter discusses how this functionality can be used for *ad hoc* network management.

For now, it is important to understand that ICMP provides a modest number of basic control messages for error-reporting. Even though IP and ICMP are both part of the internet layer, ICMP uses the delivery services of IP. If the **protocol** field of an IP datagram has the value 1, the user-data contained in the datagram is an ICMP packet. Although the format of ICMP packets varies with each control message, the first 32–bits contain the same three fields:

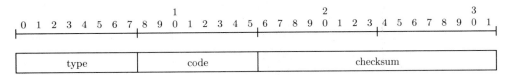

The meaning of these fields is straightforward:

type: identifies which control message is being sent (and thereby defines the format of the rest of the packet).

code: identifies a basic parameter for the control message (the semantics depends on the value of the **type** field).

checksum: a one's-complement arithmetic sum, computed over the entire ICMP packet. (Recall that the IP checksum is calculated *only* for the IP header, not the user-data.)

The control messages supported by ICMP include:

destination unreachable: to report that a datagram couldn't be delivered because a network or host was unreachable, a protocol was not running, or fragmentation was necessary but not allowed by the **flags** field.

time exceeded: to report that a datagram was discarded because its **time to live** field reached zero, or a fragment was discarded because it was on the reassembly queue too long.

parameter problem: to report an error in an IP header.

source quench: to report that a network device is discarding datagrams, especially due to lack of resources (e.g., buffers).

redirect: to report to a host the address of a router closer to a destination IP address. This is the recommended means whereby a host can learn about routers: the host starts with a default router, and performs all indirect routing through it. If the router knows of another router on the same IP network which is closer to the desired destination, it can generate an ICMP redirect message to inform the host.

echo/echo reply: to test reachability of an IP address, an echo message is sent. Upon receiving such a message, the local IP entity responds by sending an echo reply message.

timestamp/timestamp reply: to sample the delay in the network between two network devices.

information request/information reply: to determine the address of the local IP network.

address-mask request/address-mask reply: to determine the subnet-mask associated with the local IP network. (These two messages are defined in [36].)

router advertisement/router solicitation: to aid in router discovery. (These two messages are defined in [38].)

The first four of these are ICMP error messages. Note that it is a fundamental principle that an ICMP error message is never sent in response to an ICMP error message.

2.5 Transport Layer

The transport layer is responsible for providing data transfer between end-systems to the level of reliability desired by the application. That is, the transport layer provides end-to-end service.

In theory, the end-to-end needs of different applications can vary tremendously. In practice, however, there are really only two widely-used service paradigms:

reliable: in which the service offered is a "virtual pipeline":

- *stream-oriented*: rather than dealing in packet exchanges, the end-to-end service provides a sequence of octets, termed a *stream*, to the application.

- *full-duplex*: the stream provided by the end-to-end service is bi-directional in nature.

- *connection-oriented*: before the stream can be used, a virtual connection is established between the two applications.

- *application-layer addressing*: an application needs a means of identifying its peer on the remote system to which the stream should be connected.

- *in-sequence delivery*: the end-to-end service guarantees that user-data is delivered in the same order in which it was sent.

- *user-data integrity*: the end-to-end service guarantees that any user-data delivered has not been corrupted during network transmission.

- *graceful release*: because user-data may be buffered both at the hosts and in the network, the end-to-end service will make sure that *all* of the data sent by the user is successfully transmitted before the stream is released.

Note that these are general guidelines, and not fixed. In particular, the OSI CO-mode transport service, whilst offering a reliable transport paradigm, uses a packet-oriented (rather than stream-oriented) user-data paradigm, and has no graceful release mechanism (the functionality of which resides at the layer above). Regardless, the remaining characteristics are core to the concept of a reliable transport service.

unreliable: in which the service offered is virtually identical to that of the internet datagram service. The only added features are:

- *application-layer addressing*; and,

- *user-data integrity*.

It shouldn't be surprising that the reliable service paradigm corresponds closely to a connection-oriented transport service, whilst the unreliable service paradigm is similar to a connectionless-mode transport service.

The Internet suite of protocols provides two different transport protocols to meet these vastly different needs. Since both protocols use identical mechanisms to achieve application-layer addressing and user-data integrity, the simpler protocol is described first.

2.5.1   The User Datagram Protocol

The *User Datagram Protocol* (UDP) [39] is the connectionless-mode transport protocol in the Internet suite. As UDP is a transport layer protocol, for delivery, it uses the services of IP. If the **protocol** field of an IP datagram has the value 17 (decimal), the user-data contained in the datagram is a UDP packet:

source port	destination port
length	checksum
user-data	

The meaning of these fields is straightforward:

source/destination port: identifies an application running at
the corresponding IP address.

length: the length of the UDP packet (header and user-data),
measured in octets.

checksum: a one's-complement arithmetic sum, computed over
a *pseudo-header* and the entire UDP packet.

user-data: zero or more octets of data from the upper-layer
protocol. (Note that it is an artifact of the convention used
in producing the figure above that this field appears to be a
multiple of 4 octets in length. No such requirement is made
by UDP.)

The uses of these fields are now explained.

Application-layer Addressing

To achieve application-layer addressing, UDP manages 16–bit unsigned integer quantities, termed *ports*. Port numbers less than 512
are assigned by the Internet Assigned Numbers Authority (IANA)
(see Section A.5 on page 394). These are termed *well-known ports*.
In those cases when a service might be available over both TCP and
UDP, the IANA assigns the same port number to that service for both
protocols.

On Berkeley UNIX®, port numbers less than 1024 are reserved
for privileged processes (an easily spoofed, but in some environments,
useful security mechanism).

The combination of an IP address and a port number is termed an
internet *socket* which uniquely identifies an application-entity running
in an internet.

Of course, the notion of application-layer addressing is just another
example of the multiplexing operation of protocols:

- at the interface layer, each medium usually distinguishes between clients (entities at the internet layer) by using different

values in a **type** field (e.g., Ethernet uses a value of 0x0800 to indicate IP);

- at the internet layer, IP distinguishes between clients (entities at the transport layer) by using different values in a **protocol** field (e.g., IP uses a value of 17 to indicate UDP); and,

- at the transport layer, TCP and UDP distinguish between clients (entities at the application layer) by using different values in a **port** field (e.g., UDP uses a value of 161 (decimal) to indicate SNMP).

The Assigned Numbers RFC [24] lists the complete set of protocol numbers used at all layers in the Internet suite of protocols.

User-Data Integrity

To achieve both user-data integrity and modest protection against misbehavior at the layers below, UDP calculates a *pseudo-header* which is conceptually prefixed to the UDP packet. The checksum algorithm is then run over a block that looks like this:

```
                  1                   2                   3
  0 1 2 3 4 5 6 7 8 9 0 1 2 3 4 5 6 7 8 9 0 1 2 3 4 5 6 7 8 9 0 1
```

source IP address		
destination IP address		
empty	protocol	UDP length
source port		destination port
length		checksum
user-data		

pseudo-header (bracket spanning the first three rows: source IP address, destination IP address, empty/protocol/UDP length)

The fields of the pseudo-header are relatively self-explanatory: the **source** and **destination** fields are taken from the IP packet, the **empty** field is simply a zero-valued octet, the **protocol** field is the value used by IP to identify UDP (17 decimal), and the **UDP length** field is the length of the UDP packet.

TCP also uses this 96–bit pseudo-header in its checksum calculation when achieving user-data integrity.

2.5.2 The Transmission Control Protocol

The *Transmission Control Protocol* (TCP) [10] is the connection-oriented transport protocol in the Internet suite. As TCP is a connection-oriented transport protocol, it goes through three distinct phases: connection establishment, data transfer, and connection release. To keep track of a particular connection, each TCP entity maintains a *Transmission Control Block* (TCB). This is created during connection establishment, modified throughout the life of the connection, and then deleted when the connection is released.

TCP is best described as a finite state machine, which starts in the CLOSED state. As *events* occur (either activity from a user of TCP or from the network), the TCP entity performs some *action* and then enters a new state. The TCP state diagram is presented in Figure 2.4 on page 52. It is suggested that the reader study the intervening text before examining the figure.

Connection Establishment

A connection enters the LISTEN state when an application-entity tells TCP that it is willing to accept connections for a particular port number. This is termed a *passive open*.

Sometime later, another application-entity tells TCP that it wishes to establish a connection to an IP address and port number which corresponds to the application-entity which is listening. This is termed an *active open*.[12]

When two TCP entities communicate, the exchanged units of data are termed *segments*. The format of a segment is presented later on. Segments are interpreted relative to a *connection*. In TCP, a connection is defined as the pairing of the two internet sockets. This 96–bit quantity (source IP address and TCP port, destination IP address and TCP port) uniquely identifies the connection in an internet.

When an active open is attempted, the originating TCP entity computes an *initial sequence number*, which is a "starting number"

---

[12]It is possible for two application entities to simultaneously issue active opens for each other. In this case, a single TCP connection is established.

for this direction of the new connection. The sequence number must be chosen carefully so that segments from older instances of this connection, which might be floating around the network, won't cause confusion with this new connection. A SYN (synchronize) segment is then sent to the destination TCP entity. Upon receiving this segment, the destination TCP entity checks to see that an application-entity is listening on the destination TCP port. If not, the connection is aborted by sending a RST (reset) segment.[13] Otherwise, the destination TCP entity computes a sequence number for its direction, and sends this back in a SYN/ACK (synchronize/acknowledge) segment which acknowledges the sequence number for the originating TCP entity.

Upon receiving this segment, the original TCP entity makes sure that its sequence number was acknowledged and, if all is well, sends an ACK segment back to acknowledge the sequence number for the destination TCP entity.

This protocol interaction is termed a *three-way handshake*. Once the three-way handshake has been successfully concluded, the connection enters the data transfer phase.

Data Transfer

In the data transfer phase, user-data is sent as a sequence of octets, each of which is numbered, starting with the initial sequence number.

Each segment specifies a window size (in octets) which may be sent in the other direction before an acknowledgement is returned. Each segment sent by a TCP entity contains an implicit acknowledgement of all octets contiguously received thus far. Precisely stated, the acknowledgement field indicates the number of the *next* octet that is expected by a TCP entity.

This windowing strategy allows the TCP entities to achieve a *pipelining effect* in the network, while at the same time providing a flow control mechanism. The pipelining effect increases throughput by keeping more data in the network, whilst the flow control mechanism prevents either TCP entity from overrunning the connection resources (such as buffers for user-data) of the other.

---

[13]In the interest of simplicity, Figure 2.4 doesn't show this transition, or any transition, involving an RST segment.

The disadvantage of this approach is that if segments are re-ordered, this information cannot be conveyed in an acknowledgement. For example, if two segments are sent, and the first one is delayed, the receiving TCP entity cannot acknowledge the second segment until it receives the first.

Data Transfer – Retransmission

The discussion thus far has not considered loss or corruption of segments. Each time a TCP entity sends a segment, it starts a retransmission timer. At some time in the future, one of two events will happen first: either an acknowledgement for the segment will be received, and the timer can be stopped; or, the timer will expire. In this latter case, the TCP entity *retransmits* the segment and restarts the timer. Retransmission continues some number of times until eventually the TCP entity gives up and declares the transport connection to be aborted. That is, TCP emulates reliability through retransmission. The trick, of course, is knowning *when* to retransmit. If data is lost or corrupted in the network and the sending transport entity retransmits too slowly, then throughput suffers. If data is delayed or discarded due to congestion in the network and the transport entity retransmits too quickly then it merely adds to the congestion and throughput gets even worse!

The reader should appreciate that because of the service offered by IP; a TCP entity cannot distinguish between lossy or congested networks. Hence, TCP uses one of several adaptive algorithms to predict the latency characteristics of the network, which may fluctuate considerably because of other traffic.

The retransmission timeout usually varies for each segment, based on the recent history of latency and loss exhibited by the network. Work reported in [40,41] suggests some novel, common sense insights into this problem.

As might be expected, acknowledgements and retransmission interact with the window strategy. Once again, suppose two segments are sent, and the first segment is lost. The receiving TCP entity cannot acknowledge the second segment. The retransmission timer expires for the sending TCP entity. It must now decide whether to retransmit the first segment or both segments. If it retransmits both segments, then it is "guessing" that both segments were lost. If this isn't the case, then network bandwidth is being wasted. Otherwise, if it retransmits the first segment only, it must wait for an acknowledgement to see if the second segment also needs to be retransmitted. If not, it has reduced its sending throughput by waiting for a roundtrip transaction in the network.

Data Transfer – Queued Delivery

In addition to trying to optimize network traffic, a TCP entity may try to reduce the overhead of communicating with local application entities. This is usually achieved by buffering user-data in the TCP entity, both as it is received from the local application-entity, in order to efficiently use the network, and also as user-data is received from the network, in order to efficiently communicate with the local application-entity. Because of this, an application-entity might need a mechanism for ensuring that all data it has previously sent has been received.

This is accomplished using a PSH (push) function. When sending, an application-entity may indicate that data previously sent should be pushed. The local TCP entity sets a PSH bit in the next new segment it sends. Upon receiving such a segment, the remote TCP entity knows that it should push user-data up to its own application-entity.

Although the push function must be present in each TCP implementation, few implementations of applications actually use this functionality. This is because most TCP entity implementations will periodically push any queued data towards the destination. Further, it should be noted that there are no semantics associated with the push function. It is simply a way of telling TCP to deliver all data previously sent to the remote application-entity. On the remote device, the application-entity will see only the user-data and won't receive any explicit indication of the push function having been invoked. Experience has shown that the push function is largely an internal matter: application protocols should be designed so that the push function isn't used.

Data Transfer – Urgent Data

Finally, TCP supports the concept of *urgent data.* The semantics of urgent data are application-specific. What TCP does is to indicate where urgent data ends in the stream. The receiving application-entity, upon being notified that urgent data is present in the stream, can quickly read from the stream until the urgent data is exhausted.

Connection Release

When an application-entity indicates that it has finished sending on the connection, the local TCP entity will send all outstanding data, setting the FIN (finish) indication in the last segment to indicate that it is finished sending new data.

Upon receiving this indication, the remote TCP entity will send an ACK for the FIN, and will inform (using a local mechanism) the application-entity. When that application-entity indicates that it too has no more data to send, a FIN is generated in this direction also. When all data in transit and the segments containing the FINs have been acknowledged, the two TCP entities declare the connection released. In order to ensure that old, duplicate packets don't interfere with new connections being established between the two application entities, one of the TCPs will delay releasing the connection by twice the maximum segment lifetime.

Instead of requesting a graceful release, an application-entity may determine that it wishes to immediately abort the connection. In this case, the local TCP entity generates a RST (reset) segment, and the connection is immediately released. Any data in transit is lost.

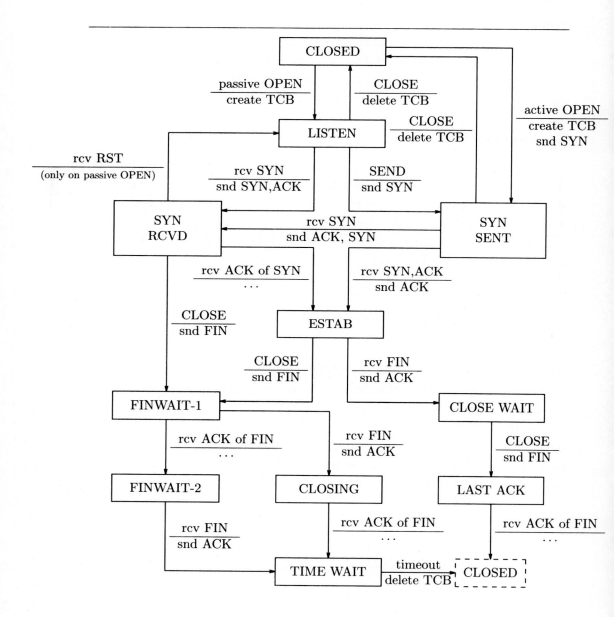

Figure 2.4: TCP State Diagram

Segment Format

When TCP wishes to send a segment, it uses the services of IP. If the **protocol** field of an IP datagram has the value 6 (decimal), the user-data contained in the datagram is a TCP segment:

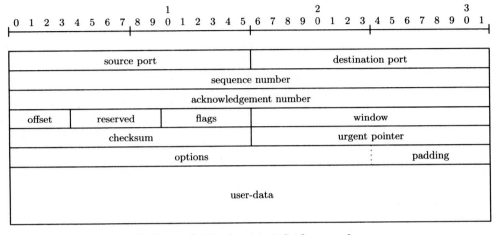

The meaning of these fields is straightforward:

source/destination port: identifies an application running at the corresponding IP address.

sequence number: the number of the first octet of user-data in this segment.

acknowledgement number: if the ACK bit is set in the **flags** field, then this field indicates the next sequence number that the TCP entity is expecting to receive.

offset: the length of the TCP segment in 32–bit words (the minimum allowed value is 5).

flags: control bits indicating special functions of this segment.

window: the number of octets of user-data (starting with the octet indicated in the **acknowledgement** field), which the TCP entity is willing to accept.

checksum: a one's-complement arithmetic sum, computed over a pseudo-header and the entire TCP segment, as discussed earlier.

urgent pointer: if the URG bit is set in the **flags** field, then this field, when added to the **sequence number** field, indicates the first octet of non-urgent data.

options: a collection of zero or more options.

padding: zero to three octets used to pad the segment header to a 32–bit boundary.

user-data: zero or more octets of data from the upper-layer protocol. (Note that it is an artifact of the convention used in producing the figure above that this field appears to be a multiple of 4 octets in length. No such requirement is made by TCP.)

2.6 Application Layer

Historically, management of the Internet suite of protocols has focused on the lower three layers (interface, internet, and transport) of the architecture. Although an effort in electronic mail management was started in late 1992, as of this writing, there is little to be gained by describing even the core application protocols. Perhaps when management of the application layer is understood and in use, a subsequent revision of *The Simple Book* will describe the corresponding protocols.

2.7   Ad Hoc Management Techniques

Even given the modest functionality provided by ICMP, it is still possible to build two tools useful in trouble-shooting connectivity problems at the internet layer. Historically, these mechanisms are the lowest common denominators available.

2.7.1   Ping

The *packet internet groper* (*ping*) program sends an ICMP echo request packet to an IP address and awaits a reply. Since implementation of ICMP is mandatory for all network devices supporting the Internet suite of protocols, this provides a crude means of seeing if "you can get there from here".

Of course, *ping* is useful only for testing the connectivity from the local network device to a remote one (typical implementations also report the time taken to receive the reply). By sending multiple requests, *ping* can report the percentage of loss. However, *ping* cannot report on the general health of an internet. Nor can it report on the path taken by an IP datagram as it traverses the networks between the local and remote network devices.

The first problem cannot be solved in the absence of general network management technology (which is the subject of the next five chapters of *The Simple Book*). However, there is a clever means by which the second problem can be solved.

2.7.2   Traceroute

The *traceroute* program sends a series of "probe packets" using UDP to an IP address and awaits, of all things, ICMP replies!

Here's how it works: the IP datagrams carrying the UDP packets are sent with monotonically increasing values in the **time to live** (TTL) field, and the UDP port number is chosen so as to most likely not be in use. For each TTL value, the *traceroute* program sends a fixed number of packets (usually 3), and reports back the IP addresses of the devices responding. This process continues until an ICMP port unreachable packet is received or some TTL threshold is reached (usually 30).

If a router receives an IP datagram and decrements the TTL to zero, then it returns an ICMP time-exceeded packet. If the IP datagram eventually reaches the network device in question, an ICMP port unreachable packet will be returned. Combining the information from all the replies, the *traceroute* program can report on the whole route.

It should be noted that *traceroute* isn't entirely foolproof in its operation: sadly, not all implementations of even IP, ICMP, and UDP operate correctly. If the probes sent by *traceroute* encounter such devices, interesting interactions result.

2.7.3 Protocol Analyzers

Both *ping* and *traceroute* work by introducing management traffic onto the network. However, a large number of management problems can be solved simply by examining the traffic generated by the protocol in question. For example, in trying to analyze the problems of a TCP connection (e.g., poor throughput), a lot can be learned by building programs which simply capture and decode the TCP segments being exchanged. These "packet monitors" have been in use since the beginning of networking and are now quite sophisticated.

The passive approach to management relies on *capture* and *analysis*. In order to capture the protocol traffic, the monitor must either be co-resident with, or attached to the same physical medium as, the device being studied. Note that if a device being monitored is multi-homed, then, in order to guarantee complete access to all traffic, the monitor must be connected to all cable segments attached to the device in question.

Indeed, quite a market has been built for devices which do nothing but monitor all traffic on a cable segment, select traffic which is interesting for the network operator, and then provide information about that traffic. Of course, given the amount of traffic that can be generated by a sender and receiver on a high-bandwidth medium, the monitor must be able to filter and store traffic at an equally fast rate. This usually argues for use of a special-purpose monitoring device, and one which can perform capture and analysis separately.

Once data has been captured, it must be analyzed. This means that the monitor must have an excellent understanding of the protocol in question, in addition to being able to understand any underlying protocols in use. Further, for connection-oriented protocols such as TCP, it must be able to maintain state for a connection being monitored, so as to be able to understand the actions of the TCP entities involved. In many cases, the difficulty of this cannot be overstated.

Analysis is, of course, dependent on the protocol being monitored. At the simplest level, the monitor can advise the network operator of duplicated packets, the timing relationships between packets, and so on.

Interestingly enough, these monitoring devices can be instrumented with a network management protocol and then controlled remotely. This is the purpose of something called the *Remote Network Monitoring* (RMON) MIB, which is briefly introduced in Section 4.2.5 starting on page 166. For now, keep in mind that one can remotely configure a monitoring device, direct it to capture a certain kind of traffic, and then retrieve the statistics which have been collated.

2.7.4   Ad Hoc doesn't mean Inadequate

Finally, it should be noted that use of the term *ad hoc* doesn't imply anything negative about the quality of these solutions. Quite the contrary.

Further, it should be noted that there is a wealth of information that can be determined by using the internet infrastructure. For example, in [42], an automated system for discovering network topology and components, uses protocols such as ARP, ICMP, and the DNS, and, as of this writing, doesn't use a "real" network management protocol. In order to maximize usefulness, a network management system must incorporate both standardized and *ad hoc* features.

Chapter 3

Concepts

Having introduced the core portions of the Internet suite of protocols, it is now time to proceed to the main focus of *The Simple Book*: network management of internets which use these protocols.

We term the framework used for network management in the Internet suite of protocols the *Internet-standard Network Management Framework*. This is primarily due to historical reasons: prior schemes were *ad hoc* and proprietary. There are actually two versions of this framework: the original framework, which consists of four documents, each a full Internet-standard having "Recommended" status; and, the successor framework, which consists of twelve documents, each having just entered onto the standards track. In time, the documents comprising the successor framework will each likely become a full Internet-standard. At that time, the original framework will be declared historic, and the Internet community will have but a single framework.

For expository purposes, the discussion in *The Simple Book* is primarily on the newer framework. To avoid confusion, for the remainder of *The Simple Book*, the term "Internet-standard Network Management Framework" will be used to refer to the original framework, whilst the term "SNMPv2 framework" will be used to refer to the new framework that will eventually displace the original framework, and the term "management framework" will be used to refer to either framework.

As it turns out, there were two intermediate steps between the original framework and the SNMPv2 framework: SNMP Security and SMP. Both of these efforts were assimilated as a part of the SNMPv2 effort. Documents which refer to either of these technologies are now of only historic interest. So, throughout *The Simple Book* we'll refer only to the original and SNMPv2 frameworks. If your readings happen to take you across these other terms, keep in mind that they were only technology snapshots along the road to SNMPv2.

3.1   A Model

A network management system contains four components:

- one or more *managed nodes*, each containing an *agent*;

- at least one *network management station* (NMS), on which one or more network management applications (which are often imprecisely termed *managers*) reside;

- a network management *protocol*, which is used by the station and the agents to exchange management information; and,

- management information.

These are now considered in turn. Readers should note that there are actually three models being introduced in this section, i.e., an information model, an operational model, and, an administrative model. Rather than attempting a rigorous taxonomical discussion, the author, hoping to present something that's easier to understand, favors a less-structured presentation.

Finally, be sure to purge the terms "client" and "server" from your vocabulary when discussing network management. The proper terms are *agent* and *manager*. The reason this is important is because the terms client and server have just too many meanings in a distributed system, depending on what part of the system is being considered.

3.1.1   Managed Nodes

A managed node refers to a device of some kind, falling into one of three categories:

- a host system, such as a workstation, mainframe, terminal server, or printer;

- a router system; or,

- a media device, such as a bridge, repeater, hub, or analyzer.

The commonality between these categories is that all devices have some sort of network capability. The first two categories are usually independent of the underlying media, whilst the primary function of devices in the third category is media-dependent. As can be seen, the potential diversity of managed nodes is quite high, spanning the spectrum from mainframes to modems.

The Fundamental Axiom

A successful network management system must take notice of this diversity and provide an appropriate framework. In the previous chapter, it was noted that the success of IP is largely due to the minimal requirements that it places on the interface layer below. A similar philosophy must be taken by the management framework:

> *The impact of adding network management to managed nodes must be minimal, reflecting a lowest common denominator.*

This *Fundamental Axiom* is mandated by the wide differences between managed nodes, and is argued quite eloquently in [43].

The Commonalities of Managed Nodes

Given the focus of the Fundamental Axiom, what commonalities between managed nodes can we exploit?

Any managed node can be conceptualized as containing three components:

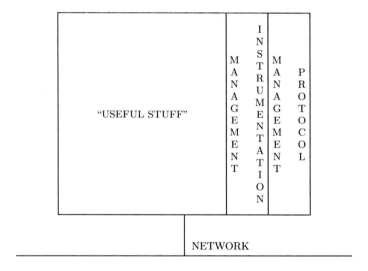

These are:

- *"useful stuff"*, which perform the functions desired by the user;

- a *management protocol*, which permits the monitoring and control of the managed node; and,

- *management instrumentation*, which interacts with the implementation of the managed node in order to achieve monitoring and control.

The interaction between these components is straightforward: the instrumentation acts as "glue" between the useful protocols and the management protocol. This is usually achieved by an internal communications mechanism in which the data structures for the useful protocols may be accessed and manipulated at the request of the management protocol.

Administrative Model

Actually, this perspective is slightly simplistic: exchanges of management information, per se, are insufficient to achieve management of the managed node. The management protocol must also provide an *administrative model*, which provides authentication and authorization policies. This allows the managed node to determine how it is managed, so that only authorized application processes may perform management.

For example, there may be several administrations responsible for management of an entire internet and some nodes therein might be managed by multiple administrations. Depending on the device in question, different administrations are likely to have vastly different levels of permissions for managing the device.

3.1.2   Network Management Stations

A network management station refers to a host system which is running:

- the network management protocol; and,

- one or more network management applications.

If the network management protocol is viewed as providing the mechanism for management, then it is the network management applications which determine the policy used for management.

Earlier it was noted that the Fundamental Axiom indicated that adding "network management" should have a minimal impact on the managed nodes. As a consequence, the burden is shifted to the management station. Thus, one should expect that the host systems supporting a management station are relatively powerful in comparison to the managed nodes. How much power is necessary? Experience shows that most workstations are quite capable of providing the resources needed to realize an effective management station. However, as with all design decisions, the trade-offs must be weighed carefully — blind adherence to dogma is no substitute for careful thought. Even so, it is good to have an underlying set of design criteria when engineering a complex system.

Note that since there are many more managed nodes than management stations in an internet, scalability favors placing the burden on the management station: it is better to require significant functionality from a small percentage of devices, rather than the vast majority.

As a final rationale, consider that because the marketplace for products using the Internet suite of protocols is fast becoming a commodity market, vendors of TCP/IP-based products are highly price-sensitive. If adding "network management" to a router implies adding another memory board or a faster processor, the vendor will balk. In contrast, since software for the management station is an unbundled item, it is more attractive, from an economic perspective, to focus development resources there.

Dual Role Entities

Thus far, management stations have been described as interacting solely with managed nodes. Suppose that the managed node is itself a management station? It is important to appreciate that the agent-manager model can directly support this by viewing the software in each management station as taking on two distinct roles: a *manager role* and an *agent role*. That is, the agent-manager model is also a peer-to-peer model.

With this in mind, one can construct hierarchical relationships between management stations. For example, one could imagine constructing a management system in which each LAN segment had a management application which kept track of the state of the devices on that segment. These management applications might report to applications running on regional management stations, which in turn might report to applications running on enterprise-wide management stations. In this example, the software in each management station takes on both a manager role when monitoring and controlling devices which are subordinate in the hierarchy, and an agent role when reporting information and acting upon the commands given from a superior in the hierarchy.

Note, however, that the key concept with dual role entities is that a hierarchical relationship is one of configuration, whilst the peer-to-peer relationship is one of architecture.

3.1.3 Network Management Protocol

Depending on the paradigm used for network management, there are several forms that a management protocol might take. For example, in a remote interpretation paradigm, the management protocol is used to exchange "program fragments" which are executed on the managed node.

Operations

In the management framework, a "remote debugging" paradigm is used. Each managed node is viewed as having several "variables". By reading the value of these variables, the managed node is monitored. By changing the value of these variables, the managed node is controlled.[1] The advantage of using this paradigm is that it is straightforward to build a simple management protocol to meet these goals.

In addition to read and write operations, there are two other operations that are required:

- a traversal operation, which allows a management station to determine which variables a managed node supports; and,

- a trap operation, which allows a managed node to report an extraordinary event to a management station.

These both require a bit more explanation.

Traversal

Since managed nodes perform different functions, it shouldn't be surprising that they might contain different management variables. In the management framework, variables related to a particular functionality are grouped together. For example, each device which implements the internet layer would be expected to provide the variables in the "internet layer" group.

---

[1]Note that this approach obviates the need for so-called *imperative* commands (e.g., "reboot the device") which are found in other management frameworks: any imperative command can be realized in terms of changing the value of a variable which has been specially defined for this purpose.

Of course, such an approach also argues for *extensibility*. As network management becomes better understood, things will change. The management framework must take this into account to provide an easy way for the new to interwork with the old.

Given that different managed nodes may support different management variables, there must be an efficient means for a management station to determine which variables are supported. Hence, the protocol must provide a means for traversing the list of variables supported by a managed node.

But, there is an even more basic need for traversal: thus far the discussion has implicitly assumed that these variables are scalar-valued, i.e., that only one instance of the variable can exist. What about the IP routing table? Clearly this isn't a scalar, but a table consisting of zero or more rows (one for each routing entry), with each row instantiating several columns. The management protocol must now provide two functions:

- a mechanism to retrieve specific cells in a table, e.g., if the management station knows which routing entry it is looking for, the management protocol should provide a means for efficiently retrieving the desired columns of that entry; and;

- a mechanism to retrieve large numbers of cells in a table, e.g., if the management station wishes to browse the routing table, the management protocol should provide a means for incrementally examining the contents of the routing table.

Traps

Since the dawn of operating systems, there has been a never-ending debate as to the merits of using either an *interrupt-driven* approach or a *polling* approach in order to learn about extraordinary events. It shouldn't be surprising that the debate has spilled over into the network management arena.

In network management parlance, the arguments are phrased in terms of *traps* and *polling*:

- With the trap-based approach, when an extraordinary event occurs (such as a link going down), the managed node sends a trap to the appropriate management stations (assuming that the device has not crashed and that there is a path in the network by which the management applications can be reached). This has the advantage of providing an immediate notification.

There are also several disadvantages: it requires resources to generate the trap. If the trap must contain a lot of information, the managed node may be spending too much time on the trap and not enough time working on useful things. For example, if traps require some sort of acknowledgement from the management station, this places further requirements on the agent's resources. Of course, when a trap is generated, the agent is assuming that the management applications are ready to receive such information. Careful design must be used in order to achieve a system in which traps can be idempotent! Further, careful configuration must be employed to make sure that only those stations interested in receiving certain traps will be recipients.

Further, if several extraordinary events occur, a lot of network bandwidth is tied up with traps, which is hardly desirable if the report is about network congestion. So, to refine the trap-based approach, a managed node might use *thresholds* in deciding when to report an event: traps are generated only when the occurrence of an event exceeds some threshold. Unfortunately, this means that the agent must often spend substantive time determining if an event should generate a trap. As a result, use of the trap-based approach has a severe impact on the performance of the agent, or the network, or both! Of course, even with thresholds, if multiple agents detect the condition, then multiple traps will be sent, again congesting the network.

In any event, the managed node has only a very limited view of the internet, so it is arguable whether it can provide "the big picture" on the problem by using traps. In fact, the management applications might have already detected the problem through some alternate means, rendering the trap redundant at best.

- With the polling-based approach, a management application periodically queries the managed node as to how things are going. This has the advantage of keeping the management application in control as it determines what "the big picture" really is.

  The disadvantage, of course, is one of timeliness. How is the management application to know which managed elements to poll and how often? If the interval is too brief, network bandwidth is wasted; if too long, the response to catastrophic events is too slow.

  A second disadvantage is that additional traffic is introduced onto the network. Correspondingly, the management application must have additional storage resources available to it.

In the management framework, the model used is one of *trap-directed polling*. When an extraordinary event occurs, the managed node sends a *single*, simple trap to the management application. The management application is then responsible for initiating further interactions with the managed node in order to determine the nature and extent of the problem. This compromise is surprisingly effective: the impact on managed nodes remains small; the impact on network bandwidth is minimized; and, problems can be dealt with in a timely fashion. Of course, since they are sent unreliably, traps serve as an early warning; low frequency polling is needed as a back-up.

`soap...` One of the myths of network management is that one can design a management protocol in which traps are reliably transmitted. This is usually accomplished by layering the management protocol on top of a connection-oriented transport protocol. Unfortunately, there is no such thing as reliability in a network. Connection-oriented transport protocols emulate reliability through *retransmission*. As noted earlier on page 49, if a timer expires before an acknowledgement is received, the segment is retransmitted. This continues until eventually an acknowledgement is received or the sending TCP gives up. There is no concept of "guaranteed reliability", it exists only as part of a confidence game being played by some telecommunications providers with an overactive marketing department.

Suppose that a managed node resides on a stub network (one for which a single link must always be used in order to reach the managed node) and that a well-known farm tool cuts through the cable which corresponds to that link. Dr. SNMP reminds us that:

> *"Even goldfish can be taught to play the piano, if you use enough voltage."*

In other words, once the cable is cut, you don't need more retransmissions, you need a **lot** more voltage.

So, one shouldn't design a system with the expectation that traps are reliable, and management protocols shouldn't make promises that they can't keep. This topic comes up time and time again in the SNMP community, and has achieved *problematic* status. (To achieve this infamous status, an issue must be raised at least six times over the course of three years, and each time the solution put forth must go down in flames.)

`...soap`

With this in mind, let us briefly consider how the network management protocol makes use of the transport service.

Transport Mappings

The choice of a transport service by the management protocol is particularly important, since the underlying mechanisms used by the transport service will have direct impact on the effectiveness of the management protocol. Consistent with the Fundamental Axiom, the smallest possible communications stack should be chosen.

Also, because a connection-oriented transport service actually tries to hide problems from the application, it is precisely this service which should be avoided. The management application, and not the transport service, should decide upon the desired level of reliability, and then implement the appropriate algorithm. Further, the managed node should be largely unburdened by the management application's choice. All of this leads to the realization that a connectionless-mode transport service is the desired choice. Such a choice implies stateless behavior on the part of the agent (which minimizes burden on the managed node), and allows the management application to control the level of reliability.

It turns out, however, that there is another good reason for choosing CL-mode transport service: in times of network stress, it is difficult to establish a connection! As noted earlier on page 48, TCP uses a three-way handshake to establish a connection. If the network is experiencing packet loss, the likelihood of a three-way handshake completion is much smaller than the likelihood of a single self-contained packet making it from the management station to the managed node. This means that, with a connection-oriented transport mapping, the delay owing to connection-establishment before the management packet can be sent may prove too high for effective management — precisely at the time when the network most needs to be managed!

3.1.4 Management Information

Finally, there must be a means for defining the management information which is exchanged by the managed node and the management station using the management protocol. The definition of a unit of management information is termed a *managed object.* A collection of related managed objects is defined in a document termed the *Management Information Base* (MIB) module.

Perhaps the most important feature of any method used to describe management information is that of extensibility. It should be easy to start with a small number of definitions, to gain experience implementing and using those definitions, and then to add new definitions based on that experience.

There is also an important side effect of extensibility, which is non-technical in nature. In addition to definitions of standard management information, vendors can also implement their own proprietary managed objects. That is, after a router vendor implements the standard objects which pertain to routing, it might choose to define and implement objects which are particular to its router products. Because this permits more effective management of its products, the vendor can view this as positive market differentiation. More importantly, this factor makes introduction of standardized management technology much more attractive to a vendor.

Managed Objects

Earlier it was noted that the management instrumentation in a managed device was responsible for acting as the "glue" between the device's useful protocols and the management protocol. More formally, the management instrumentation implements this "glue" by taking the information available in the device and making it appear as a collection of managed objects. This collection is termed "the MIB held in the agent" or, more properly, the agent's *object resources.*

Administrative Model Revisited

Earlier, the administrative model was introduced as being responsible for providing authentication and authorization policies. Having now introduced management information, we can expand on this: it is the administrative model which provides a means for determining which management applications are able to access which objects and with what operations. The management operations permitted to a management application by an agent is termed an *access policy*; the collection of managed objects which are visible to those operations is termed a *MIB view*, or simply a *view*.

Proxy Relationships

Sometimes, however, an agent has access to management information which isn't available locally, but instead is held by another device. As such, when a management request for that information is received, the agent performs some non-local interaction in order to satisfy the request. This is termed a *proxy interaction*, and the agent capable of performing such an interaction is termed a *proxy agent*.

There may be several reasons why a proxy relationship is used:

administrative firewall: It may be useful to have the proxy agent authenticate and authorize requests, so as not to burden a busy device with these tasks. In this case, the proxy agent implements an extensive administrative policy, and, in turn, the busy device will answer requests only from the proxy agent.

caching firewall: It may be useful to have the proxy agent cache information, again to minimize the burden on a busy device. Note, however, that it may be difficult to implement an efficient caching scheme to support the traversal capability mentioned earlier.

transport bridging: In a multi-protocol internet, a device may support the end-to-end services of only one protocol suite. Ideally, a management station should support the end-to-end services of all protocol suites in a multi-protocol internet. However, a proxy agent, supporting the end-to-end services of the appropriate protocol suite could be used to establish a path for management communications between the device and the management station.

protocol translation: Finally, it is possible that the device may not support the management protocol.[2] In this case, requests using the management protocol are translated into a form which is supported by the device. Similarly, responses are translated from the device-specific form back into the management protocol.

These four kinds of functionality can be viewed in terms of the complexity of the mapping required. For example, a proxy agent used as an administrative firewall or for transport bridging, performs relatively simple mappings which don't involve any semantics. In contrast, it is likely that a proxy agent used for protocol translation will involve a semantic mapping. In most cases it is hard to overestimate the complexity protocol translating: the greater the differences between the device-specific form and the management protocol, the more likely that functionality will suffer.

Fortunately, in the case of the Internet-standard Network Management Framework and the SNMPv2 framework, the management protocols are very similar. Thus, a proxy agent used to allow coexistence between the two frameworks resembles more of a bridging proxy than a translating proxy. This was no accident: when the SNMPv2 framework was developed, extraordinary consideration was given to coexistence issues — precisely to achieve this effect!

Regardless of the particulars, an important property of a proxy relationship is termed the *transparency principle*. The idea is simple: it should appear to the application as if it were communciating directly with the real agent. A management application simply specifies the desired object resources and the proxy agent is responsible for "making the right thing happen", just as if the management information were held locally by the proxy agent.

---

[2] Yet another reason why the Fundamental Axiom is crucial — by lowering the cost of entry, it is more likely that the device **will** support the management protocol.

3.1.5   In Perspective

The Fundamental Axiom of the management framework is based on the notion of universal deployment:

> *If network management is viewed as an essential aspect of an internet, then it must be universally deployed on the largest possible collection of devices in the network.*

As noted earlier, by taking a minimalist approach, the management framework enjoys significant leverage in terms of economy of scale. There are many more agents than management stations. Thus, minimizing the impact of management on the agents is the most attractive solution to the problem.

A second, though equally important, tenet is that network management is unlike all other applications:

> *When all else fails, network management must continue to function, if at all possible.*

Both the Fundamental Axiom and this tenet are argued quite eloquently in [43].

As noted earlier, this tenet mandates that many of the functions traditionally found in the transport layer (e.g., retransmission) be directly addressed by applications in the management station, since it is only the applications themselves that know the reliability requirements of each operation. Therefore, the transport service must not be "helpful". It should be the simplest possible pass-through available to the network.

The chapter now closes with a terse (but still lengthy) discussion of data representation at the application layer.

3.2 Data Representation

Throughout Chapter 2 there were numerous diagrams showing the bit-wise layout of the packets exchanged by some of the lower-layer protocols of the Internet suite. As might be expected, each implementation of these protocols has an *internal representation* which denotes these structures. The actual layout of each data structure depends on the programming language, language compiler, and machine architecture of each platform.

Because the packets are relatively simple, the only major concern is that of using a network byte ordering scheme (as discussed earlier). At the application layer, the data structures exchanged by protocol entities are potentially much more complex. Therefore, it is necessary to introduce a new formalism for describing these structures.

This new formalism is termed an *abstract syntax*, which is used to define data without regard to machine-oriented structures and restrictions. In the management framework, an OSI language termed *Abstract Syntax Notation One* (ASN.1), is used for this purpose.

It must be emphasized that ASN.1 is used for two distinct purposes by the management framework:

- defining the formats of the PDUs exchanged by the management protocol; and,

- defining the objects which are managed.

That is: abstract syntax is used to describe both the data structures exchanged at the protocol level, and the management information which is conveyed through those data structures. Note that this second use is at a conceptually higher level than the first.

Hand-in-glove with abstract syntax is the notion of a *transfer syntax*. Once data structures can be described in a machine-independent fashion, there must be some way of transmitting those data structures, unambiguously, over the network. This is the job of a transfer syntax notation. Obviously, one could have several transfer syntax notations for a single abstract syntax. But, for our purposes, only a single abstract syntax/transfer syntax pair is of interest: ASN.1 is used as the machine-independent language for data structures, and the *Basic Encoding Rules* (BER) are used as the encoding rules.

soap...

The *official* reason for using ASN.1 was to ease the eventual transition to OSI-based network management protocols. The *actual* reason is that the Internet research community got caught napping on this one, having never spent much time dealing with application-layer structuring. This is particularly humorous since ASN.1 can trace its roots back to a decade-earlier research project staffed by some of the Internet researchers! Because it fills a "well-needed gap", ASN.1 is destined, for better or worse, to become the network programming language of the 90's, just as the *C* programming language is largely seen as having been the systems programming language of the 80's.

...soap

So, the choice of ASN.1 is arguably a good one.

ASN.1 is a *formal* language, which means that it is defined in terms of a *grammar*. The language is defined in [44]. Some extensions to the language were more recently defined in [45].

It is clearly beyond the scope of *The Simple Book* to present a thorough treatment of ASN.1. The reader should consult [46] for a detailed exposition. Thus, the remainder of this chapter will introduce ASN.1 only to the extent that it is used by the management framework.

The management framework uses only a subset of the capabilities of ASN.1. The idea behind this is that whilst the general principles of abstract syntax, as embodied by the ASN.1 language, are good, many of the "bells and whistles" of ASN.1 lead to unnecessary complexity. Referring back to the Fundamental Axiom, prudence dictates using a minimalist approach in order to decrease resource requirements on the managed nodes (in terms of both code size and execution time).

Note that this chapter won't discuss how values are encoded on the network. This is postponed until the actual management protocol is discussed in Section 6.2.2 on page 295.

3.2.1 Modules

A collection of ASN.1 descriptions, relating to a common theme (e.g., a protocol specification), is termed a *module*. The high-level syntax of a module is simple:

```
<<module>> DEFINITIONS ::= BEGIN

<<linkage>>

<<declarations>>

END
```

The `<<module>>` term names the module, both informally and possibly authoritatively (uniquely) as well. Think of the authoritative designation as allowing several modules to be placed in a library and then unambiguously referenced through the `<<linkage>>` term. Thus, modules can **EXPORT** definitions for use by other modules, which in turn **IMPORT** them. Finally, the `<<declarations>>` term contains the actual ASN.1 definitions.

Three kinds of objects are defined using ASN.1:

- *types*, which define new data structures;

- *values*, which are instances (variables) of a type; and,

- *macros*, which are used to change the actual grammar of the ASN.1 language.

Each of these objects is named, using an ASN.1 word; however, ASN.1 uses an alphabetic case convention to indicate the kind of object to which the word refers:

- for a *type*, the word starts with an uppercase letter (e.g., `Gauge`);

- for a *value* (an instance of a type), the word starts with a lowercase letter (e.g., `internet`); and,

- for a *macro*, the word consists entirely of uppercase letters (e.g., `OBJECT-TYPE`).

The keywords of the ASN.1 language appear entirely in uppercase.

Types, values, and macro definitions can be exported from the module which defines them, to be later imported by another module that wants to make use of them. This latter module uses an `IMPORTS` statement which identifies both the module which made the definition, and the corresponding symbol, termed a *descriptor*. Of course, if the same descriptor (having different meanings) is imported from two different modules, there must be a way of resolving this ambiguity. The mechanism is to prefix the descriptor with the name of the appropriate module and a dot, e.g.,

```
module.descriptor
```

As might be expected, within a module, descriptors must be uniquely named.

The management framework places one other restriction on the descriptors which occur within a module. Specifically, a descriptor may not be more than 64 characters in length.

Comments in ASN.1 start with two consecutive dashes ("--") and continue until reaching another two dashes or the end of the line.

3.2.2   Types and Values

An ASN.1 type is defined using a straightforward syntax:

```
NameOfType ::=
    TYPE
```

Similarly, a value (more properly an instance of a data type) is defined as:

```
nameOfValue NameOfType ::=
    VALUE
```

That is, first the variable is named (`nameOfValue`), then it is typed (`NameOfType`), and then a value is assigned.

The management framework uses four kinds of ASN.1 types, which are now discussed in turn.

Simple Types

The simple ASN.1 types used in the management framework are now described:

INTEGER: a data type taking a cardinal number as its value. Note that since ASN.1 is describing a conceptual object, there is no limitation to the bit-level precision that may be required to represent the number. As might be expected, the management framework imposes such a limit.

In addition to defining an integer-valued data type, it is often convenient to associate symbolic names for the values that might be taken on by instances of the data type, e.g.,

```
Status ::=
    INTEGER { up(1), down(2), testing(3) }

myStatus Status ::= up      -- or 1
```

According to ASN.1, any integer-valued quantity may be assigned to `myStatus`. However, the management framework has a rule that if symbolic names for an integer-valued data type are enumerated, then only those values are valid for instances of that data type.

BIT STRING: a data type taking zero or more named bits as its value, e.g.,

```
Access ::=
    BIT STRING { read(0), write(1) }

myAccess Access ::= { read, write }   -- or '11'B
```

OCTET STRING: a data type taking zero or more octets as its value. Each byte in an octet string may take any value from 0 to 255.

OBJECT IDENTIFIER: a data type referring to an authoritative designation. This data type has such complicated (and important) semantics that it is discussed in length at the end of this section, starting on page 86.

NULL: a data type acting as a place holder.

Constructed Types

The constructed ASN.1 types used in the management framework are:

SEQUENCE: a data type denoting an ordered list of zero or more *elements*, which are other ASN.1 types. This is similar to a "structure" in most programming languages.

SEQUENCE OF TYPE: a data type denoting an ordered list of zero or more elements of the same ASN.1 type. This is analogous to the dynamic array in many programming languages: the number of elements isn't usually known until the array is created, but each element has identical syntax.

Tagged Types

In addition to using constructed types, ASN.1 provides a means for defining new types by "tagging" a previously defined type. The new and old types are distinguishable by having different tags, but they refer to the same conceptualization.

ASN.1 defines four kinds of tags, based on the identification requirements of the applications programmer:

1. The identification must be globally unique. These data types use *universal* tags. Such a tag may be defined only in the ASN.1 document or its addenda. These provide the well-known data types that have been introduced thus far. These data types, and their tags, are shown in Table 3.1.

2. The identification must be unique within a given ASN.1 module. These data types use *application-wide* tags. In any particular ASN.1 module, only one data type may be defined that uses such a tag.

3. The identification must be unique in order to satisfy a constructor type, such as a **SEQUENCE** or a **CHOICE**. In cases such as these, *context-specific* tags are used. These tags have no meaning outside of the ASN.1 type in which they are used.

Universal Tag	ASN.1 Type
1	**BOOLEAN**
2	**INTEGER**
3	**BIT STRING**
4	**OCTET STRING**
5	**NULL**
6	**OBJECT IDENTIFIER**
7	**ObjectDescriptor**
8	**EXTERNAL**
9	**REAL**
10	**ENUMERATED**
12–15	Reserved
16	**SEQUENCE, SEQUENCE OF**
17	**SET, SET OF**
18	**NumericString**
19	**PrintableString**
20	**TeletexString**
21	**VideotexString**
22	**IA5String**
23	**UTCTime**
24	**GeneralizedType**
25	**GraphicsString**
26	**VisibleString**
27	**GeneralString**
28	**CharacterString**
29–...	Reserved

Table 3.1: ASN.1 Universal Tags

4. The identification must be unique within a given enterprise, as provided by bilateral agreement. A *private-use* tag is used for these purposes.

All tags consist of a class (one of the four just introduced) and a non-negative integer. Thus, several application-wide tags might be defined in a module, each with a different number. The ASN.1 syntax used to convey the tagging information for cases 1, 2, and 4 is straightforward: when defining a data type, after entering the name and the : := symbol, the tag is entered using the [...] notation, e.g.,

```
Opaque ::=
    [APPLICATION 4]
        IMPLICIT OCTET STRING
```

To define a data type with a context-specific tag, the tag is entered using the [...] notation, but without a label, e.g.,

```
GetRequest-PDU ::=
    [0]
        IMPLICIT PDU
```

On a conceptual level, tagging a data type results in "wrapping" the existing data type, tag and all, inside a new data type. This is necessary to tell what kind of data type is really being used. If this knowledge can be derived by other means, e.g., hard-wired into the management framework, then this wrapping is unnecessary. The IMPLICIT keyword is used to denote this, as shown in the example above. (If this seems a bit vaque, don't worry — on page 307 we'll cover the details.)

Subtypes

In addition to tagging a data type to duplicate the semantics of a data object, it is also useful to refine the semantics. For example, earlier it was observed how each octet in an OCTET STRING carried a value from 0 to 255. It may be useful to create a new data type for strings using other repertoires, such as ASCII. A useful extension defined for ASN.1 is that of *subtyping*, which allows the ASN.1 programmer to make these refinements.

The ASN.1 rules for subtyping are long and complex. Instead of discussing all the details, let us look at two representative examples:

```
IpAddress ::=            -- in network-byte order
    [APPLICATION 0]
        IMPLICIT OCTET STRING (SIZE (4))


Counter32 ::=
    [APPLICATION 1]
        IMPLICIT INTEGER (0..4294967295)
```

In the first example, a new data type, **IpAddress**, which contains a string of octets is defined. Although no requirements are made on the value of each octet, the length of the string is exactly 4. Appearing with the definition is a comment indicating how an IP address is represented within the string of octets. In the second example, a new integer-valued data type, **Counter32**, is defined. Instances of this data type may take on any non-negative value less than 2^{32}.

3.2.3 Macros

Although it is beyond the scope of *The Simple Book* to discuss how an ASN.1 macro is defined, for now note that an ASN.1 macro is invoked using a straightforward syntax:

```
nameOfValue MACRO
    <<clauses>>
    ::= VALUE
```

where **MACRO** is the name of the macro being invoked, and **<<clauses>>** and **VALUE** depend on the definition of the macro.

Do not worry about this rather vague description — in the next chapter, we'll look at all the macros defined and used in the SNMPv2 framework.

3.2.4   OBJECT IDENTIFIERs

An OBJECT IDENTIFIER is a data type denoting an authoritatively named object. OBJECT IDENTIFIERs provide a means for identifying something, regardless of the semantics associated with that object (e.g., a standards document, an ASN.1 module, and so on).

An OBJECT IDENTIFIER is a sequence of non-negative integer values that traverse a tree. The tree consists of a *root* connected to a number of labeled *nodes* via edges. Each label consists of a non-negative integer value and possibly a brief textual description. Each node may, in turn, have children nodes of its own, termed *subordinates* or *sub-identifiers*, which are also labeled. This process may continue to an arbitrary level of depth. Central to the notion of the OBJECT IDENTIFIER is the understanding that administrative control of the meanings assigned to the nodes may be delegated as one traverses the tree.

When describing an OBJECT IDENTIFIER there are several formats that may be used. The most concise textual format is to list the integer values found by traversing the tree, starting at the root and proceeding to the object in question. The integer values are separated with a dot.[3] Thus,

        1.0.8571.5.1

identifies the object found by starting at the root, moving to the subordinate node with label 1, then moving to the node with label 0, and so on. The node found after traversing this list is the one being identified.

The root node has three subordinates:

- ccitt(0), which is administered by the International Telegraph and Telephone Consultative Committee (CCITT);

- iso(1), which is administered by the International Organization for Standardization and International Electrotechnical Committee (ISO/IEC); and,

---

[3]The reader shouldn't confuse the OBJECT IDENTIFIER notation with the conventions used for writing IP addresses.

- `joint-iso-ccitt(2)`, which is jointly administered by ISO/IEC and CCITT.

Thus, at the first cut, the naming tree looks like this:

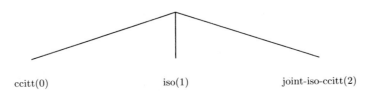

and, the administrative authority for each node is free to assign further subordinate nodes and optionally to delegate authority to others to name objects under those nodes.

In the context of the management framework, only the `iso(1)` subtree is of interest. ISO/IEC has defined four subordinates:

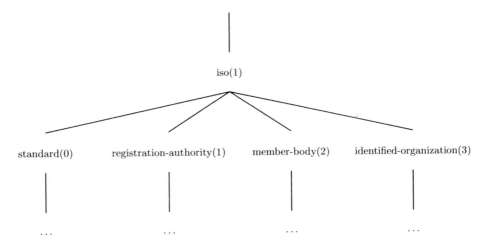

These are:

- `standard(0)`, which has a subordinate assigned to each International Standard. For example, the OSI file service, FTAM, is International Standard 8571. Thus, when FTAM defines objects, these start with the prefix `1.0.8571`. Each standard is then responsible for the naming hierarchy used under its assigned prefix.

- `registration-authority(1)`, which is reserved for use by OSI registration authorities, as they are created.

- `member-body(2)`, which has a subordinate assigned to each member body of ISO/IEC. The value of the label assigned to each node is a *decimal country code* (DCC). Each member body is then responsible for further organization of its respective naming space.

- `identified-organization(3)`, which has a subordinate assigned to any organization that ISO/IEC wishes to favor. This permits a way for any organization to name objects (even proprietary objects) without fear of collisions in the naming hierarchy.

Finally, joint committees of ISO/IEC and CCITT delegate naming authority under the `joint-iso-ccitt(2)` tree.

The `OBJECT IDENTIFIER` syntax is straightforward:

```
Document-Type-Name ::=
    OBJECT IDENTIFIER

ftam-1 Document-Type-Name ::=
    { 1 0 8571 5 1 }
```

In this example, the value declaration shows only the numeric values of the nodes. The textual values may also be used:

```
fTAM-1 Document-Type-Name ::=
    { iso standard 8571 5 1 }
```

In order to promote readability, but not risk ambiguity, these two forms can be combined, as in

```
fTAM-1 Document-Type-Name ::=
    { iso(1) standard(0) 8571 5 1 }
```

or

```
internet OBJECT IDENTIFIER ::= { iso org(3) dod(6) 1 }
directory OBJECT IDENTIFIER ::= { internet 1 }
```

3.2.5 Does Simplicity Cost?

As evidenced throughout this section, only a small subset of the ASN.1 syntax is used in the management framework. For example, a cursory comparison with Table 3.1 on page 83 shows the following data types not allowed by the framework:

```
BOOLEAN
ObjectDescriptor
EXTERNAL
REAL
ENUMERATED
SET
SET OF
```

along with over 10 refinements to the `OCTET STRING` data type. Are these serious restrictions?

In a word: *no*. At the risk of starting a soapbox, consider: one could argue that the basic data structures of computing are numbers, byte strings, and structures. One can easily emulate the semantics of the unsupported ASN.1 data types above using only

```
INTEGER
OCTET STRING
SEQUENCE
SEQUENCE OF
```

For example, a `BOOLEAN` can be represented by an `INTEGER` taking the value zero (for false) and non-zero (for true).

So, what do all these data types buy you? Primarily, they buy completeness in the language. They achieve elegance. But, there is also a cost. Adding support for another dozen data types, or worse yet, for arbitrary data types, has substantive cost, both in terms of program development, code size, and execution time. Falling back on the Fundamental Axiom, it seems wise to vastly restrict the data types supported by the framework so as to minimize the impact on managed nodes.

Interestingly enough, in the Internet-standard Network Management Framework, the enumerated `BIT STRING` data type was not allowed, as it could usually be represented by an **INTEGER** sum. However, experience in writing MIB modules showed this to be expensive in terms of human resources. It turned out to be fairly costly to educate engineers as to what the intent was! So, in the SNMPv2 framework, this restriction was relaxed.

RFC	Name	Chapter
1441	Introduction to SNMPv2	3
1442	SMI for SNMPv2	4
1443	Textual Conventions for SNMPv2	4
1444	Conformance Statements for SNMPv2	4
1445	Administrative Model for SNMPv2	5
1446	Security Protocols for SNMPv2	5
1447	Party MIB for SNMPv2	5, 6
1448	Protocol Operations for SNMPv2	6
1449	Transport Mappings for SNMPv2	6
1450	MIB for SNMPv2	4, 5, 6
1451	Manager-to-Manager MIB	6
1452	Coexistence between SNMPv1 and SNMPv2	4, 6

Table 3.2: Components of the Framework

3.3 Components of the Framework

Table 3.2 shows the components of the SNMPv2 framework, and identifies the chapters in *The Simple Book* which discuss the components in considerable detail. Believe it or not, in this chapter, we have briefly touched on the primary issues involved with each component!

Chapter 4

Information Model

It is now time to examine the role of management information in the management framework. Discussion is divided into five parts:

- the rules for defining management information;

- several examples of existing collections of definitions;

- the rules for defining conformance requirements;

- how these facilities are accessed when defining management information; and,

- coexistence between the original framework and the SNMPv2 framework.

Before starting, however, we need to discuss one small matter of terminology: it is now time to clarify the relationship between variables, objects, and object types. The terms *object* and *object type* are used in both the original and SNMPv2 management frameworks as a means of object-oriented expression: that is, a management object has associated with it a syntax and semantics which are purposefully abstract. In contrast, a *variable* refers to a particular instance of a particular object. The term more commonly used for this is *object instance*, since this conveys the desired meaning and isn't easily confused with programmatic terminology.

4.1   Structure of Management Information

The *Structure of Management Information* (SMI) defines the rules for describing management information. Specifically, its job is to allow management information to be described in such a way as to be largely independent of the implementation "details".

If one views the collection of managed objects as residing in a virtual store, such as a database, the SMI defines the *schema* for that database. In fact, there is a precise name for this database; it is called the *Management Information Base* (MIB).

The SMI is defined using ASN.1. Rather than present the entire SMI definition in one figure, we'll gradually introduce it as we consider its different components.

4.1.1   Information Modules

Generally, three different kinds of ASN.1 modules, termed *information modules*, are defined using the SMI:

- *MIB modules*, which define a collection of related managed objects;

- *compliance statements*, which define a set of requirements of managed nodes with respect to one or more MIB modules; and,

- *capability statements*, which describe how well a particular managed node is able to implement the objects defined in one or more MIB modules.

Of course, these functions might be combined into a single module. For example, a committee writing a "standard" information module would include the definition of several managed objects, and perhaps a compliance statement which refers to those objects. Similarly, a vendor writing an "enterprise-specific" information module might include the definition of several proprietary managed objects, and in a product-specific module, provide a capability statement. These capability statements, one for each of the vendor's products, would

---

MODULE-IDENTITY MACRO ::=
BEGIN
  TYPE NOTATION ::=
            `"LAST-UPDATED"` value(Update UTCTime)
            `"ORGANIZATION"` Text
            `"CONTACT-INFO"` Text
            `"DESCRIPTION"` Text
            RevisionPart

  VALUE NOTATION ::=   10
            value(**VALUE OBJECT IDENTIFIER**)

RevisionPart ::=
          Revisions
        | empty
Revisions ::=
          Revision
        | Revisions Revision
Revision ::=
          `"REVISION"` value(Update UTCTime)   20
          `"DESCRIPTION"` Text

−− uses the NVT ASCII character set
Text ::= `""""` string `""""`
−− that's four double−quotes on either side...
END

Figure 4.1: Definition of the MODULE-IDENTITY macro

---

explain how well that particular product realized the MIB modules
that it implemented.

Identifying an Information Module

Each information module must begin with an indication of the module's identity and its revision history. The SMI defines a special macro,
MODULE-IDENTITY, for this purpose. Figure 4.1 shows the definition
of this macro.

The best way to understand the definition is to look at an example of its invocation:

```
snmpMIB MODULE-IDENTITY
    LAST-UPDATED "9303040000Z"
    ORGANIZATION "IETF SNMPv2 Working Group"
    CONTACT-INFO
           "         Marshall T. Rose

               Postal: Dover Beach Consulting, Inc.
                       420 Whisman Court
                       Mountain View, CA  94043-2186
                       US

                  Tel: +1 415 968 1052
                  Fax: +1 415 968 2510

               E-mail: mrose@dbc.mtview.ca.us"
    DESCRIPTION
            "The MIB module for SNMPv2 entities."
    ::= { snmpModules 1 }
```

Recall from the discussion on ASN.1 macros on page 85, that a macro is invoked as:

```
nameOfValue MACRO
    <<clauses>>
    ::= VALUE
```

where `MACRO` is the name of the macro being invoked, and `<<clauses>>` and `VALUE` depend on the definition of the macro. So, the data type "snmpMIB" is being defined to have the value "{ snmpModules 1 }", and everything else appearing in between must be the `<<clauses>>`.

To understand the clauses, let's go through this example step by step. The macro is defined in three parts: a `TYPE NOTATION`, which gives the syntax of the clauses; a `VALUE NOTATION`, which indicates the data type that will be used for the value; and, a collection of auxiliary productions.

The `TYPE NOTATION` for this macro says that four clauses must appear:

```
LAST-UPDATED
ORGANIZATION
CONTACT-INFO
DESCRIPTION
```

The first of these contains a local variable of type `UTCTime`. This is a universal timestamp defined in the ASN.1 standard. In our case,

```
LAST-UPDATED "9303040000Z"
```

refers to Wednesday, December 23rd, 1992, in the morning as the clock strikes midnight. The other three clauses are followed by simple text, which starts and ends with a double-quote ("""). The text can be multi-line, and an ASN.1 comment indicates that the characters are taken from the NVT ASCII repertoire, commonly referred to as US ASCII [47]. Following these four clauses, revision information may be present. Information on each revision consists of two clauses:

```
REVISION
DESCRIPTION
```

where the first clause contains a `UTCTime`, and the second clause contains simple text.

This example illustrates how the ASN.1 macro notation can be used to structure a collection of information related to an object. What it doesn't convey is the semantics associated with that structure. Thus, after using the ASN.1 macro notation to define each macro, the SMI contains a section of text explaining the semantics behind each clause. So, in this case:

LAST-UPDATED: the timestamp when this information module was lasted edited;

ORGANIZATION: contact information for the organization responsible for this information module;

CONTACT-INFO: contact information for the editor of this information module; and,

-- *the path to the root*

internet   **OBJECT IDENTIFIER** ::= { iso 3 6 1 }

directory   **OBJECT IDENTIFIER** ::= { internet 1 }

mgmt   **OBJECT IDENTIFIER** ::= { internet 2 }

experimental   **OBJECT IDENTIFIER** ::= { internet 3 }

private   **OBJECT IDENTIFIER** ::= { internet 4 }
enterprises   **OBJECT IDENTIFIER** ::= { private 1 }

security   **OBJECT IDENTIFIER** ::= { internet 5 }

snmpV2   **OBJECT IDENTIFIER** ::= { internet 6 }

-- *transport domains*
snmpDomains   **OBJECT IDENTIFIER** ::= { snmpV2 1 }

-- *transport proxies*
snmpProxys   **OBJECT IDENTIFIER** ::= { snmpV2 2 }

-- *module identities*
snmpModules   **OBJECT IDENTIFIER** ::= { snmpV2 3 }

Figure 4.2: OBJECT IDENTIFIER prefixes used for management

DESCRIPTION: a textual explanation of this information module.

For our purposes, the only thing left to explain is the significance of the value of an invocation of the `MODULE-IDENTITY` macro. This value, an `OBJECT IDENTIFIER`, is used to unambiguously identify the information module.

Use of **OBJECT IDENTIFIERs**

As noted in Section 3.2.4 on page 86, an `OBJECT IDENTIFIER` is an authoritatively assigned name. As shown in Figure 4.2, the SMI defines the `OBJECT IDENTIFIERs` which are used in the management framework. Let's consider each in turn.

The prefix used in the Internet is:

```
internet       OBJECT IDENTIFIER ::= { iso 3 6 1 }
```

which is concisely written as:

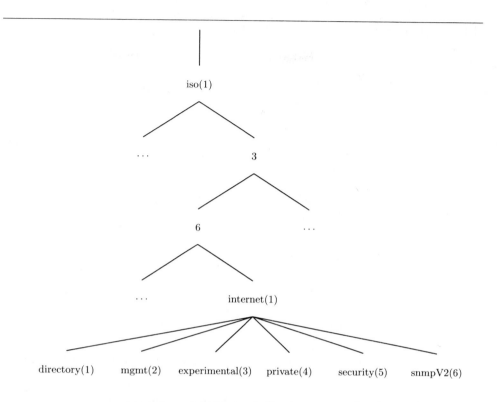

Figure 4.3: OBJECT IDENTIFIER prefix for the Internet

```
1.3.6.1
```

Do not confuse this with the dotted quad notation used to write IP-addresses — for readability purposes, we use dots, rather than spaces, to separate the components in an OBJECT IDENTIFIER.

As shown in Figure 4.3, several nodes have been defined beneath the internet subtree, and four are of interest for management purposes.

The mgmt subtree

Objects defined under the subtree

```
mgmt              OBJECT IDENTIFIER ::= { internet 2 }
```

are registered by the Internet Assigned Numbers Authority:

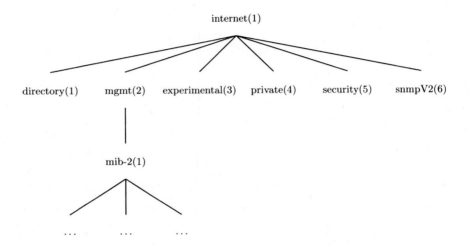

At present, only one subtree is defined, `mib-2(1)`.

The experimental subtree

Objects defined under the subtree

```
experimental OBJECT IDENTIFIER ::= { internet 3 }
```

are registered by the Internet Assigned Numbers Authority:

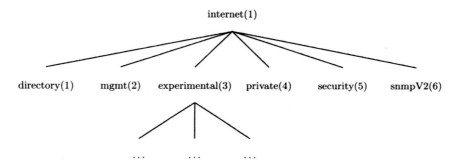

Each management experiment is assigned a new number by the IANA.

The private subtree

Objects defined under the subtree

```
      private      OBJECT IDENTIFIER ::= { internet 4 }
```

are registered by the Internet Assigned Numbers Authority:

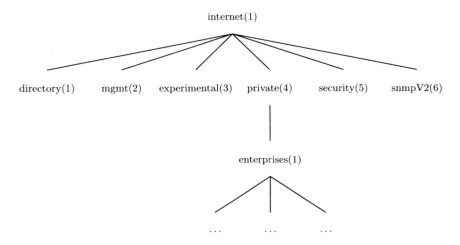

At present, only one subtree is defined, `enterprises(1)`. This is where vendor-specific objects are registered.

The snmpV2 subtree

Finally, the `snmpV2` subtree is used for "house-keeping" purposes in SNMPv2. (A figure isn't shown for this subtree — after three examples, you should have the hang of it by now.)

```
OBJECT-IDENTITY MACRO ::=
BEGIN
  TYPE NOTATION ::=
          "STATUS" Status
          "DESCRIPTION" Text
          ReferPart

  VALUE NOTATION ::=
          value(VALUE OBJECT IDENTIFIER)
                                                              10
  Status ::=
          "current"
        | "obsolete"

  ReferPart ::=
          "REFERENCE" Text
        | empty

  Text ::= """" string """"
END                                                           20
```

Figure 4.4: Definition of the OBJECT-IDENTITY macro

Identifying a Registration Point

Because OBJECT IDENTIFIERs are used so frequently in the SNMPv2 framework, there is another macro which can be used to associate some textual information with an OBJECT IDENTIFIER assignment, the OBJECT-IDENTITY macro. Figure 4.4 shows the definition of this macro.

As can be seen, there are two mandatory clauses and one optional clause when this macro is invoked:

STATUS: a keyword indicating whether this definition is current or obsolete;

DESCRIPTION: a textual explanation of this OBJECT IDENTIFIER assignment; and,

REFERENCE: if this assignment relates to some other OBJECT IDENTIFIER, then this clause is present and includes text which identifies the other assignment.

For example,

```
fizbin69 OBJECT-IDENTITY
    STATUS   current
    DESCRIPTION
            "The authoritative identity of the Fizbin 69
            chipset."
    ::= { fizbinChipSets 1 }
```

might register `fizbin69` in the object tree as referring to a particular chipset offered by a manufacturer. (Although this particular example doesn't use the REFERENCE clause, the next example will.)

Revising an Information Module

As we shall see, information modules are meant to be extensible: we'll be able to add new managed object definitions, and to remove old ones. Nevertheless, it is important to impose a few rules in order to avoid ambiguity.

Consider the skeletal MIB module:

```
SNMPv2-MIB DEFINITIONS ::= BEGIN

snmpMIB MODULE-IDENTITY
    ...
    ::= { snmpModules 1 }


...

END
```

If this module is revised, then it is critically important that neither its label (SNMPv2-MIB), nor its identity ({ snmpModules 1}) be changed. Instead, REVISION information should be added.

When revising the module, new objects can be added or deleted, but under no circumstances can an OBJECT IDENTIFIER be reused. To do so would cause tremendous confusion. Besides, OBJECT IDENT- IFIERs offer the management framework an extensible name space. Because there is no effective limit to the depth of the tree, nor on the magnitude of non-negative integers assigned to labels, an infinite number of names are available for authoritative use.

4.1.2   Object Definitions

Each managed object is described using the **OBJECT-TYPE** macro, the definition of which is shown in Figure 4.5 starting on page 106.

Before describing how this macro is used, consider a simple example:

```
snmpStatsPackets OBJECT-TYPE
    SYNTAX      Counter32
    MAX-ACCESS  read-only
    STATUS      current
    DESCRIPTION
            "The total number of packets received by the
             SNMPv2 entity from the transport service."
    REFERENCE
            "Derived from RFC1213-MIB.snmpInPkts."
    ::= { snmpStats 1 }
```

which describes a managed object called **snmpStatsPackets**. Each "clause" of the **OBJECT-TYPE** macro is now described.

SYNTAX

The syntax for a managed object defines the data type which models the object. According to the macro definition, this is taken from the data type **ObjectSyntax**. Rather than delve into the details, a discussion is postponed for a few pages (until Section 4.1.3 starting on page 110). For now, just think of the syntax as being taken from the ASN.1 subset described earlier in Section 3.2.2 on page 80, with a few restrictions on the use of **SEQUENCE** and **SEQUENCE OF**.

UNITS

If present, this is a textual indication of the units associated with a value of the syntax, e.g., **seconds**. The purpose of this clause is solely to aid the human implementor.

OBJECT-TYPE MACRO ::=
BEGIN
  TYPE NOTATION ::=
          `"SYNTAX"` type(Syntax)
          UnitsPart
          `"MAX-ACCESS"` Access
          `"STATUS"` Status
          `"DESCRIPTION"` Text
          ReferPart
          IndexPart   10
          DefValPart

  VALUE NOTATION ::=
          value(**VALUE** ObjectName)

  UnitsPart ::=
          `"UNITS"` Text
        | empty

  Access ::=   20
          `"not-accessible"`
        | `"read-only"`
        | `"read-write"`
        | `"read-create"`

  Status ::=
          `"current"`
        | `"deprecated"`
        | `"obsolete"`

Figure 4.5: Definition of the OBJECT-TYPE macro

```
ReferPart ::=
        "REFERENCE" Text
      | empty

IndexPart ::=
        "INDEX"    "{" IndexTypes "}"
      | "AUGMENTS" "{" Entry      "}"
      | empty
IndexTypes ::=
        IndexType                                              10
      | IndexTypes "," IndexType

IndexType ::=
        "IMPLIED" Index
      | Index
Index ::=
            -- use the SYNTAX value of the
            -- correspondent OBJECT-TYPE invocation
        value(Indexobject ObjectName)
Entry ::=                                                     20
            -- use the INDEX value of the
            -- correspondent OBJECT-TYPE invocation
        value(Entryobject ObjectName)

DefValPart ::=
        "DEFVAL" "{" value(Defval Syntax) "}"
      | empty

-- uses the NVT ASCII character set
Text ::= """" string """"                                     30
END


ObjectName ::=
OBJECT IDENTIFIER
```

Figure 4.5: Definition of the OBJECT-TYPE macro (cont.)

MAX-ACCESS

The `MAX-ACCESS` clause defines the level of access that makes "protocol sense" for the managed object, from highest to lowest, one of:

- `read-create`, indicating that instances of the object may be read, written, and created;

- `read-write`, indicating that instances of the object may be read or written, but not created;

- `read-only`, indicating that instances of the object may be read, but not written or created; or,

- `not-accessible`, indicating that instances of the object may not be directly read, written, or created.

This level of access is the intended maximum. Note that other factors, such as the inability of an agent to set new values, or the access control policy, may result in the actual level of access being different.

STATUS

The status of this managed object definition, one of:

- `current`, indicating that the definition is current;

- `deprecated`, indicating that the definition will soon be made obsolete and need no longer be implemented; or,

- `obsolete`, indicating that managed nodes shouldn't implement this object.

DESCRIPTION

A textual description of the managed object. This is where all of the semantics of the managed object are detailed.

REFERENCE

If this managed object is somehow derived from another managed object, then this clause is present and includes text which identifies the other managed object.

INDEX/AUGMENTS

These clauses (which are mutually exclusive) indicate how instances of the object are identified. We'll postpone discussion of this for a few pages (until Section 4.1.7 starting on page 128).

DEFVAL

If this clause is present, it gives advice to the agent implementor as to the initial default value to be used when creating an instance of this managed object. In addition, this clause is also useful as an example data value so that implementors can better understand the object.

4.1.3   Object Syntax

Earlier it was noted that managed objects have a syntax defined by the ASN.1 data type called `ObjectSyntax`. As shown in Figure 4.6, this is defined as a `CHOICE` in the ASN.1 language, meaning that the actual type can be one of any of the types defined in the `CHOICE`.

There are three kinds:

- *simple*, which refers to the four primitive ASN.1 types described earlier in Section 3.2.2 on page 80;

- *application-wide*, which refers to special data types defined by the SMI; or,

- *simply constructed*, which refers to the two constructed ASN.1 types described earlier in Section 3.2.2.

Each is now described in turn.

Simple Types

As shown in Figure 4.6, the four simple types are:

```
INTEGER
OCTET STRING
OBJECT IDENTIFIER
BIT STRING
```

The only tricky part is that the SMI "redefines" the `INTEGER` data type to refer to a quantity which can be represented in 32 bits using two's-complement arithmetic. Although ASN.1's `INTEGER` can have arbitrary precision, when using the management framework, it has bounded precision. In order to reinforce this, the data type `Integer32` is defined.

The SMI also places a limit on the width and depth that an `OBJECT IDENTIFIER` may take:

- there may be at most 128 sub-identifiers; and,

- each sub-identifier must be in the range $[0,\ 2^{32} - 1]$.

```
-- syntax of objects

ObjectSyntax ::=
    CHOICE {
        simple
            SimpleSyntax,

            -- note that SEQUENCEs for conceptual tables and
            -- rows are not mentioned here...                          10

        application-wide
            ApplicationSyntax
    }


-- built-in ASN.1 types

SimpleSyntax ::=
    CHOICE {
        -- INTEGERs with a more restrictive range                     20
        -- may also be used
        integer-value
            INTEGER (-2147483648..2147483647),

        string-value
            OCTET STRING,

        objectID-value
            OBJECT IDENTIFIER,
                                                                       30
        -- only the enumerated form is allowed
        bit-value
            BIT STRING
    }

-- indistinguishable from INTEGER, but never needs more than
-- 32-bits for a two's complement representation
Integer32 ::=
    [UNIVERSAL 2]
        IMPLICIT INTEGER (-2147483648..2147483647)            · 40
```

Figure 4.6: Definition of the Simple Types

Application-Wide

Figure 4.7 starting on page 113 shows the new data types defined by the SMI.

These new data types are:

IpAddress: a data type representing an IP address:

```
IpAddress ::=               -- in network byte order
    [APPLICATION 0]
        IMPLICIT OCTET STRING (SIZE (4))
```

Counter32: a data type representing a non-negative integer, which monotonically increases until it reaches a maximum value $(2^{32} - 1)$, when it wraps back to zero:

```
Counter32 ::=
    [APPLICATION 1]
        IMPLICIT INTEGER (0..4294967295)
```

In order to "make sense" of such an object, you must sample two values. The delta between the values has meaning — any one value has no meaning. By dividing the delta by the time-interval between samples, one can calculate a rate with respect to the managed object. It is important that objects having this syntax don't have arbitrary discontinuities introduced, thus the `MAX-ACCESS` of these objects is `read-only` — the agent, and only the agent, is responsible for maintaining the value of such objects.

Gauge32: a data type representing a non-negative integer, which may increase or decrease, but which may never exceed a maximum value $(2^{32} - 1)$:

```
Gauge32 ::=
    [APPLICATION 2]
        IMPLICIT INTEGER (0..4294967295)
```

If the value of this object ever exceeds $2^{32} - 1$ then this maximum value will be returned by the agent; if the value later drops beneath $2^{32} - 1$, then the actual value will be returned.

-- *application--wide types*

ApplicationSyntax ::=
    CHOICE {
        ipAddress--value
            IpAddress,

        counter--value
            Counter32,

        gauge--value
            Gauge32,

        timeticks--value
            TimeTicks,

        arbitrary--value
            Opaque,

        nsapAddress--value
            NsapAddress,

        big--counter--value
            Counter64,

        unsigned--integer--value
            UInteger32
    }

10

20

Figure 4.7: Definition of the Application-wide Types

```
-- in network-byte order
-- (this is a tagged type for historical reasons)
IpAddress ::=
    [APPLICATION 0]
        IMPLICIT OCTET STRING (SIZE (4))

-- this wraps
Counter32 ::=
    [APPLICATION 1]
        IMPLICIT INTEGER (0..4294967295)                          10

-- this doesn't wrap
Gauge32 ::=
    [APPLICATION 2]
        IMPLICIT INTEGER (0..4294967295)

-- hundredths of seconds since an epoch
TimeTicks ::=
    [APPLICATION 3]
        IMPLICIT INTEGER (0..4294967295)                          20

-- for backward-compatibility only
Opaque ::=
    [APPLICATION 4]
        IMPLICIT OCTET STRING

-- for OSI NSAP addresses
-- (this is a tagged type for historical reasons)
NsapAddress ::=
    [APPLICATION 5]
        IMPLICIT OCTET STRING (SIZE (1 | 4..21))                  30

-- for counters that wrap in less than one hour with only 32 bits
Counter64 ::=
    [APPLICATION 6]
        IMPLICIT INTEGER (0..18446744073709551615)

-- an unsigned 32-bit quantity
UInteger32 ::=
    [APPLICATION 7]
        IMPLICIT INTEGER (0..4294967295)                          40
```

Figure 4.7: Definition of the Application-wide Types (cont).

TimeTicks: a data type representing a non-negative integer, which counts the time in hundredths of a second since some epoch, modulo $2^{32} - 1$:

```
TimeTicks ::=
    [APPLICATION 3]
        IMPLICIT INTEGER (0..4294967295)
```

The definition of each object with a syntax of `TimeTicks` must identify the corresponding epoch.

Opaque: a data type representing an arbitrary encoding:

```
Opaque ::=              -- arbitrary ASN.1 value,
    [APPLICATION 4]     -- "double-wrapped"
        IMPLICIT OCTET STRING
```

This data type is used as an escape mechanism, to bypass the limitations of the restrictive data typing used by the SMI, and is included only for compatibility with the original framework. An instance of an arbitrary ASN.1 data type is encoded using the *Basic Encoding Rules* (described in Section 6.2.2 on page 295). The resultant string of octets forms the value for the `Opaque` type.

It is important to appreciate that such a scheme works only with bilateral agreement between the managed node and the management station, as the only requirement placed on either device is the ability to recognize and accept opaquely-encoded data. A device needn't be able to unwrap the data and interpret the contents.

NsapAddress: a data type representing an OSI network address (NSAP) [48]:

```
NsapAddress ::=
    [APPLICATION 5]
        IMPLICIT OCTET STRING (SIZE (1 | 4..21))
```

The first octet of the octet string indicates the length of the NSAP which follows, from three to twenty octets. In addition, some objects use a zero-length NSAP to refer to a "default" address.

Counter64: a data type used only when a `Counter32` would wrap in less than one hour.

```
Counter64 ::=
    [APPLICATION 6]
        IMPLICIT INTEGER (0..18446744073709551615)
```

Objects having this data type wrap after reaching $2^{64} - 1$. It is important that objects having this syntax don't have arbitrary discontinuities introduced, therefore, the `MAX-ACCESS` of these objects is `read-only`.

UInteger32: a data type equivalent to 32–bits of unsigned precision.

```
UInteger32 ::=
    [APPLICATION 7]
        IMPLICIT INTEGER (0..4294967295)
```

This data type is used when an `Integer32` would be inappropriate (i.e., when up to 32–bits of precision are needed, but the values are always non-negative).

Simply Constructed

The SMI defines two kinds of constructed types. Both are purposely limited in scope.

row: a data type of the form

```
<row> ::=
    SEQUENCE {
        <type1>,
        ...
        <typeN>
    }
```

in which each `<type>` resolves to a primitive type (simple or application-wide). These are used to form a row in a table. Whilst ASN.1 allows some or all of the elements in a `SEQUENCE` to be `OPTIONAL`, this isn't allowed by the SMI.

table: a data type of the form

```
<table> ::=
    SEQUENCE OF
        <row>
```

It should be clear from the above that all tables defined in the management framework are two-dimensional in nature: a table, when fully instantiated, consists of zero or more rows, each row having the same number of columns. Once again, this seemingly strange restriction is motivated by the Fundamental Axiom.

Of course, two-dimensional tables are not limiting — one can emulate an n-dimensional table by having $n - 1$ indexing columns (a subject discussed momentarily in Section 4.1.7).

```
TEXTUAL-CONVENTION MACRO ::=
BEGIN
  TYPE NOTATION ::=
          DisplayPart
          "STATUS" Status
          "DESCRIPTION" Text
          ReferPart
          "SYNTAX" type(Syntax)

  VALUE NOTATION ::=
          value(VALUE Syntax)

DisplayPart ::=
          "DISPLAY-HINT" Text
        | empty

Status ::=
          "current"
        | "deprecated"
        | "obsolete"

ReferPart ::=
          "REFERENCE" Text
        | empty

-- uses the NVT ASCII character set
Text ::= """" string """"
END
```
                                                                              10

                                                                              20

Figure 4.8: Definition of the TEXTUAL-CONVENTION macro

4.1.4   Textual Conventions

Although the application-wide types defined in the SMI are useful, experience in writing MIB modules has shown that it is often useful to define new data types having a similar syntax to the "standard" types, but with more precise semantics. (Further, such new definitions are needed on an ongoing basis more frequently than the SMI can be updated.)

These newly defined types are termed *textual conventions*. Their encoding on the wire is identical to that of the standard types from which they are derived. However, within the MIB module they have special semantics. To capture this, the TEXTUAL-CONVENTION macro, the definition of which is shown in Figure 4.8, is used.

The **TEXTUAL-CONVENTION** macro isn't invoked like any other macro in the SNMPv2 framework. Instead of the usual

```
nameOfValue MACRO
    <<clauses>>
    ::= VALUE
```

the form

```
NameOfType ::= TEXTUAL-CONVENTION
    <<clauses>>
    SYNTAX TYPE
```

is used instead, e.g.,

```
DisplayString ::= TEXTUAL-CONVENTION
    DISPLAY-HINT "255a"
    STATUS        current
    DESCRIPTION
            "Represents textual information taken from
            the NVT ASCII character set, as defined on
            pages 4, 10-11 of RFC 854.  Any object
            defined using this syntax may not exceed
            255 characters in length."
    SYNTAX        OCTET STRING (SIZE (0..255))
```

The reason for this is that a textual convention defines a refinement of a data type, instead of defining a new value.

The clauses in the **TEXTUAL-CONVENTION** macro are:

DISPLAY-HINT: an indication of how an integer- or string-value corresponding to this textual convention might be rendered for display purposes;

STATUS: an indication of the status of this textual convention definition, one of **current**, **deprecated**, or **obsolete**;

DESCRIPTION: a textual explanation of this textual convention;

REFERENCE: if this textual convention is somehow derived from another textual convention, then this clause is present and includes text which identifies the other textual convention; and,

SYNTAX: the syntax associated with the data type.

These clauses are all straightforward with one exception: `DISPLAY-HINT` clause. For integer-values, a hexadecimal, decimal, octal, or binary format may be selected. For string-values, the format indication divides the value into one or more fields, each field containing one or more octets. For each field, a hexadecimal, decimal, octal, or ASCII format may be selected, along with a separator character. This allows complex data types to be encoded as a single string-value. The `DateAndTime` textual convention, described momentarily, will be used to demonstrate this.

Pre-defined Textual Conventions

There are several textual conventions initially defined. We'll look briefly at each, not only to introduce them, but also to give examples of the `DISPLAY-HINT` clause:

DisplayString: an NVT ASCII string of up to 255 characters:

```
OCTET STRING (SIZE (0..255))
```

The associated `DISPLAY-HINT` is `255a`, which is interpreted as: print this value as an ASCII string.

PhysAddress: an arbitrary media address:

```
OCTET STRING
```

The associated `DISPLAY-HINT` is `1x:`, which is interpreted as: print each octet of the value as a hexadecimal number, and separate each value with a colon-character (":"), e.g., `08:00:20:00:38:ba`.

MacAddress: an IEEE 802 media address, represented in canonical order:

```
OCTET STRING (SIZE (6))
```

TruthValue: a boolean value:

```
INTEGER { true(1), false(2) }
```

TestAndIncr: an integer-value used for coarse-coordination between management applications:

```
INTEGER (0..2147483647)
```

When set by the management protocol, the supplied value must be identical to the actual value, or an error occurs. Otherwise, if the set operation succeeds, then the value is incremented by one unless it reaches the maximum value (in which case it wraps back to zero).

AutonomousType: a value which points to an `OBJECT IDENTIFIER` assignment. For example, if a managed object defined the chipset associated with a processor, it might take on a value like `fizbin69`, which was used in an earlier example on page 104.

InstancePointer: an `OBJECT IDENTIFIER`-value which identifies a particular instance of a managed object.

RowStatus: the value used for the status column of a conceptual row:

```
INTEGER {
    active(1), notInService(2), notReady(3),
    createAndGo(4), createAndWait(5),
    destroy(6)
}
```

All discussion of this textual convention is deferred until Section 6.1.4 starting on page 268.

TimeStamp: the time when an event occurred, as measured in `TimeTicks`, from the time that the agent was last re-initialized:

> `TimeTicks`

The object `sysUpTime`, introduced later on page 146, indicates how long ago the agent was last re-initialized.

TimeInterval: the delta between two events, or the value to which a countdown timer is initialized, expressed in hundredths of a second:

> `INTEGER (0..2147483647)`

(Usually, this is the delta of two `TimeTicks` values.)

DateAndTime: a date-time specification:

> `OCTET STRING (SIZE (8 | 11))`

(This is an example of subtyping — it says the string may be either 8 or 11 characters in length.) The associated `DISPLAY-HINT` is

> `2d-1d-1d,1d:1d:1d.1d,1a1d:1d`

which is interpreted as:

> take the first two octets, treat them as an integer expressed in network-byte order, and print them in decimal format followed by a hyphen-character ("-");
>
> print the third octet as a decimal number followed by a hyphen-character ("-");
>
> print the fourth octet as a decimal number followed by a comma-character (",");
>
> and so on.

The DESCRIPTION clause indicates the semantics of each of these fields:

field	octets	contents	range
1	1-2	year	0..65536
2	3	month	1..12
3	4	day	1..31
4	5	hour	0..23
5	6	minutes	0..59
6	7	seconds	0..60
		(use 60 for leap-second)	
7	8	deci-seconds	0..9
8	9	direction from UTC	"+" / "−"
9	10	hours from UTC	0..11
10	11	minutes from UTC	0..59

For example,

```
Tuesday May 26, 1992 at 1:30:15 PM EDT
```

would be encoded as the OCTET STRING

```
'07c8051a0d1e0f002d0400'H
```

which might be displayed as:

```
1992-5-26,13:30:15.0,-4:0
```

Note that if only local time is known, then time-zone information (fields 8-10) isn't present.

object syntax	range	enumeration	size	repertoire
INTEGER	√	√		
Integer32	√			
UInteger32	√			
Gauge32	√			
BIT STRING		√		
OCTET STRING			√	√
IpAddress				
Counter32				
OBJECT IDENTIFIER				
TimeTicks				
NsapAddress				
Counter64				

Table 4.1: Rules for Refining Syntax

4.1.5   Syntax Refinement

When defining the SYNTAX clause of an object type or a textual convention, a "refined" version of ObjectSyntax may be used. A refinement is simply a more restricted form of a data type. Table 4.1 shows the rules for refining an object syntax.

There are four kinds of refinements:

range refinement: which reduces the range of possible values of an integer-valued syntax.

For example, if a textual convention is defined as:

```
TimeInterval ::= TEXTUAL-CONVENTION
...
    SYNTAX INTEGER (0..2147483647)
```

then another textual convention might be defined as:

```
ShortInterval ::= TEXTUAL-CONVENTION
...
    SYNTAX INTEGER (0..65535)
```

Note that the refinement could have been expressed as:

```
SYNTAX TimeInterval (0..65535)
```

enumeration refinement: which reduces the choice of possible values of an integer-valued or bitstring-valued syntax.

For example, if a textual convention is defined as:

```
IfStatus ::= TEXTUAL-CONVENTION
    ...
    SYNTAX INTEGER { up(1), down(2), testing(3) }
```

then another textual convention might be defined as:

```
LimitedIfStatus ::= TEXTUAL-CONVENTION
    ...
    SYNTAX INTEGER { up(1), down(2) }
```

Note that in this case, the refinement may **not** be expressed as:

```
SYNTAX IfStatus { up, down }
```

since the meaning of an enumeration (e.g., **up**) is bound only during the definition of the ASN.1 type (**INTEGER {...}**).

size refinement: which reduces the range of possible sizes of a string-valued syntax, e.g.,

```
SYNTAX OCTET STRING (SIZE (0..255))
```

repertoire refinement: which simplifies the character set used in a string-valued syntax. (This is done by adding text to the **DESCRIPTION** clause of the object's definition.)

It must be emphasized that refinements are used solely to add clarity to the definitions of the values which an object can take. While implementors may infer "storage hints" for the restrictions, this is a side effect, not a goal.

4.1.6   Object Groups

Related objects are defined together into an *object group*. This grouping is performed for two reasons:

- first, to focus the attention of implementors; and,

- second, to provide one means for making `OBJECT IDENTIFIER` assignments to object types.

Let's look at each in turn.

Implementation Focus

Implementation experience with many protocols over the years has shown that optional facilities usually receive poor "overlap of implementation". That is, if two people independently implement a protocol, experience teaches us that the likelihood of both people implementing many of the same optional facilities is quite low. This often results in poor interoperability in fielded products.

So, designers and implementors of MIB modules are encouraged to view an object group as a unit of implementation. In a perfect world, an implementor will code zero or all of the objects contained within the group. (Of course, it isn't a perfect world, and later on in Section 4.3.2 we'll see how deviations from this perspective can be documented.)

Identifying an Object Type

`OBJECT IDENTIFIER` assignments for the object types in a MIB module are made according to this procedure:

1. Object types are placed into object groups.

2. An `OBJECT IDENTIFIER` is assigned to each object group, e.g.,

   ```
   snmpOR       OBJECT IDENTIFIER ::= { snmpMIBObjects 3 }
   ```

   The `OBJECT IDENTIFIER` is subordinate to the one that's used to identify the information module, e.g.,

```
snmpMIB MODULE-IDENTITY
    ...
    ::= { snmpModules 1 }

snmpMIBObjects OBJECT IDENTIFIER ::= { snmpMIB 1 }
```

So, one might reasonably expect that **snmpOR** is the third object group assigned in the MIB module.

3. Non-tabular objects are then assigned an **OBJECT IDENTIFIER** sequentially under that group, e.g.,

```
snmpORLastChange OBJECT-TYPE
    ...
    ::= { snmpOR 1 }
```

4. Tabular objects are also assigned an **OBJECT IDENTIFIER** sequentially under that group, e.g.,

```
snmpORTable OBJECT-TYPE
    SYNTAX SEQUENCE OF SnmpOREntry
    ...
    ::= { snmpOR 2 }
```

(a) The row object is then registered under the tabular object, e.g.,

```
snmpOREntry OBJECT-TYPE
    SYNTAX SnmpOREntry
    ...
    ::= { snmpORTable 1 }
```

(b) Each columnar object is then assigned an **OBJECT IDENT-IFIER** sequentially under that row, e.g.,

```
snmpORIndex OBJECT-TYPE
    ...
    ::= { snmpOREntry 1 }
```

4.1.7   Identifying an Object Instance

It should also be noted that more than just the name of an object is needed in order to access that object on a managed node. Objects, per se, are only templates. It is the *instances* of objects which are manipulated by a management protocol. Hence, in addition to knowing the object name, the *instance-identifier* must also be specified.

In order to provide an efficient means for traversing the management information, the management framework employs a rather clever method for identifying instances: an `OBJECT IDENTIFIER`, formed by concatenating the name of the object type with a suffix, is used. By naming instances using `OBJECT IDENTIFIER`s, a *lexicographic ordering* is enforced over all object instances. This means that, for instance names a and b, one of three conditions consistently holds: either $a < b$, $a = b$, or $a > b$.

The rules for instance identification (determining the suffix) depend on the object type in question. If the object type isn't part of a table, then there is exactly one instance of the object type in a particular device. To identify it, simply append ".0" to the object name. For example, to identify the only instance of `snmpORLastChange`,

```
snmpORLastChange.0
```

is used.

If the object is a part of a table, then there are three possibilities:

- the object type is the table;

- the object type is a row in the table; or,

- the object type defines a column in the row.

The management framework doesn't allow manipulation of aggregate variables — only instances of the columnar objects which form the cells of a table may be manipulated with SNMP. As such, the `MAX-ACCESS` for table- and row-objects is always `not-accessible`.

The INDEX clause

For the columnar objects, there are potentially multiple instances, each corresponding to a cell in a given row in the table. In order to distinguish between different rows, the **INDEX** or **AUGMENTS** clause is used. This clause is found in the object type definition of a row in the table.

For example, consider this skeletal table definition:

```
ifTable OBJECT-TYPE
    SYNTAX SEQUENCE OF IfEntry
    ...
    ::= { interfaces 1 }

ifEntry OBJECT-TYPE
    SYNTAX IfEntry
    ...
    INDEX { ifIndex }
    ::= { ifTable 1 }

IfEntry ::=
    SEQUENCE {
        ifIndex INTEGER,
        ifDescr DisplayString,
        ...
    }

ifIndex OBJECT-TYPE
    SYNTAX INTEGER
    ...
    ::= { ifEntry 1 }

ifDescr OBJECT-TYPE
    SYNTAX DisplayString
    ...
    ::= { ifEntry 2 }


    ...
```

which shows a table with two columns. In this example, the **INDEX** clause says that the value of **ifIndex** uniquely identifies each row in the table. Because **ifIndex** is integer-valued, a single component consisting of the particular integer value of **ifIndex** is appended to the name of the column to form the desired instance. For example,

```
ifDescr.3
```

refers to the value of the `ifDescr` column in the only row in which the `ifIndex` column has the value 3.

The `INDEX` clause identifies one or more objects in order to uniquely identify a particular row. The `OBJECT IDENTIFIER`-fragments associated with each are simply appended onto the desired column's name. To complicate matters, non-integer-valued objects can be used as index objects. The rules are:

integer-valued: a single sub-identifier taking the integer value (only non-negative integers may be used);

string-valued, fixed-length strings: n sub-identifiers, where n is the length of the string (each octet of the string is encoded in a separate sub-identifier);

string-valued, variable-length strings: $n+1$ sub-identifiers, where n is the length of the string (the first octet is n itself; following this, each octet of the string is encoded in a separate sub-identifier); or,

OBJECT IDENTIFIER-valued: $n+1$ sub-identifiers, where n is the number of sub-identifiers in the value (the first octet is n itself; following this, each sub-identifier in the value is copied).

If an object having some other syntax is used as an index, then the appropriate rule above is followed (e.g., if an `IpAddress`-valued object is used for indexing, then the rules for a fixed-length string object are employed).

Let's look at an example. Suppose we have:

```
printQEntry OBJECT-TYPE
    ...
    INDEX { printQName }

printQName OBJECT-TYPE
    SYNTAX DisplayString
    ...
```

```
printQEntries OBJECT-TYPE
    SYNTAX Gauge32
    ...
```

The number of entries in the print queue called "**barney**" is identified by the variable:

```
printQEntries.6.98.97.114.110.101.121
```

Because **printQName** refers to a variable-length string, the first sub-identifier to be added refers to the length of the string (6), and the remaining sub-identifiers each correspond to an octet taken from the string.

This example points out a rather undesirable side effect of the instance-identification rules. Suppose we have two print queues, one named "**barney**" and another named "**fred**". One would expect that the natural ordering of these would be alphabetical, so that the instance of **printQEntries** for "**barney**" would appear before the instance which corresponds to "**fred**". Not so! Because "**fred**" has fewer characters than "**barney**", it occurs earlier in the lexicographic ordering,

$$\text{"fred"} \quad \mapsto \quad .4.102.114.101.100$$
$$\text{"barney"} \quad \mapsto \quad .6.98.97.114.110.101.121$$

To avoid this, a special keyword **IMPLIED** may occur before the last variable-length object (string or **OBJECT IDENTIFIER**) in the **INDEX** clause.[1] For example,

```
printQEntry OBJECT-TYPE
    ...
    INDEX { IMPLIED printQName }
```

which indicates that n sub-identifiers are used, one for each octet or sub-identifier, e.g.,

$$\text{"barney"} \quad \mapsto \quad .98.97.114.110.101.121$$
$$\text{"fred"} \quad \mapsto \quad .102.114.101.100$$

would be the instance-identifiers.

---

[1] There is one exception: the **IMPLIED** keyword may not be used on a variable-length string object if that string might have a value of zero-length.

Auxiliary-objects

Sometimes a column may be placed in a table solely for the purpose of instance-identification. For example, remember `ifIndex` from the example back on page 129? Well, this object is simply an integer which uniquely identifies a given row in `ifTable`. Because auxiliary-objects convey no information by themselves, the **MAX-ACCESS** for auxiliary-objects is `not-accessible`, e.g.,

```
ifIndex OBJECT-TYPE
    SYNTAX      INTEGER
    MAX-ACCESS not-accessible
    ...
    ::= { ifEntry 1 }
```

Note that the value of such an object can be derived from the instance information of an associated object. For example, if the object instance

```
ifDescr.3
```

exists, then, by definition, the value of the `ifIndex` column in that row has the value 3.

The AUGMENTS clause

Sometimes it is useful to define extensions to an existing table. For example, a "standard" MIB module might define a table which describes the TCP connections currently in use on a managed node. That device might have additional information about the TCP connections which isn't present in the standard MIB module. The device's vendor might define that information in an "enterprise-specific" MIB module. The **AUGMENTS** clause is used to provide the linkage between the table in the "standard" MIB module and the vendor-defined table.

For example, consider:

```
unixTcpConnEntry OBJECT-TYPE
    SYNTAX      UnixTcpConnEntry
    MAX-ACCESS not-accessible
    ...
```

```
        AUGMENTS    { tcpConnEntry }
        ::= { unixTcpConnTable 1 }

    unixTcpConnSendQ OBJECT-TYPE
        SYNTAX      INTEGER (0..2147483647)
        ...
        ::= { unixTcpConnEntry 1 }
```

which says that the columns in the **unixTcpConnTable** augment the columns in the **tcpConnTable**, using the same rules for instance identification. Note however, that these new columns aren't named under the **tcpConnTable**; they reside in a different part of the object tree.

The **AUGMENTS** clause is used when one table is a logical extension of another table. Because of this, for each row which is instantiated in the primary table, a corresponding row must be instantiated in the secondary table. If this isn't the case, then an augmentation isn't appropriate. Instead, when defining a secondary table, it is permissible to simply duplicate the **INDEX** clause from the primary table. For example, when defining a table that had information about a specific kind of interface, one could use:

```
    fooEntry OBJECT-TYPE
        SYNTAX FooEntry
        ...
        INDEX { ifIndex }
        ...
```

which indicates that the cells in this table are instantiated using the same semantics as the **ifTable** sketched out earlier. In this example, we would expect that there may be instances in the **ifTable** which have no corresponding instance in the **fooTable**.

```
NOTIFICATION-TYPE MACRO ::=
BEGIN
  TYPE NOTATION ::=
          ObjectsPart
          "STATUS" Status
          "DESCRIPTION" Text
          ReferPart

  VALUE NOTATION ::=
          value(VALUE OBJECT IDENTIFIER)                        10

ObjectsPart ::=
          "OBJECTS" "{" Objects "}"
        | empty
Objects ::=
          Object
        | Objects "," Object
Object ::=
          value(Name ObjectName)
                                                                 20
Status ::=
          "current"
        | "deprecated"
        | "obsolete"

ReferPart ::=
          "REFERENCE" Text
        | empty

  -- uses the NVT ASCII character set                            30
  Text ::= """" string """"
END
```

Figure 4.9: Definition of the NOTIFICATION-TYPE macro

4.1.8   Notification Definitions

In addition to object type definitions, the SMI also allows for the definition of notifications. It turns out that there are two kinds of notifications: *traps*, which are used sparingly by agents to report extraordinary events, and *confirmed events*, which are used by managers when communicating with other managers. The SMI provides the NOTIFICATION-TYPE macro, whose definition is shown in Figure 4.9, to define both kinds of notifications.

The clauses in the NOTIFICATION-TYPE macro are straightforward:

OBJECTS: if present, this identifies one or more objects which are carried in the notification;

STATUS: an indication of the status of this notification definition, one of `current`, `deprecated`, or `obsolete`;

DESCRIPTION: a textual explanation of this notification; and,

REFERENCE: if this notification is somehow derived from another notification, then this clause is present and includes text which identifies the other notification.

A notification is identified by an `OBJECT IDENTIFIER`. Later on, in Section 6.1.5 starting on page 279, we'll see how this can be used when configuring the management applications to which notifications should be sent.

For now, let's just look at a simple example:

```
linkUp NOTIFICATION-TYPE
    OBJECTS { ifIndex }
    STATUS  current
    DESCRIPTION
            "A linkUp trap signifies that the SNMPv2
            entity, acting in an agent role,
            recognizes that one of the communication
            links has come up."
    ::= { snmpTraps 4 }
```

This says that the `linkUp` notification will contain an instance of one object, `ifIndex`, which can be used to determine which interface has suddenly become active.

4.1.9   Revising a MIB Module

Back on page 104, the general rules for revising an information module were given. When the information module contains object types and notification types, there are a few more rules:

Modifying Object Definitions

When modifying an existing object type definition, there are certain changes which may be made without changing the `OBJECT IDENT-IFIER` assignment:

- If the `SYNTAX` clause uses an enumerated integer, e.g.,

    `SYNTAX INTEGER { up(1), down(2) }`

    then additional enumerations may be added, e.g.,

    `SYNTAX INTEGER { up(1), down(2), testing(3) }`

    and the labels associated with existing enumerations may be changed.

- A `UNITS` clause may be added.

- The `STATUS` clause may be changed:

    - from `current` to either `deprecated` or `obsolete`; or,
    - from `deprecated` to `obsolete`.

- A `REFERENCE` clause may be added, or, if present, it may be changed.

- A `DEFVAL` clause may be added, or, if present, it may be changed.

- Finally, changes of an "editorial" nature may be made.

Any other changes require that a new object type be defined with a different `OBJECT IDENTIFIER` assignment. Note that since other information modules may reference object type definitions, if the descriptor (the word to the left of `OBJECT-TYPE`) changes, then the `OBJECT IDENTIFIER` assignment must also change.

Of course, new object type definitions may be made, having new descriptors and different OBJECT IDENTIFIER assignments; and, as expected, new columns can be added to the "right" of a table. But, under no circumstances may an OBJECT IDENTIFIER assignment be reused, even if the old definition has been declared obsolete.

Modifying Notification Definitions

The rules for modifying an existing notification definition are simpler: a REFERENCE clause may be added or changed, but if any other non-editorial change is made, then a new notification type must be defined.

4.1.10   In Perspective

The SNMPv2 framework uses several ASN.1 macros in an effort to allow for concise definitions of information modules. It must be noted, however, that this concise notation is good at capturing only the syntax (or "sugar-coating") of the concepts. The semantics must be conveyed via text. Although a compiler familiar with the SMI can do wonders with the concise definitions, the `DESCRIPTION` clause must still be interpreted by a human, who must be knowledgeable with respect to the functions being managed.

soap...

It should also be noted that, although these macros make it easy to define many managed objects, they can't promote effective management without:

- implementation of the managed objects in agents; and,

- intelligent use of the information in management applications.

Although the next section will demonstrate the success of the SMI as a definition language, interested readers will have to skip to page 376 ...soap to appreciate the irony of this soapbox.

4.2   MIB Modules

We now look at some of the MIB modules which have been defined.

4.2.1   The Different Kinds of MIB Modules

There are three kinds of MIB modules:

standard: These MIB modules are developed by a working group of the IETF and then declared standard by the IESG. The prefix for the `OBJECT IDENTIFIER` assignments for these MIBs is under the `mgmt` subtree, discussed back on page 100.

experimental: While a working group is developing a MIB module, it is assigned a temporary `OBJECT IDENTIFIER` under the `experimental` subtree, discussed back on page 101. If the MIB module ever achieves standardization status, then, when it is placed onto the standards track, it is assigned a new prefix under the `mgmt` subtree. Note that as long as the MIB module is under the `experimental` subtree, it shouldn't be "shipping" as product.

enterprise-specific: The "standard" MIB modules are designed to capture the core aspects of a particular technology, e.g., a "standard" MIB module dealing with routing should list only those objects which are *essential* for managing the routing subsystem. However, individual products may have additional features which also require management. Vendors are strongly encouraged to develop their own product-specific MIBS under the `enterprises` subtree, discussed back on page 102.

Section A.4 on page 392 tells how to find the registry of the various subtree assignments.

Table 4.2 starting on page 140 shows the Internet MIB modules which, as of this writing, are standardized or are approaching standardization. All told, these MIB modules represent over 2000 standard object definitions.

Area	Standard			Exp.	Work in Progress
	Full	Draft	Proposed		
General	MIB-II		DECnet Phase-IV	CLNS	DNS
			AppleTalk®		Host resources
			User Identity		
Media		Ether-like	Interface extensions		PPP
			RMON		Chassis
			802 bridges		MAU
			802.3 repeaters		TRMON
			Token Ring		
			FDDI		
			DS1, DS3		
			SIP, FR-DTE		
			Character (serial, parallel, ports)		
			X.25 (PLP, LAPB)		
Routing			OSPF v2		IS-IS
			BGP v3		IDPR
			RIP v2		IDRP
			IP forwarding		

Table 4.2: Internet MIB Modules

Acronyms	
BGP	Border Gateway Protocol
CLNS	OSI Connectionless-mode Network Service
DNS	Domain Name System
FDDI	Fiber Distributed Data Interface
IDPR	Inter-Domain Policy Routing Protocol
IDRP	ISO Inter-Domain Routing Protocol
IS-IS	OSI Intermediate-System to Intermediate-System Protocol
LAPB	X.25 link layer
MAU	Media Access Unit
OSPF	Open Shortest Path First
PLP	X.25 Packet Layer Protocol
PPP	Point-to-Point Protocol
RIP	Routing Information Protocol
RMON	Remote Network Monitoring
SIP	SMDS Interface Protocol
TRMON	Token Ring RMONn

Table 4.2: Internet MIB Modules (cont.)

4.2.2   The Philosophy of Writing a MIB Module

When writing a MIB module, it is important to remember that new definitions can always be added later. Thus, initially, one should focus on the core aspects. This fosters interoperability and lowers the cost of entry. Because of this, one can learn how the MIB module is used, and this knowledge can be applied when the MIB module is revised.

Consistent with the Fundamental Axiom, the objects defined should have a minimal impact on the critical loop of a device. That is, it is less harmful to count error conditions than good conditions. And this leads us to consider a tool used by some MIB module designers.

Case Diagrams

It is often useful to pictorially represent the relationship between MIB objects in a protocol entity. A useful tool, the *Case Diagram*, was developed for this purpose [49].[2]

When designing a MIB module, it is often considered good practice to avoid defining objects which are derivable from other objects. In the case of objects with a `Counter` syntax, this means that the objects must not be (easily) related arithmetically. Case Diagrams are used to visualize the flow of management information in a layer and thereby mark where counters are incremented. This helps to decide if an object meets the arithmetic-derivability criterion.

Consider an example of a Case Diagram shown in Figure 4.10. According to this diagram, two invariants hold:

- the number of packets received from the layer below is equal to:

$$inErrors + forwPackets + inDelivers$$

- the number of packets sent to the layer below is equal to:

$$outRequests + forwPackets$$

In addition, the diagram also indicates that inErrors is checked before forwPackets, and so on.

---

[2]The term Case Diagram is named after the eminent Professor Case. The term was coined by Craig Partridge, then-chair of the working group which produced MIB-I.

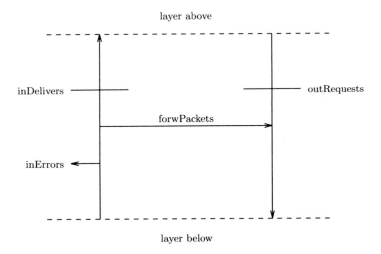

layer above

inDelivers   outRequests

forwPackets

inErrors

layer below

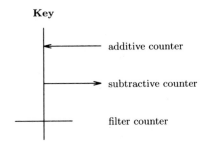

Key

additive counter

subtractive counter

filter counter

Figure 4.10: Example of a Case Diagram

The limitation of Case Diagrams is that they imply a sequential flow. Many error-counting objects can be incremented from anywhere inside a protocol entity. From a visual perspective, however, the error counter is incremented only in one place. Of course, since they are meant to be pictorially simple, they cannot convey any complex semantics. Thus, a Case Diagram is an aid to, not a substitute for, a textual MIB description.

group	no.	objects for
system	7	the managed node itself
interfaces	23	network attachments
at	3	IP address translation
ip	42	the Internet Protocol
icmp	26	the Internet Control Message Protocol
tcp	19	the Transmission Control Protocol
udp	6	the User Datagram Protocol
egp	20	the Exterior Gateway Protocol
transmission	0	used for media-specific MIBs
snmp	29	the Simple Network Management Protocol
total	175	

Table 4.3: The Internet-standard MIB

4.2.3 The Internet-standard MIB

It is now time to present a summary of the objects in the Internet-standard MIB, MIB-II [50]. Table 4.3 summarizes the groups in the Internet-standard MIB. As indicated by its name, this is the first major revision of the Internet-standard MIB. MIB-I [51] was the original Internet-standard MIB. Further, MIB-II was written using the SMI of the original management framework, so some of the object definitions may appear slightly strange. Later on, in Section 4.5 starting on page 186, these differences will be explained.

The System Group

The system group contains generic configuration information:

```
system          OBJECT IDENTIFIER ::= { mib-2 1 }
```

sysDescr: description of device

sysObjectID: identifies the agent's hardware, software, resources, etc.

sysUpTime: how long ago the agent (re-)started

sysContact: name of contact person

sysName: device name

sysLocation: device's physical location

sysServices: services offered by device

Of these, it is perhaps instructive to consider the description of two in greater detail.

The value of the `sysObjectID` object is an `OBJECT IDENTIFIER` that indicates the object resources available in the agent. That is, it is somehow supposed to summarize the particular MIB modules which are implemented by the managed node. In practice, a different `OBJECT IDENTIFIER` value is assigned to each version of each product. In retrospect, perhaps a table of `OBJECT IDENTIFIER` values would have been a better choice. Later on, in Section 4.3.2 starting on page 178, we'll see how the `sysObjectID` object can be used to help tailor a management application's behavior.

The `sysServices` object is a concise means of determining the set of services which corresponds to the device's primary purpose. It is an integer-value, initially zero. Then for each layer, L, in the range 1 through 7, for which the device performs transactions, the number 2^{L-1} is added to the value. For example, a device which performs

only routing functions would have a value of $2^{3-1} = 4$. The layers
are:

layer	functionality	2^{L-1}
1	physical (e.g., repeaters)	1
2	data-link (e.g., bridges)	2
3	internet (e.g., supports IP)	4
4	end-to-end (e.g., supports TCP)	8
7	application (e.g., supports SMTP)	64

Obviously, this object was defined prior to the SNMPv2 framework.
If defined today, the SYNTAX clause would probably be:

```
BIT STRING {
    physical(0), datalink(1), network(2), transport(3),
    session(4), presentation(5), application(6)
}
```

instead of the summed-integer nonsense.

A "dump" of the object instances in the system group might look
like this:

```
sysDescr        "4BSD/ISODE SNMPv2"
sysObjectID     1.3.6.1.4.1.4.1.2.8.6
sysUpTime       22843440
                (2 days, 15 hours, 27 minutes, 14.40 seconds)
sysContact      "Marshall Rose ... <mrose@dbc.mtview.ca.us>"
sysName         dbc.mtview.ca.us
sysLocation     "upstairs machine room"
sysServices     0x48 (transport, application)
```

The Interfaces Group

The interfaces group contains generic information on the entities at
the interface layer, either physical or logical.[3] This group contains two
top-level objects: the number of interface attachments on the device,
and a single table containing information on those interfaces:

```
interfaces    OBJECT IDENTIFIER ::= { mib-2 2 }

ifNumber OBJECT-TYPE
    SYNTAX INTEGER
    ...
    ::= { interfaces 1 }

ifTable OBJECT-TYPE
    SYNTAX SEQUENCE OF IfEntry
    ...
    ::= { interfaces 2 }

ifEntry OBJECT-TYPE
    SYNTAX IfEntry
    ...
    INDEX { ifIndex }
    ::= { ifTable 1 }
```

Each row of the table contains several columns:

ifIndex: interface number

ifDescr: description of the interface

ifType: type of interface

ifMtu: MTU size

ifSpeed: transmission rate in bits/second

ifPhysAddress: media-specific address

---

[3]It is widely agreed that the interfaces group is poorly-defined because it doesn't
accommodate relationships between interfaces. Thus, at some time in the future, a
new model will likely be proposed for standardization.

ifAdminStatus: desired interface state

ifOperStatus: current interface state

ifLastChange: the time when the interface last changed state

ifInOctets: total octets received from the media

ifInUcastPkts: unicast packets delivered above

ifInNUcastPkts: broadcast/multicast packets delivered above

ifInDiscards: packets discarded due to resource limitations

ifInErrors: packets discarded due to any error

ifInUnknownProtos: packets destined for unknown protocols

ifOutOctets: total octets sent on the media

ifOutUcastPkts: unicast packets from above

ifOutNUcastPkts: broadcast/multicast packets from above

ifOutDiscards: packets discarded due to resource limitations

ifOutErrors: packets discarded due to error

ifOutQLen: size of output packet queue

ifSpecific: media-specific MIB pointer

All of these objects are generic in that they apply to all interfaces regardless of the interface type. Support for interface type-specific objects is possible by using the `ifSpecific` object as a "pointer" to some interface-specific MIB.

The `ifAdminStatus` object is a means for conveying an imperative action to the agent. For example, if the value is changed from **down** to **up**, the agent understands this to mean that the interface should be initialized and brought into the ready state, if possible.

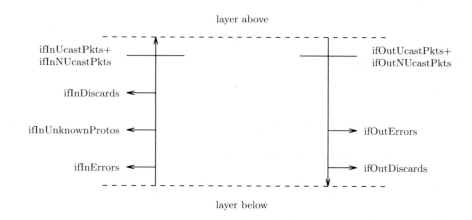

Figure 4.11: Case Diagram for the Interfaces Group

Figure 4.11 shows a Case Diagram relating many of the objects in the interfaces group.

A "dump" of the object instances in the row corresponding to the first interface on the managed node might look like this:

```
ifIndex          1
ifDescr          "le0"
ifType           6 (ethernet-csmacd)
ifMtu            1500
ifSpeed          10000000
ifPhysAddress    08:00:20:00:38:ba
ifAdminStatus    1 (up)
ifOperStatus     1 (up)
ifInUcastPkts    986357
ifInErrors       94
ifOutUcastPkts   887098
ifOutDiscards    0
ifOutErrors      0
ifOutQLen        0
ifSpecific       0.0
```

Note that not all of the columns defined earlier are present. This is because it is simply not possible for some implementations to support those objects. In this case, the correct behavior is for the managed node to consider those variables as having a *not-accessible* level of access. Under no circumstances, should a managed node make up values for objects which it doesn't implement! Instead, SNMP provides a well-defined set of exceptions that can be returned to inform the management application that the agent "just doesn't know".

The Address Translation Group

The address translation group contains address resolution information. In fact, the group contains a single table used for mapping IP addresses into media-specific addresses:

```
at                OBJECT IDENTIFIER ::= { mib-2 3 }

atTable OBJECT-TYPE
    SYNTAX SEQUENCE OF AtEntry
    ...
    ::= { at 1 }

atEntry OBJECT-TYPE
    SYNTAX AtEntry
    ...
    INDEX { atIfIndex, atNetAddress }
    ::= { atTable 1 }
```

Each row of the table contains three columns:

atIfIndex: interface number

atPhysAddress: media address of mapping

atNetAddress: IP address of mapping

The address translation group is marked *deprecated*, as information on address resolution was moved (in the evolution of MIB-I to MIB-II) to each network protocol group (e.g., the IP group).

The IP Group

The IP group contains information about the IP subsystem of a managed node. The group contains several scalars and four tables.

```
ip              OBJECT IDENTIFIER ::= { mib-2 4 }
```

The scalars are:

ipForwarding: acting as a router or a host

ipDefaultTTL: default TTL for IP packets

ipInReceives: total datagrams from below

ipInHdrErrors: datagrams discarded due to format error

ipInAddrErrors: datagrams discarded due to misdelivery

ipForwDatagrams: datagrams forwarded

ipInUnknownProtos: datagrams for unknown protocols

ipInDiscards: datagrams discarded due to resource limitations

ipInDelivers: datagrams delivered above

ipOutRequests: datagrams from above

ipOutDiscards: datagrams discarded due to lack of resource

ipOutNoRoutes: datagrams discarded due to no route

ipReasmTimeout: timeout value for reassembly queue

ipReasmReqds: fragments received needing reassembly

ipReasmOKs: datagrams successfully reassembled

ipReasmFails: reassembly failures

ipFragOKs: datagrams successfully fragmented

ipFragFails: datagrams needing fragmentation when not allowed

ipFragCreates: fragments created

Figure 4.12 shows a Case Diagram relating many of these objects.

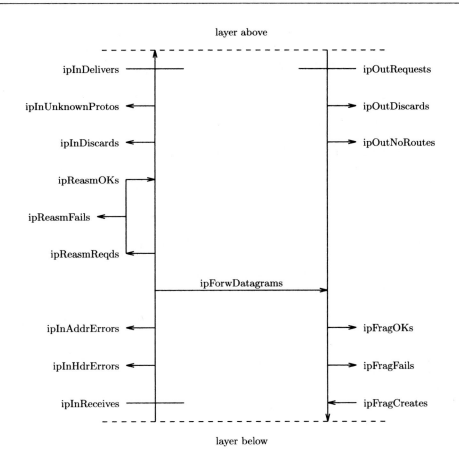

Figure 4.12: Case Diagram for the IP Group

The IP address table keeps track of the IP addresses associated with the managed node:

```
ipAddrTable OBJECT-TYPE
    SYNTAX SEQUENCE OF IpAddrEntry
    ...
    ::= { ip 20 }

ipAddrEntry OBJECT-TYPE
    SYNTAX IpAddrEntry
    ...
    INDEX { ipAdEntAddr }
    ::= { ipAddrTable 1 }
```

Each row of the table contains several columns:

ipAdEntAddr: the IP address of this entry

ipAdEntIfIndex: interface number

ipAdEntNetMask: subnet-mask for IP address

ipAdEntBcastAddr: the least significant bit of IP broadcast address

ipAdEntReasmMaxSize: the largest IP datagram that can be reassembled

A "dump" of the object instances in a row of this table might look like this:

```
ipAdEntAddr           192.33.4.20
ipAdEntIfIndex        1
ipAdEntNetMask        255.255.255.0
ipAdEntBcastAddr      1
ipAdEntReasmMaxSize   65535
```

The IP routing table keeps track of the IP routes associated with the managed node (but has subsequently been obsoleted by a new table discussed in Section 4.2.4 starting on page 165):

```
ipRoutingTable OBJECT-TYPE
    SYNTAX SEQUENCE OF IpRoutingEntry
    ...
    ::= { ip 21 }

ipRouteEntry OBJECT-TYPE
    SYNTAX IpRouteEntry
    ...
    INDEX { ipRouteDest }
    ::= { ipRoutingTable 1 }
```

Each row of the table contains several columns:

ipRouteDest: destination IP address

ipRouteIfIndex: interface number

ipRouteMetric1: routing metric #1

ipRouteMetric2: routing metric #2

ipRouteMetric3: routing metric #3

ipRouteMetric4: routing metric #4

ipRouteMetric5: routing metric #5

ipRouteNextHop: next hop (router IP address for indirect routing)

ipRouteType: type (direct, remote, valid, invalid)

ipRouteProto: mechanism used to determine route

ipRouteAge: age of route in seconds

ipRouteMask: subnet-mask for route

ipRouteInfo: routing protocol-specific MIB pointer

If the value of the `ipRouteType` is set to "`invalid`", then the corresponding row is invalidated.

A "dump" of the object instances in this table might look like this:

```
    Dest        IfIndex      NextHop       Type          Mask
  0.0.0.0          1      192.44.33.3    4 (remote)  0.0.0.0
192.44.33.0        1      192.44.33.20   3 (direct)  255.255.255.0
```

(The routing metrics, protocol, and age fields have been omitted.) The first entry is the default route used by the managed node.

The IP address translation table keeps track of the mapping between IP and media-specific addresses:

```
ipNetToMediaTable OBJECT-TYPE
    SYNTAX SEQUENCE OF IpNetToMediaEntry
    ...
    ::= { ip 22 }

ipNetToMediaEntry OBJECT-TYPE
    SYNTAX IpNetToMediaEntry
    ...
    INDEX { ipNetToMediaIfIndex,
            ipNetToMediaNetAddress }
    ::= { ipNetToMediaTable 1 }
```

Each row of the table contains four columns:

ipNetToMediaIfIndex: interface number

ipNetToMediaPhysAddress: media address of mapping

ipNetToMediaNetAddress: IP address of mapping

ipNetToMediaType: how mapping was determined (other, invalid, dynamic, static)

If the value of the `ipNetToMediaType` is set to "`invalid`", then the corresponding row is invalidated.

A "dump" of the object instances in this table might look like this:

```
                        ipNetToMedia
IfIndex         PhysAddress        NetAddress        Type
    1        08:00:20:00:38:ba    192.33.4.20    3 (dynamic)
    1        00:00:c0:d5:8f:13    192.33.4.3     3 (dynamic)
    1        00:00:22:08:2a:c3    192.33.4.4     3 (dynamic)
```

The ICMP Group

The ICMP group consists of 26 counters.

```
icmp            OBJECT IDENTIFIER ::= { mib-2 5 }
```

In the interest of brevity, this group can be summarized as:

- for each ICMP message type, two counters exist, one counting the number of times this message type was generated by the local ICMP entity; the other counting the number of times this message type was received by the local ICMP entity.

- there are four additional counters which keep track of the total number of ICMP messages received, sent, received in error, or not sent due to error.

Figure 4.13 shows a Case Diagram relating these objects.

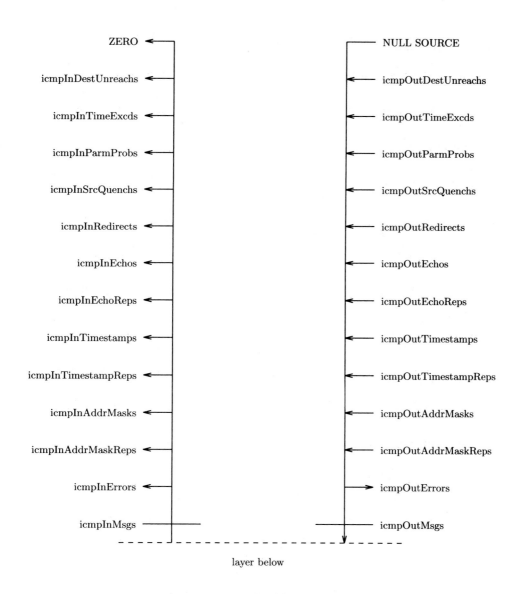

Figure 4.13: Case Diagram for the ICMP Group

The TCP Group

The TCP group contains several scalars and a table.

```
tcp             OBJECT IDENTIFIER ::= { mib-2 6 }
```

The scalars are:

tcpRtoAlgorithm: identifies retransmission algorithm

tcpRtoMin: minimum retransmission timeout in milliseconds

tcpRtoMax: maximum retransmission timeout in milliseconds

tcpMaxConn: maximum number of simultaneous TCP connections allowed

tcpActiveOpens: number of active opens

tcpPassiveOpens: number of passive opens

tcpAttemptFails: number of failed connection attempts

tcpEstabResets: number of connections reset

tcpCurrEstab: number of current connections

tcpInSegs: number of segments received

tcpOutSegs: number of segments sent

tcpRetransSegs: number of segments retransmitted

tcpInErrs: number of segments discarded due to format error

tcpOutRsts: number of resets generated

Figure 4.14 shows a Case Diagram relating some of these objects.

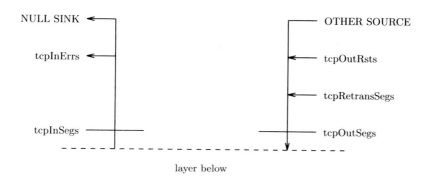

Figure 4.14: Case Diagram for the TCP Group

The table is used to keep track of the application entities which are using TCP:

```
tcpConnTable OBJECT-TYPE
    SYNTAX SEQUENCE OF TcpConnEntry
    . . .
    ::= { tcp 13 }

tcpConnEntry OBJECT-TYPE
    SYNTAX TcpConnEntry
    . . .
    INDEX    { tcpConnLocalAddress,
              tcpConnLocalPort,
              tcpConnRemAddress,
              tcpConnRemPort }
    ::= { tcpConnTable 1 }
```

Each row of the table contains five columns:

tcpConnState: state of connection

tcpConnLocalAddress: local IP address

tcpConnLocalPort: local TCP port

tcpConnRemAddress: remote IP address

tcpConnRemPort: remote TCP port

The distinguished value 0.0.0.0 is used for IP addresses when this information isn't yet bound for the connection.

A "dump" of the object instances in this table might look like this:

```
                       tcpConnLocal         tcpConnRemote
    tcpConnState    Address      Port    Address     Port
    2 (listen)      0.0.0.0        21    0.0.0.0         0
   11 (timewait)    127.0.0.1    4459    127.0.0.1     111
    5 (estab)       192.33.4.20    23    192.33.4.4   1803
          . . .
```

The UDP Group

The UDP group contains four counters and a table.

```
    udp             OBJECT IDENTIFIER ::= { udp 7 }
```

The scalars are:

udpInDatagrams: datagrams delivered above

udpNoPorts: datagrams destined for unknown ports

udpInErrors: datagrams discarded due to format errors

udpOutDatagrams: datagrams sent from above

Figure 4.15 shows a Case Diagram relating these objects.

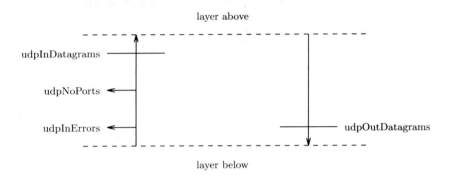

Figure 4.15: Case Diagram for the UDP Group

The table is used to keep track of the application entities which are using UDP:

```
udpTable OBJECT-TYPE
    SYNTAX SEQUENCE OF UdpEntry
    ...
    ::= { udp 5 }

udpEntry OBJECT-TYPE
    SYNTAX UdpEntry
    ...
    INDEX    { udpLocalAddress,
               udpLocalPort }
    ::= { udpTable 1 }
```

Each row of the table contains two columns:

udpLocalAddress: local IP address

udpLocalPort: local UDP port

The distinguished value 0.0.0.0 is used for IP addresses when this information isn't yet bound.

A "dump" of the object instances in this table might look like this:

```
udpLocalAddress        udpLocalPort
     0.0.0.0                42
     0.0.0.0                53
     0.0.0.0               111
...
   127.0.0.1               53
 192.33.4.20               53
 192.33.4.20             1024
```

The EGP Group

The EGP group is mandatory for those managed nodes which implement the *Exterior Gateway Protocol* which, as described earlier, is a reachability protocol used between Autonomous Systems. Space limitations prevent this group from being described here.

The Transmission Group

The transmission group is a place holder for media-specific MIB modules. Looking back at Table 4.2 starting on page 140, most of the MIB modules in the **media** area are registered here.

The SNMP Group

The SNMP group contains objects that related to version 1 of SNMP.

```
ipForward OBJECT IDENTIFIER ::= { ip 24 }

ipForwardNumber OBJECT-TYPE
    SYNTAX   Gauge
    ...
    ::= { ipForward 1 }

ipForwardEntry OBJECT-TYPE
    SYNTAX   IpForwardEntry
    ...
    INDEX { ipForwardDest, ipForwardProto,
        ipForwardPolicy, ipForwardNextHop }
    ::= { ipForwardTable 1 }

IpForwardEntry ::= SEQUENCE {
    ipForwardDest       IpAddress,
    ipForwardMask       IpAddress,
    ipForwardPolicy     INTEGER,
    ipForwardNextHop    IpAddress,
    ipForwardIfIndex    INTEGER,
    ipForwardType       INTEGER,
    ipForwardProto      INTEGER,
    ipForwardAge        INTEGER,
    ipForwardInfo       OBJECT IDENTIFIER,
    ipForwardNextHopAS  INTEGER,
    ipForwardMetric1    INTEGER,
    ipForwardMetric2    INTEGER,
    ipForwardMetric3    INTEGER,
    ipForwardMetric4    INTEGER,
    ipForwardMetric5    INTEGER
}
```

Figure 4.16: The IP Forwarding Table MIB

4.2.4   The IP Forwarding Table MIB

Refinements in the IP routing algorithm led to MIB-II's IP routing table being inadequate for its intended task. So, the IP Forwarding Table MIB module [52] was defined as a replacement. Figure 4.16 gives a synopsis of this MIB module. There are two top-level objects: the number of entries in the routing table, and a single table containing information on those routes.

group	no.	objects for
statistics	21	statistics on LAN usage
history	22	historical samples of statistics
alarm	12	alarm generation objects
hosts	26	source/destination traffic matrix
hostTopN	14	ordered traffic matrix
matrix	18	conversation statistics
filter	23	frame filtering
capture	20	frame capture
event	11	event generation
total	167	

Table 4.4: The Remote Network Monitoring MIB

Most of these columns have definitions similar to their counterparts in MIB-II. Here are the ones which are new:

ipForwardPolicy: the policy associated with this route, used when there are multiple routes to the same destination. By default, the policy refers to the IP type of service field (introduced way back on page 37).

ipForwardNextHopAs: the autonomous system number associated with the next hop (introduced way back on page 33).

Note that there are four objects specified in the `INDEX` clause. This is to allow for routing configurations in which there may be multiple routes for the same destination, each having a different policy or routing protocol.

4.2.5   The RMON MIB

The Remote Network Monitoring MIB module [53] is used to remotely configure a passive monitoring device to capture and analyze information. Table 4.4 summarizes the groups in the RMON MIB module.

Let's briefly look at the function of each group:

statistics: contains utilization and error statistics measured by the monitor for each monitored interface on this device (at present, only Ethernet information is measured, however, work is currently underway to measure token ring information);

history: records periodic statistical samples from a network and stores them for later retrieval;

alarm: periodically takes statistical samples from variables in the monitor and compares them to previously configured thresholds — if a monitored variable crosses a threshold, then a hysteresis mechanism is used to determine if an event should be generated;

hosts: contains statistics associated with each host discovered on the network (by observing source and destination medium addresses);

hostTopN: prepares reports that describe the hosts that top a list ordered by one of their statistics;

matrix: stores statistics for conversations between pairs of addresses;

filter: allows packets that matched a filter equation to be either captured or used in event generation;

capture: captures packets matched by a filter and allows them to be downloaded; and,

event: controls the generation and notification of events.

4.2.6   The SNMPv2 MIB

This MIB module is part of the instrumentation for an SNMPv2 entity. There are six groups:

> **snmpStats:** the SNMPv2 statistics group;
>
> **snmpV1:** the SNMPv1 statistics group;
>
> **snmpOR:** the object resources group;
>
> **snmpTrap:** the traps group;
>
> **snmpTraps:** well-known traps; and,
>
> **snmpSet:** the SNMPv2 set group.

Of these, three we can discuss now. The other three will be introduced as necessary.

The snmpOR Group

The definition of `sysObjectID` assumes that the agent's object resources, "the MIB held by an agent", is rather static. Some agents, however, are able to dynamically acquire new object resources. The `snmpOR` group contains two top-level objects to model this: a timestamp indicating the last time the table of dynamic object resources changed, and a single table containing information on those dynamic object resources:

```
snmpOR          OBJECT IDENTIFIER ::= { snmpMIBObjects 3 }

snmpORLastChange OBJECT-TYPE
    SYNTAX INTEGER
    ACCESS read-only
    STATUS current
    ::= { snmpOR 1 }

snmpORTable OBJECT-TYPE
    SYNTAX SEQUENCE OF SnmpOREntry
    ...
    ::= { snmpOR 2 }

snmpOREntry OBJECT-TYPE
    SYNTAX SnmpOREntry
    ...
    INDEX { snmpORIndex}
    ::= { snmpORTable 1 }
```

Each row of the table contains several columns:

snmpORIndex: the index of this entry in the table

snmpORID: the `OBJECT IDENTIFIER` associated with the object resources, analogous to `sysObjectID`

snmpORDescr: a textual description associated with the object resources, analogous to `sysDescr`

In an agent which can't acquire new object resources, this table is always empty.

The snmpTraps Group

```
snmpTraps        OBJECT IDENTIFIER ::= { snmpMIBObjects 5 }
```

This group defines the "standard" traps:

coldStart: the agent is (re-)initializing itself, and objects in its view may be altered (e.g., the protocol entities on the managed node are starting);

warmStart: the agent is re-initializing itself, but the objects in its view won't be altered (other than `sysUpTime` and its counters);

linkDown: an attached interface has changed from the `up` to the `down` state (the first variable identifies the interface);

linkUp: an attached interface has changed to the `up` state (the first variable identifies the interface);

authenticationFailure: an SNMP message has been received which was deemed unauthentic; and,

egpNeighborLoss: an EGP peer has transitioned to the `down` state (the first variable identifies the IP address of the EGP peer).

Refer back to page 135 for an example of how these traps are defined.

The snmpSet Group

This group defines one object which is used to allow several cooperating management applications to coordinate their use of the set operation:

```
snmpSet          OBJECT IDENTIFIER ::= { snmpMIBObjects 6 }


snmpSetSerialNo OBJECT-TYPE
    SYNTAX      TestAndIncr
    MAX-ACCESS  read-write
    STATUS      current
    DESCRIPTION
            "An advisory lock used to allow several
             cooperating SNMPv2 entities, all acting
             in a manager role, to coordinate their
             use of the SNMPv2 set operation.

             This object is used for coarse-grain
             coordination.  To achieve fine-grain
             coordination, one or more similar
             objects might be defined within each
             MIB group, as appropriate."
    ::= { snmpSet 1 }
```

(The **TestAndIncr** textual convention was described back on page 121.)

4.3   Conformance Statements

In the original management framework, each object group carried with it an ASN.1 comment indicating the conformance level associated with the group. For example,

```
-- Implementation of the TCP group is mandatory
-- for all systems that implement the TCP.
```

Although this was useful, there were also some unsatisfactory results, as different environments have different requirements.

In order to move towards a more general solution, conformance information is no longer contained in an ASN.1 commentary. Instead, a new macro, the OBJECT-GROUP macro, whose definition is shown in Figure 4.17, is used.

The clauses in the OBJECT-GROUP macro are straightforward:

OBJECTS: identifies which objects from the enclosing MIB module are part of the conformance group.

STATUS: an indication of the status of this conformance group definition, one of current, or obsolete.

DESCRIPTION: a textual explanation of this conformance group; and,

REFERENCE: if this conformance group is somehow derived from another conformance group, then this clause is present and includes text which identifies the other conformance group.

For example,

```
snmpV1Group OBJECT-GROUP
    OBJECTS { snmpV1BadCommunityNames,
              snmpV1BadCommunityUses }
    STATUS  current
    DESCRIPTION
            "A collection of objects providing basic
             instrumentation of an SNMPv2 entity which
             also implements SNMPv1."
    ::= { snmpMIBGroups 2 }
```

OBJECT-GROUP MACRO ::=
BEGIN
  TYPE NOTATION ::=
        ObjectsPart
        "STATUS" Status
        "DESCRIPTION" Text
        ReferPart

  VALUE NOTATION ::=
        value(**VALUE OBJECT IDENTIFIER**)   10

ObjectsPart ::=
        "OBJECTS" "{" Objects "}"
Objects ::=
        Object
       | Objects "," Object
Object ::=
        value(Name ObjectName)

Status ::=   20
        "current"
       | "obsolete"

ReferPart ::=
        "REFERENCE" Text
       | empty

  -- uses the NVT ASCII character set
  Text ::= """" string """"
END   30

Figure 4.17: Definition of the OBJECT-GROUP macro

---

defines a conformance group containing two objects. Note that an object may be listed in zero, one, or more conformance groups.

A conformance group is identified by an `OBJECT IDENTIFIER`, and is used in one of two ways: in definitions of compliance requirements, and in definitions of the extent to which an agent implements a MIB module. Let's look at each in turn.

4.3.1 Module Compliance

The `MODULE-COMPLIANCE` macro, the definition of which is shown in Figure 4.18 starting on page 175, is used to concisely detail the expectations placed on an agent.

MODULE-COMPLIANCE MACRO ::=
BEGIN
  TYPE NOTATION ::=
        "STATUS" Status
        "DESCRIPTION" Text
        ReferPart
        ModulePart

  VALUE NOTATION ::=
        value(**VALUE OBJECT IDENTIFIER**)   10

Status ::=
      "current"
    | "obsolete"

ReferPart ::=
      "REFERENCE" Text
    | empty

ModulePart ::=   20
      Modules
    | empty
Modules ::=
      Module
    | Modules Module
Module ::=
      -- name of module --
      "MODULE" ModuleName
      MandatoryPart
      CompliancePart   30

ModuleName ::=
      identifier ModuleIdentifier
      -- must not be empty unless contained
      -- in MIB Module
    | empty
ModuleIdentifier ::=
      value(ModuleID **OBJECT IDENTIFIER**)
    | empty
                                     40

Figure 4.18: Definition of the MODULE-COMPLIANCE macro

```
MandatoryPart ::=
        "MANDATORY-GROUPS" "{" Groups "}"
    | empty
Groups ::=
        Group
    | Groups "," Group
Group ::=
        value(Group OBJECT IDENTIFIER)

CompliancePart ::=                                                      10
        Compliances
    | empty

Compliances ::=
        Compliance
    | Compliances Compliance
Compliance ::=
        ComplianceGroup
    | Object
                                                                        20
ComplianceGroup ::=
        "GROUP" value(Name OBJECT IDENTIFIER)
        "DESCRIPTION" Text
```

Figure 4.18: Definition of the MODULE-COMPLIANCE macro (cont.)

Object ::=
   "OBJECT" value(Name ObjectName)
   SyntaxPart
   WriteSyntaxPart
   AccessPart
   "DESCRIPTION" Text

−− must be a refinement for object's SYNTAX clause
SyntaxPart ::=
   "SYNTAX" type(**SYNTAX**)   10
   | empty

−− must be a refinement for object's SYNTAX clause
WriteSyntaxPart ::=
   "WRITE-SYNTAX" type(WriteSYNTAX)
   | empty

AccessPart ::=
   "MIN-ACCESS" Access
   | empty   20
Access ::=
   "not-accessible"
   | "read-only"
   | "read-write"
   | "read-create"

−− uses the NVT ASCII character set
Text ::= """" string """"
END

Figure 4.18: Definition of the MODULE-COMPLIANCE macro (cont.)

When invoked, zero or more modules are identified. For each
module, the MANDATORY-GROUPS clause identifies those groups which
must be implemented. Similarly, the GROUPS clause identifies those
groups which must be implemented if some condition is met.   In
addition, if some refinement for an object is allowed, then the OBJECT
clause is used to identify the object and the refinement. For example,
an OBJECT clause could be used to indicate that an object with a
MAX-ACCESS of read-write may be implemented as read-only.

Here's a rather straightforward example which shows a group that
must be conditionally implemented:

```
snmpMIBCompliance MODULE-COMPLIANCE
    STATUS   current
    DESCRIPTION
            "The compliance statement for SNMPv2
             entities which implement the SNMPv2 MIB."
    MODULE   RFC1213-MIB
        MANDATORY-GROUPS { system }

    MODULE   -- this module
        MANDATORY-GROUPS { snmpStatsGroup,
                           snmpORGroup,
                           snmpTrapGroup,
                           snmpSetGroup }
        GROUP    snmpV1Group
        DESCRIPTION
            "The snmpV1 group is mandatory only
             for those SNMPv2 entities which also
             implement SNMPv1."
    ::= { snmpMIBCompliances 1 }
```

4.3.2   Agent Capabilities

The AGENT-CAPABILITIES macro, the definition of which is shown in
Figure 4.19 starting on page 179, is used to concisely detail how a
specific agent behaves.

AGENT-CAPABILITIES MACRO ::=
BEGIN
  TYPE NOTATION ::=
          `"PRODUCT-RELEASE"` Text
          `"STATUS"` Status
          `"DESCRIPTION"` Text
          ReferPart
          ModulePart

  VALUE NOTATION ::=   10
          −− agent's sysObjectID [3] or snmpORID [4]
          value(**VALUE OBJECT IDENTIFIER**)

Status ::=
          `"current"`
      | `"obsolete"`

ReferPart ::=
          `"REFERENCE"` Text
      | empty   20

ModulePart ::=
          Modules
      | empty
Modules ::=
          Module
      | Modules Module
Module ::=
          −− name of module −−
          `"SUPPORTS"` ModuleName   30
          `"INCLUDES"` `"{"` Groups `"}"`
          VariationPart

ModuleName ::=
          identifier ModuleIdentifier
ModuleIdentifier ::=
          value(ModuleID **OBJECT IDENTIFIER**)
      | empty

Figure 4.19: Definition of the AGENT-CAPABILITIES macro

Groups ::=
         Group
         | Groups "," Group
Group ::=
         value(Name **OBJECT IDENTIFIER**)

VariationPart ::=
         Variations
         | empty
Variations ::=   10
         Variation
         | Variations Variation

Variation ::=
         "VARIATION" value(Name ObjectName)
         SyntaxPart
         WriteSyntaxPart
         AccessPart
         CreationPart
         DefValPart   20
         "DESCRIPTION" Text

−− *must be a refinement for object's SYNTAX clause*
SyntaxPart ::=
         "SYNTAX" type(**SYNTAX**)
         | empty

−− *must be a refinement for object's SYNTAX clause*
WriteSyntaxPart ::=
         "WRITE-SYNTAX" type(WriteSYNTAX)   30
         | empty

Figure 4.19: Definition of the AGENT-CAPABILITIES macro (cont.)

```
AccessPart ::=
          "ACCESS" Access
        | empty

Access ::=
          "not-implemented"
        | "read-only"
        | "read-write"
        | "read-create"
        -- following is for backward-compatibility only              10
        | "write-only"

CreationPart ::=
          "CREATION-REQUIRES" "{" Cells "}"
        | empty

Cells ::=
          Cell
        | Cells "," Cell
                                                                      20
Cell ::=
          value(Cell ObjectName)

DefValPart ::=
          "DEFVAL" "{" value(Defval ObjectSyntax) "}"
        | empty

-- uses the NVT ASCII character set
Text ::= """" string """"
END                                                                   30
```

Figure 4.19: Definition of the AGENT-CAPABILITIES macro (cont.)

When invoked, zero or more modules are identified. For each module, the conformance groups implemented are listed. For each of these, any variations are noted. These variations include:

- some objects in a conformance group not implemented;

- some objects not "completely" implemented, e.g.,

  - there might be fewer choices for an enumerated integer; or,

  - some objects may be read-only instead of read-write;

  and,

- some objects may be created only in conjunction with others.

The invocation of the AGENT-CAPABILITIES macro is intended to capture the gist of these variations. Figure 4.20 shows an example of a capability statement.

A capability statement is identified by an OBJECT IDENTIFIER. This corresponds to the value of the sysObjectID object, or to a value stored in the snmpORTable, both of which were described earlier. This allows a management application to maintain a database of capability statements and then to dynamically compare the value associated with those statements to the value of a device's sysObjectID.

exampleAgent **AGENT-CAPABILITIES**
    PRODUCT-RELEASE   "ACME Agent release 1.1 for 4BSD"
    STATUS   current
    DESCRIPTION   "ACME agent for 4BSD"

    SUPPORTS   RFC1213−MIB
      INCLUDES   { systemGroup, interfacesGroup, atGroup, ipGroup,
              icmpGroup, tcpGroup, udpGroup, snmpGroup }

      VARIATION   ifAdminStatus   10
        SYNTAX   **INTEGER** { up(1), down(2) }
      DESCRIPTION "Unable to set test mode on 4BSD"

      VARIATION   atEntry
      CREATION-REQUIRES { atPhysAddress }
      DESCRIPTION "Address mappings on 4BSD must be complete"

      VARIATION   ipDefaultTTL
        SYNTAX   **INTEGER** (255..255)
      DESCRIPTION "Hard-wired on 4BSD"   20
      VARIATION   ipInAddrErrors
        ACCESS   not−implemented
      DESCRIPTION "Information not available on 4BSD"

      VARIATION   ipRouteType
        SYNTAX   **INTEGER** { direct(3), indirect(4) }
      WRITE-SYNTAX INTEGER { invalid(2), direct(3),
                indirect(4) }
      DESCRIPTION "Information limited on 4BSD"

                                             30
      VARIATION   tcpConnState
        ACCESS   read−only
      DESCRIPTION "Unable to set this on 4BSD"

    SUPPORTS   EVAL−MIB
      INCLUDES   { functions, expressions }
      VARIATION   exprEntry
      CREATION-REQUIRES { evalString }
      DESCRIPTION "Conceptual row creation supported"

                                             40
::= { acme−agents 1 }

Figure 4.20: An example capability statement

4.3.3   In Perspective

The relationship between object definitions, compliance statements, and capability statements is rather straightforward:

- an object definition indicates the maximum expectations;

- a compliance statement indicates the minimum expectations; and,

- a capabilities statement indicates the actual implementation.

Note that both the `MODULE-COMPLIANCE` and `AGENT-CAPABILITIES` macros are invoked as "deltas" against MIB modules. As such, a single invocation of the `AGENT-CAPABILITIES` macro can be compared to each of several different compliance statements.

Finally, it must be strongly emphasized that the whole notion of compliance and capability statements is rather new in the SNMPv2 framework. For example, none of these facilities capture any information about notifications. In fact, there are several aspects of the management framework which these facilities are unable to describe. As such, these features are likely to undergo revision as the documents which define them progress along the standards track.

4.4 Importing Macro Definitions

The ASN.1 macros described in this chapter are defined in three separate ASN.1 modules. To use one of these macros in your own information modules, use the `IMPORTS` statement accordingly:

module	macros
SNMPv2-SMI	MODULE-IDENTITY
	OBJECT-IDENTITY
	OBJECT-TYPE
	NOTIFICATION-TYPE
SNMPv2-TC	TEXTUAL-CONVENTION
SNMPv2-CONF	OBJECT-GROUP
	MODULE-COMPLIANCE
	AGENT-CAPABILITIES

In addition, the `SNMPv2-SMI` module defines all of the object syntaxes:

IpAddress	Counter32	Gauge32
TimeTicks	Opaque	NsapAddress
Counter64	UInteger32	

along with `Integer32` and the `OBJECT IDENTIFIER` values for well-known registration points.

The `SNMPv2-TC` module defines the initial set of textual conventions:

DisplayString	PhysAddress	MacAddress
TruthValue	TestAndIncr	AutonomousType
InstancePointer	RowStatus	TimeStamp
TimeInterval	DateAndTime	

4.5   Coexistence

> **NOTE:**   Read this section only if you are familiar with the
> original Internet-standard Network Management
> Framework.

The SMI for the original framework is defined in two documents
[54,55].

4.5.1   Object Definitions

The original framework uses an early version of the `OBJECT-TYPE`
macro. This section summarizes the difference between the old and
new versions of the macro:

SYNTAX: this clause was more restrictive than the current
clause and did not allow these object syntaxes:

```
BIT STRING
NsapAddress
Counter64
UInteger32
```

Further, the `Integer32` syntax was called `INTEGER`, the
`Counter32` syntax was called `Counter`, and the `Gauge32`
syntax was called `Gauge`.

UNITS: this clause was not present in the old definition.

MAX-ACCESS: this clause was called the `ACCESS` clause. In
addition, there was a `write-only` value allowed, but no
`read-create` value.

STATUS: this clause implied something about the implementation status of the object rather than the currency of the
object's definition. Thus, instead of `current`, the value
`mandatory` was used. There was also an `optional` value
allowed.

DESCRIPTION: the use of this clause was identical to the current clause, but was optional.

REFERENCE: the use of this clause was identical to the current clause.

INDEX: this clause was optional, and lacked the `IMPLIED` keyword.

AUGMENTS: this clause was not present in the old definition.

DEFVAL: the use of this clause was identical to the current clause.

Given these relatively few changes, it is straightforward to upgrade a MIB module that was defined using the original framework.

4.5.2 Notification Definitions

The original framework never had a standard mechanism for defining traps. (An informational document was available instead.)

The technique used in the original framework was very similar, e.g., compare

```
linkUp TRAP-TYPE
    ENTERPRISE  snmp
    VARIABLES   { ifIndex }
    DESCRIPTION
            "A linkUp trap signifies that the sending
            protocol entity recognizes that one of
            the communication links represented in
            the agent's configuration has come up."
    ::= 3
```

with the example given on page 135. The differences are:

- the macro name changed from **TRAP-TYPE** to **NOTIFICATION-TYPE**;

- the **VARIABLES** clause is now called the **OBJECTS** clause; and,

- the identity of the trap changed from the combination of an `OBJECT IDENTIFIER` and an integer (e.g., **snmp** and 3), to an `OBJECT IDENTIFIER`.

4.5.3   Conformance Statements

In the original framework, all compliance information was "buried" in ASN.1 commentary associated with an object group. Other than this, there was no mechanism in the original framework corresponding to the conformance mechanism in the SNMPv2 framework.

4.5.4 In Perspective

The strategy for transition from the original framework to the SNMPv2 framework is quite simple: it's called *coexistence*. Throughout the SNMPv2 design process, coexistence with the original framework was given substantive attention. Many design decisions were made by favoring coexistence over other goals.

For users, a good strategy for the transition to SNMPv2 goes something like this:

- first, keep existing agents in the field;

- next, upgrade existing management stations to add support for SNMPv2; and,

- finally, start buying SNMPv2 agents as they become available.

SNMPv2 was carefully designed so that construction of bilingual management stations is straightforward and inexpensive.[4] This allows for a focus on preserving the existing (and continuing) investment in the original framework, allowing for a lengthy period of coexistence.

Hence, for vendors of management applications, the strategy is simple: support both versions of SNMP at run-time. In contrast, for agent vendors, the strategy is to have both SNMPv1 and SNMPv2 available in the product line, allowing the user to select which of the two versions will be running in the agent when deployed.[5]

---

[4]In fact, one can easily construct an API for management applications which allows transparent access to both SNMPv1 and SNMPv2 — allowing the management application to be unconcerned with which version of SNMP is in use!

[5]In some environments, the user might opt to have both versions running concurrently in an agent, if some of the user's management applications are monolingual. Hopefully, this will be the exception, and not the rule, for the majority of user environments. Even so, this should really be viewed as a "stop gap" as management applications are upgraded to become bilingual.

Chapter 5

Administrative Model

We now consider how one defines the administrative policy for agents and management applications. This part of the management framework has undergone the most revision since the introduction of SNMP.

In the original SNMP, the administrative relationship between an agent and one or more management applications was identified by a *community*. The community relationship involved three aspects:

- identification of the entities authorized to request management operations;

- identification of the type of management operation that's allowed; and,

- identification of management information available to the operations.

The identity of the community — a simple string of octets — was sent with the management operation, in plaintext form, between entities participating in the same community.

Owing to its weak authentication properties, one side effect of the original administrative model was that it encouraged designers of MIB modules to make sure that any control objects had weak properties. An unfortunate side effect, however, was that it gave some vendors the opportunity to avoid implementing control functions in their agents. The public position of these vendors was that because of the lack of strong authentication, a third-party might learn the community string

soap...

and take control of the network. Instead, the vendors would let their customers use TELNET to the device's console, which was password protected. Dr. SNMP reminds us to

> *"Spread the manure where you are going to grow the vegetables."*

meaning that use of TELNET and a plaintext password is no more secure than use of SNMP and a plaintext community string. The correct behavior for these vendors is to implement SNMP's control functions and then allow each customer to enable or disable these functions according to their own requirements. In addition, it should be noted that because TELNET uses a connection-oriented transport service, it is poorly suited for crisis management (e.g., recall the discussion on transport mappings back on page 71). There are many real-life anecdotes about users who suffered greatly because of a device which offered password-protected TELNET but not SNMP's control functions, even though the vendor claimed that the device supported SNMP.

`...soap`

With that bit of historical perspective out of the way, let's consider the administrative model used in the SNMPv2 framework.

There are three core concepts in the administrative model:

- the *party* concept, which refers to entities that communicate via a management protocol and a transport service using authentication and privacy facilities;

- the *context* concept, which refers to collections of management information; and,

- the *access policy* concept, which determines the operations that may be performed when one party asks another party to perform an operation on the objects in a context.

Here's how a management application might relate these concepts: first, the application determines that it wants to perform a given operation on a particular collection of managed objects; second, it determines the level of authentication and privacy that should be used when making the request; third, it looks at its access policies to find out which parties to use which minimally meet its requirements.

The fundamental concept is that of a dichotomy between communications and objects.

5.1   Parties

An SNMPv2 party, or simply a party, is an execution environment residing in an agent or management application. It has associated with it three sets of attributes:

- *transport* attributes;

- *authentication* attributes; and,

- *privacy* attributes.

In order for an SNMPv2 entity to communicate with another, it must have information on at least two SNMP parties: one for itself and the other for the remote entity. In order to allow for remote configuration and maintenance, all of these attributes are available as managed objects for each party known to an agent. But, before considering each in turn, let's look at the message format used by parties.

Figure 5.1 shows the message format used when two SNMPv2 parties communicate. There are three nested structures:

SnmpPrivMsg: the structure used to transmit a message via the transport service. The `privDst` field identifies the party for which the message is intended. The `privData` field contains an `SnmpAuthMsg` structure which has been serialized into a string of octets, and then possibly encrypted. (Serialization is the process of taking a structure and transforming it into a string of octets for unambiguous transmission on the network. This process is discussed, in great detail, in Section 6.2.2 starting on page 295.)

SnmpAuthMsg: an intermediate structure containing authentication credentials (`authInfo`) and information about the management operation and its execution environment (`authData`).

SnmpMgmtCom: an intermediate structure identifying the party which originated the message (`srcParty`), the party which is intended to receive the message (`dstParty`), the managed objects visible to the operation (`context`),

```
SnmpPrivMsg ::=
   [1] IMPLICIT SEQUENCE {
      privDst
         OBJECT IDENTIFIER,
      privData -- SnmpAuthMsg, possibly encrypted
         [1] IMPLICIT OCTET STRING
   }

SnmpAuthMsg ::=
   [1] IMPLICIT SEQUENCE {                                               10
      authInfo
         ANY, -- depends on authentication used
      authData
         SnmpMgmtCom
   }

SnmpMgmtCom ::=
   [2] IMPLICIT SEQUENCE {
      dstParty
         OBJECT IDENTIFIER,                                             20
      srcParty
         OBJECT IDENTIFIER,
      context
         OBJECT IDENTIFIER,
      operation
         PDUs
   }
```

Figure 5.1: **SNMPv2 Message Format**

and the desired operation (`operation`). (For the impatient
reader, the `PDUs` data type is defined much later in Figure 6.1 starting on page 244.)

This figure tells us two important things:

- parties and contexts are identified by **OBJECT IDENTIFIER** values; and,

- privacy and authentication are separate functions, with authentication layered inside privacy.

The one thing this figure doesn't tell us is what an operation looks
like. That will be the topic of the next chapter. (If you're impatient,
you might want to glance at the ASN.1 definition found in Figure 6.1
starting on page 244.)

5.1.1   Transport Attributes

Since the purpose of a party is communication, it must have associated with it information regarding how it uses the underlying transport service.

The specific transport attributes of a party are:

partyTDomain: the party's *transport domain* identifies the management protocol (normally SNMPv2) and transport service (normally UDP) which the party uses when communicating.

partyTAddress: the party's *transport address* identifies the address used with the transport service specified by the transport domain; and,

partyMaxMessageSize: the party's *maximum message size* identifies the size, in octets, of the largest message that the party will accept.

Within a single entity, more than one party can use the same transport address. For example, when several parties execute in an agent, traffic to all of them will probably be sent to the same transport address.

It is important to appreciate that the transport address associated with a party is used *only* when originating traffic to that party. Responses are always sent back to the originating address, regardless of the transport address associated with the original party.

Transport Domains

At present, there are several transport domains defined:

domain	protocol	transport
snmpUDPDomain	SNMPv2	UDP
snmpCLNSDomain	SNMPv2	OSI CLTS (using CLNS)
snmpCONSDomain	SNMPv2	OSI CLTS (using CONS)
snmpDDPDomain	SNMPv2	AppleTalk® DDP
snmpIPXDomain	SNMPv2	Novell IPX

All of these are discussed in greater detail in Section 6.2.1 starting on page 291. There is also a transport domain defined — for coexistence purposes — for the original SNMP. (It's discussed in Section 6.3.1.)

5.1.2   Authentication Attributes

When a party originates a communication, it may be configured to supply authentication credentials as a part of the communication. Depending on the authentication facilities provided by the entity, three kinds of services might be available:

- *origin identification*, in which a message can be associated with an originating party with great certainty;

- *message integrity*, in which an altered message can be detected with great certainty; and,

- *limited replay protection*, in which a message that had been duplicated or delayed by the network or a third-party can be detected outside the message's lifetime.

Note that preventing *denial of service*, in which a third-party interrupts a communication, isn't a goal of the administrative framework. The specific authentication attributes of a party are:

partyAuthProtocol: the party's *authentication protocol* identifies the algorithm used to supply credentials when this party generates a message;

partyAuthClock: the party's *authentication clock* is used to attach timestamps to messages generated by the party;

partyAuthPrivate: the party's *private authentication key* is the "secret information" used by the party's authentication algorithm;

partyAuthPublic: the party's *public authentication key* is the "public information" used by the party's authentication algorithm; and,

partyAuthLifetime: the party's *message lifetime* is the number of seconds that a message sent by the party can remain in transit and still be considered valid on receipt.

```
AuthInformation ::=
    [2] IMPLICIT SEQUENCE {
        authDigest
            OCTET STRING (SIZE (16)),
        authDstTimestamp
            UInteger32,
        authSrcTimestamp
            UInteger32
    }
```

Figure 5.2: v2md5AuthProtocol Credentials

As can be seen, the party's authentication protocol is the important attribute, as it defines how the other attributes are used, and also the structure of the credentials used when a party generates a message.

At present, there are two authentication protocols defined: `noAuth` and `v2md5AuthProtocol`. Let's look at each in turn.

The noAuth Protocol

The `noAuth` protocol has identical authentication properties to the old community-based authentication scheme, i.e., trivial! This means that any entity knowing the identity of a source party which uses the `noAuth` protocol can generate messages as that entity. When a `noAuth` party generates a message, it supplies an empty octet string as its credentials. (Knowledge of the originating and recipient parties' identities is equivalent to knowledge of a community string under the old scheme.)

The v2md5AuthProtocol

The `v2md5AuthProtocol` is intended to provide origin identification, message integrity, and limited replay protection services. Figure 5.2 shows the format of the credentials employed when a party using this authentication protocol generates a message.

During the generation of a message, a party will construct an instance of the `SnmpAuthMsg` structure, shown earlier on page 195. The `authData` field will contain an `SnmpMgmtCom` structure providing complete information about the operation and its execution environment. The party then constructs the `authInfo` field by initializing a credentials structure thusly:

authDigest: a copy of the originating party's private authentication key (`partyAuthPrivate`);

authDstTimestamp: a copy of the recipient party's authentication clock (`partyAuthClock`); and,

authSrcTimestamp: a copy of the originating party's authentication clock.

The `SnmpAuthMsg` structure is then serialized into a string of octets, which is saved. This string of octets is then supplied as input to the MD5 message-digest algorithm [56], which outputs an octet string of length sixteen, termed a *digest*. The originating party then writes the digest over the `authDigest` field in the saved string of octets, replacing the private authentication key.

When a message is received, a similar set of steps is followed. First, the receiving entity takes the `authSrcTimestamp` field and adds the originating party's authentication lifetime (`partyAuthLifetime`) and compares the sum to its notion of the originating party's authentication clock (`partyAuthClock`). If the sum is less than its notation of the authentication clock, the message has either been delayed or duplicated (by the network or a third-party). A "not in lifetime" counter is incremented and the message is discarded. Otherwise, the location of the `authDigest` field in the string of octets corresponding to the received `SnmpAuthMsg` is determined. The sixteen octets starting at that location are saved and then replaced by the originating party's private authentication key (`partyAuthPrivate`). The modified string of octets is then input to the MD5 message-digest algorithm and the result is compared with the sixteen octets saved earlier. If they don't match, then either the message has been corrupted or it really wasn't from the originating party. Either way, a "digest mismatch" counter is incremented and the message is discarded. Otherwise, the message is considered authentic. In this case, the receiving entity checks its access policy to see if any form of communication is allowed between the originating and recipient parties. If so, then:

- if the value of the `authSrcTimestamp` field is greater than the originating party's authentication clock, this authentication clock is advanced to the greater value; and,

- if the value of the `authDstTimestamp` field is greater than the recipient party's authentication clock, this authentication clock is advanced to the greater value.

That is, upon receipt of an authentic message, the receiving entity automatically advances its notion of the authentication clocks of the originating and recipient parties so they are at least as large as the originating entity's notion.

So, how does this provide a basis for authentication? The answer is simple: *magic*. Actually, security experts conjecture that it is computationally infeasible to calculate any input string to the MD5 message-digest algorithm that will produce a specific output string.[1] Hence, only an entity which knows the party's private authentication key can generate or verify the message-digest value. As a consequence, any tampering with either the credentials (`authInfo`) or the `SnmpMgmtCom` structure (`authData`) will be detected by the receiver.

Of course, for this authentication algorithm to work, the originating and recipient entities must have a shared knowledge of (at least) two attributes of the originating party: the authentication clock and private authentication key. Let's look at each.

Authentication Clocks

A party's authentication clock is monotonically increasing and measured in seconds. Unlike a counter, however, when an authentication clock reaches its maximum (over 4 billion seconds or slightly over 136 years), it latches — neither increasing nor wrapping back to zero.

Because decreasing the authentication clock might allow a replay attack, a protocol operation may reset a party's authentication clock only if that same protocol operation also changes the party's private authentication key.

---

[1] The operative term here is "conjecture". As such, the administrative framework allows for the definition of future authentication protocols and algorithms.

As implied by the algorithm above, the value of a party's authentication clock must be known to both the originating and receiving entities. The technical term for this is a *loosely-coupled clock*. It is possible that, over time, the clocks used by the two entities might become skewed. As this skew increases, the message lifetime for the party becomes warped. If the lifetime decreases as a result of this warping, then authentic messages will be mistakenly deemed as "not in lifetime" and discarded; instead, if the lifetime increases, then there is a greater window for replay attacks.

It turns out that the authentication algorithm automatically corrects most skews. Remember the automatic synchronization that occurs at the end of the algorithm? Because of this, there is only one condition that requires a management application to periodically issue an authentication clock synchronization operation: if the agent's notion of the authentication clock for a party executing in the management application is larger than the application's notion by more than `partyAuthLifetime`. In this case, messages sent using this party will be considered unauthentic by the agent. The management application will encounter a timeout, and may decide to employ this algorithm:

1. The management application, using a pair of `noAuth` parties, retrieves the agent's notion of the authentication clock associated with the party.

   If for some reason the value cannot be ascertained, the algorithm terminates.

2. If the value of the authentication clock retrieved is larger than the management application's notion, then the locally-held value is saved, and then updated to the value just retrieved from the agent.

   Otherwise, clock skew isn't the cause of the timeout, and the algorithm terminates.

3. The management application, retrieves the authentication clock associated with the party, using a pair of `v2md5AuthProtocol` parties.

If for some reason the value cannot be ascertained, the old authentication clock value is restored, and the algorithm terminates.

This algorithm illustrates an important point — one we'll see time and time again — namely, that the management protocol is used to maintain the objects which are present in the administrative model.

Finally, one might think that the authentication clock is tied to a smoothly advancing clock. Although helpful to implementation, this isn't necessary: an authentication clock must be monotonically increasing, but it needn't increase smoothly. The minimum requirement is that the value used by the party needs to be kept in stable storage and updated at some frequency. When a device re-initializes itself, these values can be retrieved and incremented by an amount greater than the frequency of updating stable storage. In doing so, any traffic sent (and possibly captured) during the device's down time will be considered unauthentic.

Finally, we should briefly re-consider the relationship between the authentication clock and the timestamp of a message. This is best summarized as:

partyAuthClock		minimum acceptable
from	**to**	`authSrcTimestamp`
0	`partyAuthLifetime`	0
`partyAuthLifetime+1`	maximum-1	`partyAuthClock` $-$`partyAuthLifetime`
maximum	maximum	`partyAuthClock`

or pictorially as:

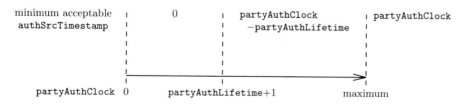

Secrets

In brief: secrets must be kept secret.[2] Any entity knowing the private authentication key of a party is able to generate credentials for that party which are likely to be considered authentic. Of course, an entity has to know the private authentication key of a party in order to authenticate the credentials of messages generated by that party. Even within an entity though, great care should be taken in order to minimize access to secret information.

Finally, secrets must be maintained in non-volatile storage.

5.1.3 Privacy Attributes

When a party receives a communication, it may be configured to require privacy enhancement as a part of the communication. The term "privacy enhancement" refers to encipherment.

The specific privacy attributes of a party are:

partyPrivProtocol: the party's *privacy protocol* identifies the algorithm used to decipher information when this party receives a message;

partyPrivPrivate: the party's *private privacy key* is the "secret information" used by the party's privacy algorithm; and,

partyPrivPublic: the party's *public privacy key* is the "public information" used by the party's privacy algorithm.

As can be seen, the party's privacy protocol is the important attribute, as it defines how the other attributes are used.

At present, there are two privacy protocols defined: `noPriv` and `desPrivProtocol`. Let's look at each in turn.

The noPriv Protocol

The `noPriv` protocol has no non-disclosure properties — the `privData` field is simply a serialized copy of an `SnmpAuthMsg` structure. Thus, a

---

[2]In general, administrative laxity in selecting, distributing, and maintaining the secrecy of secrets tends to be the biggest weakness in security processes.

third-party can observe messages sent to a `noPriv` party and view their contents. (Of course, since authentication is separate from privacy, the message can still be protected from other threats.)

The desPrivProtocol

The `desPrivProtocol` is intended to provide privacy enhancement.

During the generation of a message, a party will construct an instance of the `SnmpPrivMsg` structure, shown earlier on page 195. The `privDst` field will identify the intended recipient party, and the `privData` field will contain the serialized and then enciphered representation of an `SnmpAuthMsg` structure.

To generate this latter field, the recipient party's private privacy key (`partyPrivPrivate`) is split into two eight-octet long strings. The first of these is used as the secret key, and the second as the initialization vector, for the Cipher Block Chaining (CBC) mode of the Data Encryption Standard (DES) [57,58], a symmetric enciphering algorithm. The serialized representation of an `SnmpAuthMsg` structure is padded to a multiple of eight octets and enciphered using the DES-CBC. Finally, the resulting string of octets is placed in the `privData` field.

When a message is received, a similar set of steps is followed: the receiving entity takes the recipient party's private privacy key, splits it into a secret key and an initialization vector, and then deciphers the `privData` field using the DES-CBC. After removing any padding that might be at the end of the output, the resulting string of octets should be the serialized representation of an `SnmpAuthMsg`. (If not, then the message has been altered or damaged during transit — a fact which is easily detected.)

Again, any entity knowing the private privacy key of a party is able to decipher messages intended for that party. So the earlier concerns about keeping secret values secret are also echoed here.

5.1.4   The Party Database Group

The party database group in the `SNMPv2-PARTY-MIB` module defines a party table which represents information about all of the parties known to an entity. Figure 5.3 summarizes this group.

Most of the attributes associated with a party have already been introduced, so let's just fill in the gaps:

partyIdentity: the identity of the party, defined using the `Party` textual convention;

partyIndex: a unique integer assigned to this party by the agent, which remains constant between re-initializations of the entity, used to index other tables;

partyLocal: indicates whether the party executes locally or in a remote entity;

partyCloneFrom: used when creating a party;

partyStorageType: describes this entry in the `partyTable`;

```
          StorageType ::= TEXTUAL-CONVENTION
              ...
          SYNTAX    INTEGER {
                        other(1),
                        volatile(2),
                        nonVolatile(3),
                        permanent(4)
                    }
```

(volatile parties are lost on reboot, whilst permanent parties cannot be changed or deleted); and,

partyStatus: describes the status of this entry in the `partyTable`, defined using the `RowStatus` textual convention.

The only object requiring additional explanation is `partyStatus`. This indicates whether the objects corresponding to a party are valid. For example, if a party is in the process of being created, not all

Party ::= **TEXTUAL-CONVENTION**
...
   SYNTAX   **OBJECT IDENTIFIER**

TAddress ::= **TEXTUAL-CONVENTION**
...
   SYNTAX   **OCTET STRING**

Clock ::= **TEXTUAL-CONVENTION**
...   10
   SYNTAX   UInteger32

snmpParties   **OBJECT IDENTIFIER** ::= { partyMIBObjects 1 }

partyTable **OBJECT-TYPE**
   SYNTAX   **SEQUENCE OF** PartyEntry
...
   ::= { snmpParties 1 }   20

partyEntry **OBJECT-TYPE**
   SYNTAX   PartyEntry
...
   INDEX   { **IMPLIED** partyIdentity }
   ::= { partyTable 1 }

PartyEntry ::=
   SEQUENCE {
      partyIdentity   Party,   30
      partyIndex   **INTEGER** (1..65535),
      partyTDomain   **OBJECT IDENTIFIER**,
      partyTAddress   TAddress,
      partyMaxMessageSize **INTEGER** (484..65507),
      partyLocal   TruthValue,
      partyAuthProtocol   **OBJECT IDENTIFIER**,
      partyAuthClock   Clock,
      partyAuthPrivate   **OCTET STRING**,
      partyAuthPublic   **OCTET STRING**,
      partyAuthLifetime   **INTEGER** (0..2147483647),   40
      partyPrivProtocol   **OBJECT IDENTIFIER**,
      partyPrivPrivate   **OCTET STRING**,
      partyPrivPublic   **OCTET STRING**,
      partyCloneFrom   Party,
      partyStorageType   StorageType,
      partyStatus   RowStatus
   }

Figure 5.3: The Party Database Group

information, e.g., the secrets, may have been supplied. Until this information is supplied, the party cannot be used. Section 6.1.4 starting on page 268 discusses the `RowStatus` textual convention. The details are unimportant in the current discussion.

5.1.5   Party Creation and Modification

Because it is represented as a collection of objects, the attributes of a party can be created and modified using the management protocol. However, there is one hitch: how can the secret information for a party — the private authentication key and the private privacy key — be initialized or updated?

Well, at first glance, the answer is: you have to use a party on the agent which has privacy enhancement. Fortunately, this isn't the case. (When security is involved, it seems that nothing is as it appears at first glance!)

Before looking at party creation, let's look at modification.

Party Modification

It turns out that for updating secret information, the definition of the `partyAuthPrivate` and `partyPrivPrivate` objects contains a little bit of wizardry to avoid the use of privacy enhancement:

- when instances of these objects are retrieved, an octet string of length zero is returned; and,

- when instances of these objects are set, the value supplied in the protocol set operation is exclusive-OR'd with the current value (the latter being padded with zeros as appropriate).

The first rule is straightforward. The second rule requires a bit of explanation. When a management application decides to change the secret information for a party, it must pseudo-randomly generate a new secret. It then XOR's this new secret with the current value, and sends the resulting octet string in the management request. When the agent applies the XOR again, it gets back the new secret to store.

Does this make the system less secure? The answer is probably not, because the new secret can be calculated only if the old secret is known to a third-party. If the old secret is known, then the system has already been compromised.

There are two other concerns involved when modifying a party's attributes:

- if a party's authentication protocol can be altered, then another party can usurp its privileges; and,

- if a party's message lifetime can be altered, then it can be made more susceptible to replay attacks.

Here's why: suppose there's an authenticated party, "Wheeler", which is allowed to access a context containing sensitive management information. If another party, "Woolsey", is able to change Wheeler's authentication protocol to `noAuth`, then Woolsey can start sending messages on Wheeler's behalf. Similarly, if Woolsey can increase Wheeler's message lifetime to a big number (e.g., 150 years), then any time Woolsey wants to get some information which Wheeler has asked for in the past, Woolsey can simply replay the message.

Finally, it turns out that if Woolsey can change some of the other attributes associated with Wheeler (e.g., the private authentication key), then Woolsey can prevent Wheeler from being able to authenticate itself.[3]

The straightforward way to avoid such attacks is to make sure that each party can modify only its own attributes, e.g., for clock maintenance. In some cases, however, it may be impractical to configure a device to this level of granularity. To avoid the biggest problems, once a party's authentication protocol, message lifetime, or privacy protocol attributes have been created, their values may not be changed.

---

[3]Woolsey can't masquerade as Wheeler after changing Wheeler's private authentication key because of the XOR rule — when Woolsey changes the value of Wheeler's private authentication key, the new value supplied by Woolsey is XOR'd with the original value, which Woolsey presumably doesn't know, creating a new value which Woolsey also doesn't know.

Party Creation

So, what about party creation? The XOR rule works fine when a party
has already had its secrets initialized, since there are old secrets with
which to XOR new secrets, but how do those secrets get initialized?
The answer is that when a party is created, a template is provided
which contains default information for these attributes:

```
partyAuthProtocol
partyAuthPublic
partyAuthLifetime
partyPrivProtocol
partyPrivPublic
```

Before a party can be used, the party's `partyCloneFrom` attribute
must be set. This identifies the template party. If any of the five
attributes above haven't been set for the new party, then the appropriate values are copied from the template party. In addition, the new
party's

```
partyAuthPrivate
partyPrivPrivate
```

attributes are updated from the template party using the XOR rule.
Unless these attributes are also present in a protocol set operation,
then the secrets for the new party are identical to those in the template
party. Because of this, the new party cannot be used until a protocol
set operation updates these two attributes in the new party. And,
once again, the XOR rule is used.

5.2 Contexts

An SNMPv2 context, or simply a context, is a collection of managed object resources accessible by an SNMPv2 entity. The object resources identified by a context are either local or remote.

If the entity uses local mechanisms to access the objects, then the context defines a MIB view; otherwise, if the objects reside in a remote entity, then the context defines a proxy relationship.

Let's look at each kind of context, in turn.

5.2.1 MIB Views

A MIB view is a collection of managed objects, a (usually proper) subset of all the managed objects held by an entity. A MIB view is defined in terms of one or more *subtree families.*

A subtree family consists of an arbitrary OBJECT IDENTIFIER and a bit-mask. To determine if a particular instance is a member of a family, the bit-mask is used to determine which sub-identifiers in the family's OBJECT IDENTIFIER are significant. Those sub-identifiers are then compared to the corresponding sub-identifiers in the instance.

Let's look at an example. Suppose we have these families:

	subtree	bit-mask
system	1.3.6.1.2.1.1	1 1 1 1 1 1 1
interfaces	1.3.6.1.2.1.2	1 1 1 1 1 1 1
ifEntry.0.5	1.3.6.1.2.1.2.2.1.0.5	1 1 1 1 1 1 1 1 1 0 1

and we want to see if the instance `ifIndex.7` is a member of any of these families. For the first family:

```
1.3.6.1.2.1.1            -- subtree
1 1 1 1 1 1 1            -- bit-mask
1.3.6.1.2.1.2.2.1.1.7    -- ifIndex.7
            *            -- mismatch on 7th sub-identifier
```

we see that `ifIndex.7` isn't a member. For the second family:

```
1.3.6.1.2.1.2            -- subtree
1 1 1 1 1 1 1            -- bit-mask
1.3.6.1.2.1.2.2.1.1.7    -- ifIndex.7
```

we see that `ifIndex.7` is a member, even though it has more sub-identifiers than the family's subtree. Finally, for the third family:

```
1.3.6.1.2.1.2.2.1.0.5      -- subtree
1 1 1 1 1 1 1 1 1 0 1      -- bit-mask
1.3.6.1.2.1.2.2.1.1.7      -- ifIndex.7
                  *        -- mismatch on 11th sub-identifier
```

we see that `ifIndex.7` isn't a member.

Before the example, a MIB view was said to be defined in terms of one or more subtree families. What wasn't explained was the relationship between these families. Associated with each family is something that indicates whether the family is included in, or excluded from, the MIB view. Because of this, the order in which families are evaluated can influence whether an instance is considered to be within a MIB view. So, here's the final definition:

> *A MIB view is an ordered collection of subtree families, in which each family is either included in, or excluded from, the MIB view.*

And how are the subtree families ordered? Lexicographically, of course, using the same ordering rules as the rest of the management framework. (Observant readers will recall lexicographical ordering being introduced back on page 128.)

Combining the three families in the earlier example, we might construct this MIB view.

	subtree	bit-mask	status
system	1.3.6.1.2.1.1	1 1 1 1 1 1 1	included
interfaces	1.3.6.1.2.1.2	1 1 1 1 1 1 1	included
ifEntry.0.5	1.3.6.1.2.1.2.2.1.0.5	1 1 1 1 1 1 1 1 1 0 1	excluded

In this new example, `ifIndex.7` would be included in the MIB view, but `ifIndex.5` would not.

Spatial and Temporal Localities

Experience has shown that some devices may have multiple local
entities residing within them. For example, a "chassis" might house
several repeater cards, each a distinct physical entity, but with only
one agent in the entire device. In order to distinguish between the
MIB views for the different entities, the context's local entity attribute
(`contextLocalEntity`) may be used. This is simply a `DisplayString`
of local significance, e.g.,

> `Repeater1`

Note that by representing the local entity as an attribute of a context,
rather than of a MIB view, it is possible to have several contexts all
referring to the same MIB view, but with different local entities. If
the MIB view is complex, then this results in a significant savings.

In addition, there is some indication that it may be useful to
represent a temporal domain as an attribute of a context,

> `contextLocalTime`

which at present can take on one of three values:

currentTime: this refers to management information at the
current time;

restartTime: this refers to management information used upon
the next re-initialization of the device; and,

cacheTime.N: this refers to management information that is at
most "N" seconds old.

Obviously, `currentTime` makes a lot of sense, but what about the
other two? Well, `restartTime` is used when you want to modify the
"boot parameters" of a device. In contrast, `cacheTime` could be used
when talking to a device which collects and collates information from
a number of sources.

It should be noted that these last two temporal domains are new to
the management framework, and while there is hope for their utility,
they will have to prove themselves.

5.2.2 Proxy Relationships

A proxy relationship exists when an entity must communicate with a remote entity in order to access a collection of managed objects. Some of the reasons a proxy relationship might be used were explained back on page 74.

For now, we need only consider that a proxy relationship has three attributes: a proxy destination party (`contextProxyDstParty`), a proxy source party (`contextProxySrcParty`), and a remote context (`contextProxyContext`). Of these, the transport domain associated with the proxy destination party attribute determines if the other two attributes are used and, if so, how.

For example, if the proxy destination party uses SNMPv2, then the proxy relationship can be satisfied by simply constructing a new `SnmpMgmtCom` structure initialized as follows:

dstParty: the proxy destination party;

srcParty: the proxy source party;

context: the remote context; and,

operation: copied from the original message.

and the usual procedures are followed!

Let's look at an example. Table 5.1 shows a portion of the party and context databases that might be held by a proxy agent in which:

- α-1 and α-2 are parties executing at the proxy agent;

- β-1 is a party executing at the management application;

- γ-1 is a party executing on the remote entity which holds the management information;

- δ-1 is the context referencing the proxy relationship when the management application makes requests; and,

- δ-2 is the context used by the proxy agent when talking to the remote entity.

partyIdentity	β-1	α-1
partyIndex	10	11
partyTDomain	snmpUDPDomain	snmpUDPDomain
partyTAddress	u.x.y.z, 2000	a.b.c.d, 161
partyLocal	false	true
partyAuthProtocol	v2md5AuthProtocol	v2md5AuthProtocol
partyAuthClock	0	0
partyAuthPrivate	(secret)	(secret)
partyAuthPublic	"H	"H
partyAuthLifetime	300	300
partyPrivProtocol	noPriv	noPriv
partyPrivPrivate	"H	"H
partyPrivPublic	"H	"H

partyIdentity	γ-1	α-2
partyIndex	12	13
partyTDomain	snmpUDPDomain	snmpUDPDomain
partyTAddress	p.q.r.s, 161	
partyLocal	false	true
partyAuthProtocol	v2md5AuthProtocol	v2md5AuthProtocol
partyAuthClock	0	0
partyAuthPrivate	(secret)	(secret)
partyAuthPublic	"H	"H
partyAuthLifetime	300	300
partyPrivProtocol	noPriv	noPriv
partyPrivPrivate	"H	"H
partyPrivPublic	"H	"H

contextIdentity	δ-1	δ-2
contextIndex	100	101
contextViewIndex	0	0
contextLocalEntity	"H	"H
contextLocalTime	0.0	0.0
contextProxyDstParty	γ-1	β-1
contextProxySrcParty	α-2	α-1
contextProxyContext	δ-2	δ-1

Table 5.1: **Party and Context Databases held by Proxy Agent**

When the management application wants to access information on the remote entity, it sends the proxy agent a management communication like this:

dstParty=α-1, srcParty=β-1, context=δ-1

Assuming that everything checks out, the proxy agent will take the operation contained within that communication, wrap it in a new management communication like this:

dstParty=γ-1, srcParty=α-2, context=δ-2

and then send it to the remote entity. The remote entity's response will be sent back to the proxy agent in a management communication like this:

dstParty=α-2, srcParty=γ-1, context=δ-2

and the proxy agent will take the operation contained within that communication, wrap it in a new management communication like this:

dstParty=β-1, srcParty=α-1, context=δ-1

and then send it to the management application.

Observant readers probably have two questions:

1. How much of the information in Table 5.1 is known to the management application and the remote entity?

   The answer is that the management application knows only about parties α-1 and β-1, and context δ-1, but the management application doesn't know about the two parties or the context that makes up the proxy relationship defined by δ-1. Similarly, the remote entity knows only about parties α-2 and γ-1, and context δ-2.

2. Is the context δ-2 really necessary?

   The proxy agent doesn't really have to know anything about δ-2 other than it is the value in the `contextProxyContext` field of the proxy relationship defined by the context δ-1. As such, the proxy agent doesn't have to assign any meaning to δ-2. Similarly, the management application has no special reason to know anything about δ-2. In contrast, the remote entity must know all about context δ-2.

However, there is a reason why the proxy agent might need to have an entry for δ-2 in its context database — if the remote entity generates notifications, then the proxy agent might be configured to propagate these to the management application.

Finally, note that depending on the nature of the proxy, all three fields in the proxy relationship may not be useful. For example, when discussing proxy relationships to a device implementing SNMPv1, only the `contextProxyDstParty` attribute is of interest. (This is discussed in greater detail later on in Section 6.3.1 starting on page 315.)

5.2.3   The Context Database Group

The context database group in the `SNMPv2-PARTY-MIB` module defines a context table which represents information about all of the contexts known to an entity. Figure 5.4 summarizes this group.

Let's look at the attributes which are common to all contexts:

contextIdentity: the identity of the context, defined using the `Context` textual convention;

contextIndex: a unique integer assigned to this context by the agent, which remains constant between re-initializations of the entity, used to index other tables;

contextLocal: indicates whether this context is realized by the entity;

contextViewIndex: identifies whether this context refers to object resources that are either local (a MIB view) or remote (a proxy relationship);

contextStorageType: describes this entry in the `contextTable`; and,

contextStatus: describes the status of this entry in the `contextTable`.

The only object requiring additional explanation is

```
contextViewIndex
```

If the value of this object for a particular context is greater than zero, then the context refers to a MIB view and, for that context, these objects are meaningless:

```
contextProxyDstParty
contextProxySrcParty
contextProxyContext
```

Otherwise, if the value of `contextViewIndex` is equal to zero, then the context refers to a proxy relationship and, for that context, these objects are meaningless:

```
contextLocalEntity
contextLocalTime
```

Context ::= **TEXTUAL-CONVENTION**
    ...
    SYNTAX   OBJECT IDENTIFIER

snmpContexts   **OBJECT IDENTIFIER** ::= { partyMIBObjects 2 }

contextTable **OBJECT-TYPE**
    SYNTAX   SEQUENCE OF ContextEntry   10
    ...
    ::= { snmpContexts 1 }

contextEntry **OBJECT-TYPE**
    SYNTAX   ContextEntry

    ...
    INDEX   { **IMPLIED** contextIdentity }
    ::= { contextTable 1 }

ContextEntry ::=   20
    SEQUENCE {
        contextIdentity   Context,
        contextIndex   **INTEGER** (1..65535),
        contextLocal   TruthValue,
        contextViewIndex   **INTEGER** (0..65535),
        contextLocalEntity   **OCTET STRING**,
        contextLocalTime   **OBJECT IDENTIFIER**,
        contextProxyDstParty Party,
        contextProxySrcParty Party,
        contextProxyContext **OBJECT IDENTIFIER**,   30
        contextStorageType   StorageType,
        contextStatus   RowStatus
    }

Figure 5.4: The Contexts Database Group

5.2.4   The MIB View Database Group

The MIB view database group in the `SNMPv2-PARTY-MIB` module defines a view table which represents information about all of the MIB views known to an entity. Figure 5.5 summarizes this group.

Each row in this table defines a subtree family. Let's look at the columns in this table:

viewIndex: the identity of the MIB view which includes or excludes this subtree family (this corresponds to the value of the `contextViewIndex` object for the context defining a MIB view);

viewSubtree: the `OBJECT IDENTIFIER` associated with the subtree family;

viewMask: the bit-mask associated with the subtree family, expressed as a string of octets;

viewType: an indication of whether this subtree family is included in or excluded from its MIB view;

viewStorageType: describes this entry in the `viewTable`; and,

viewStatus: describes the status of this entry in the `viewTable`.

The only object that requires additional discussion is `viewMask`. Earlier, when we discussed subtree families, a bit-mask was used to determine which sub-identifiers in the subtree family's `OBJECT IDENTIFIER` were of interest. To provide for a compact representation, the `SNMPv2-PARTY-MIB` module uses an `OCTET STRING` for its syntax. Looking back to the earlier example on page 211, we might represent the `viewMask` column as follows:

	subtree	mask
system	1.3.6.1.2.1.1	'fe'H
interfaces	1.3.6.1.2.1.2	'fe'H
ifEntry.0.5	1.3.6.1.2.1.2.2.1.0.5	'ffa0'H

where zero-valued bits were used to pad the mask, both to be long enough for the subtree, and to be an integral number of octets in

snmpViews   **OBJECT IDENTIFIER** ::= { partyMIBObjects 4 }

viewTable **OBJECT-TYPE**
   SYNTAX   **SEQUENCE OF** ViewEntry
   ...
   ::= { snmpViews 1 }

viewEntry **OBJECT-TYPE**
   SYNTAX   ViewEntry   10
   ...
   INDEX   { viewIndex, **IMPLIED** viewSubtree }
   ::= { viewTable 1 }

ViewEntry ::=
   SEQUENCE {
      viewIndex   **INTEGER** (1..65535),
      viewSubtree   **OBJECT IDENTIFIER**,
      viewMask   **OCTET STRING** (**SIZE** (0..16))
      viewType   **INTEGER** { included(1), excluded(2) },   20
      viewStorageType   StorageType,
      viewStatus   RowStatus
   }

Figure 5.5: The MIB View Database Group

length. Finally, as a further optimization, if the mask is the empty string, then it is treated as if it were a string filled with one-valued bits. Hence, the canonical form for this example would be:

	subtree	mask
system	1.3.6.1.2.1.1	"H
interfaces	1.3.6.1.2.1.2	"H
ifEntry.0.5	1.3.6.1.2.1.2.2.1.0.5	'ffa0'H

5.3   Access Policies

An SNMPv2 access policy or, simply, an access policy, defines the operations that may be performed when a source party communicates with a destination party and references a particular context. Recalling the definition of the `SnmpAuthMsg` structure shown back on page 195, in order for the operation contained within this structure to be executed, the receiving entity must have an access policy entry which relates `dstParty`, `srcParty`, and `context` and allows the operator specified in the `operation` field to be performed.

Given that there are a small number of SNMP operations, one would expect that privileges associated with an access policy be a string of bits, e.g.,

```
BIT STRING {
    get(0), get-next(1), response(2),
    set(3), get-bulk(4), inform(5),
    snmpV2-trap(6)
}
```

Well, for historical reasons, an integer sum is used instead.

operation	value
get	1
get-next	2
response	4
set	8
get-bulk	32
inform	64
snmpV2-trap	128

So, the value 35 represents these three operations:

```
get
get-next
get-bulk
```

As might be expected, the value zero(0) represents no operations whatsoever.

There is also one very important rule about access policies: the principals (originating and receiving parties) must use the same authentication protocol. There are three primary reasons for this:

- the `v2md5AuthProtocol` references clocks from both the originating and receiving parties;

- if the originating party didn't use either authentication or privacy, and the recipient party used both authentication and privacy, then a response would use privacy without authentication, which is nonsensical; and,

- if the two parties use the same authentication protocol, then their credentials will be roughly of the same size. (This makes it easier for the protocol engine to estimate what the size of a response will be!)

snmpAccess   **OBJECT IDENTIFIER** ::= { partyMIBObjects 3 }

aclTable **OBJECT-TYPE**
  SYNTAX   **SEQUENCE OF** AclEntry

   ...
  ::= { snmpAccess 1 }

aclEntry **OBJECT-TYPE**
  SYNTAX   AclEntry   10

   ...
  INDEX   { aclTarget, aclSubject, aclResources }
  ::= { aclTable 1 }

AclEntry ::=
  SEQUENCE {
    aclTarget   **INTEGER**, $--$ *dstParty's partyIndex*
    aclSubject   **INTEGER**, $--$ *srcParty's partyIndex*
    aclResources   **INTEGER**, $--$ *context's contextIndex*
    aclPrivileges   **INTEGER** (0..255),   20
    aclStorageType   StorageType,
    aclStatus   RowStatus
  }

Figure 5.6: The Access Privileges Database Group

5.3.1   The Access Privileges Database Group

The access privileges database group in the `SNMPv2-PARTY-MIB` module defines an access control table which represents information about all of the access policies known to an entity. Figure 5.6 summarizes this group.

Let's look at the columns in this table:

aclTarget: identifies the `partyIndex` of a recipient party;

aclSubject: identifies the `partyIndex` of an originating party;

aclResources: identifies the `contextIndex` of a context;

aclPrivileges: identifies the allowed operations;

aclStorageType: describes this entry in the `aclTable`; and,

aclStatus: describes the status of this entry in the `aclTable`.

aclTarget	11	10	12	13
aclSubject	10	11	13	12
aclResources	100	100	101	101
aclPrivileges	35	132	35	132
	get	response	get	response
	get-next	snmpV2-trap	get-next	snmpV2-trap
	get-bulk		get-bulk	

Table 5.2: Access Privileges Database held by Proxy Agent

The only thing tricky about this table is that it is indexed by three integers which refer to the principals and the context. The alternative was a table indexed by three **OBJECT IDENTIFIER**s which some might find excessive. The disadvantage to using integers is rather subtle: because they are indirect pointers, a single protocol set operation cannot be used to create parties, contexts, and access policy entries — you have to create the parties and contexts first, then retrieve the indexes which are automatically created for them, and finally issue a second protocol set operation to create access policy entries.

Briefly, let's reconsider the example of a proxy agent which was introduced starting on page 214. Table 5.2 shows a portion of the access privileges database that might be held by that proxy agent. In terms of information held by the management application, it has entries only for parties α-1 and β-1. Similarly, the remote entity has entries only for parties α-2 and γ-1.

5.4   Procedures

Well, we've spent a lot of time looking at parties, contexts, and access policies. Let's put it all together. In order to make things easier to follow, refer to Figure 5.7 when reading the rest of this section.

5.4.1   Originating a Message

Using local knowledge, the originating entity begins by selecting the appropriate originating and recipient parties which have the required access privileges and security properties for the context of the operation. An `SnmpMgmtCom` structure is then initialized from this information and copied into the `authData` field of an `SnmpAuthMsg` structure.

Next, the authentication algorithm for the originating party is applied in order to fill in the `authInfo` field with the originating party's credentials:

- If the algorithm is `noAuth`, then the `authInfo` field is set to a zero-length string of octets;

- otherwise, if the algorithm is `v2md5AuthProtocol`, an `AuthInformation` structure is used.

The `SnmpAuthMsg` structure is then serialized.

Then, an `SnmpPrivMsg` structure is initialized, using the recipient party's identity to fill in the `privDest`. The privacy algorithm for the recipient party is then invoked in order to generate the `privData` field of an `SnmpPrivData` structure using the serialized representation of the `SnmpAuthMsg` structure.

Finally, the `SnmpPrivMsg` structure is serialized and this is sent to the transport address of the recipient party.

5.4.2   Receiving a Message

When a packet is received from the transport service, the

`snmpStatsPackets`

```
SnmpPrivMsg ::=
    [1] IMPLICIT SEQUENCE {
        privDst
            OBJECT IDENTIFIER,
        privData -- SnmpAuthMsg, possibly encrypted
            [1] IMPLICIT OCTET STRING
    }

SnmpAuthMsg ::=
    [1] IMPLICIT SEQUENCE {                                         10
        authInfo
            CHOICE {
                noAuth
                    OCTET STRING (SIZE (0)),

                v2md5AuthProtocol
                    [2] IMPLICIT SEQUENCE {
                        authDigest
                            OCTET STRING (SIZE (16)),
                        authDstTimestamp                           20
                            UInteger32,
                        authSrcTimestamp
                            UInteger32
                    }
            },

        authData
            SnmpMgmtCom
    }
                                                                   30
SnmpMgmtCom ::=
    [2] IMPLICIT SEQUENCE {
        dstParty
            OBJECT IDENTIFIER,
        srcParty
            OBJECT IDENTIFIER,
        context
            OBJECT IDENTIFIER,
        operation
            PDUs                                                   40
    }
```

Figure 5.7: SNMPv2 Message Format (revisited)

counter is incremented. (This counter, along with another dozen or so counters, will be defined momentarily, starting on page 232.) Then the packet is examined to see if it is a serialized representation of an SnmpPrivMsg structure.

If not, then one of two counters is incremented:

- snmpStats30Something, if the first octet of the packet is hexadecimal 30;[4] or,

- snmpStatsEncodingErrors,

and the packet is discarded. Otherwise, the packet is converted into an SnmpPrivMsg structure, and the party identified in the privDest field is looked up in the receiving entity's party database.

If information on the party isn't present (or doesn't refer to a party which executes locally at the entity), then the

snmpStatsUnknownDstParties

counter is incremented and the message is discarded. Otherwise, the privacy algorithm associated with the recipient party is invoked in order to decipher the privData field.

If the resulting string of octets isn't a serialized representation of an SnmpPrivMsg structure, then the

snmpStatsEncodingErrors

counter is incremented and the packet is discarded. (Note that there are many possible reasons for this error, including, e.g., mismatch of the privacy key.) Otherwise, the resulting string of octets is converted into an SnmpAuthMsg structure.

If the values in the privDest field and the dstParty field don't match, then the

snmpStatsDstPartyMismatches

counter is incremented and the packet is discarded. Otherwise, the party identified in the srcParty field is looked up in the receiving entity's party database.

If information on the party isn't present, then the

---

[4]The first octet of an SNMPv1 message has a hexadecimal value of 30.

snmpStatsUnknownSrcParties

counter is incremented and the message is discarded. Otherwise, the authentication algorithm associated with the originating party is invoked in order to evaluate the validity of the credentials contained in the authInfo field.

If the SnmpAuthMsg structure is deemed unauthentic, then the appropriate counter is incremented:

- snmpStatsBadAuths, if the credentials were of an inappropriate type;

- snmpStatsNotInLifetimes, if the communication was "not in lifetime"; or,

- snmpStatsWrongDigestValues, if there was a "digest mismatch".

authorizationFailure traps are generated (if the

snmpV2EnableAuthenTraps

object allows), and the message is discarded. Otherwise, the context identified in the context field of the SnmpMgmtCom structure contained within the SnmpAuthMsg structure is looked up in the receiving entity's context database.

If information on the context isn't present (or, if the operation contained within the SnmpMgmtCom structure is get, get-next, set, or get-bulk, and the context isn't realized by the receiving entity), then the

snmpStatsUnknownContexts

counter is incremented and the message is discarded. Otherwise, the receiving entity's access privileges database is consulted to see what operations are allowed when the principals communicate referring to the specified context.

If the operation contained within the SnmpMgmtCom structure is not allowed, then:

- if the operation is a **response** or an **snmpV2-trap**, then the

    snmpStatsBadOperations

  counter is incremented; otherwise,

- an **authorizationError** response is returned to the originating party.

In either event, the message is discarded.

Finally, if the context refers to local object resources, then the operation is performed with respect to the MIB view identified by the context. If a response is generated to the request, the steps above in Section 5.4.1 are followed, with the originating and recipient parties swapped. In addition, the response is sent to the transport address from which the request was received, not the transport address found in the party database.

Instead, if the context refers to remote object resources, then:

- if the operation is a **response**, then it is correlated with a previous request, and a response is sent to the party which originated that request (the steps above in Section 5.4.1 are followed, with the originating and recipient parties swapped, and with the response sent to the transport address from which the request was received);

- if the operation is an **snmpV2-trap**, then the trap is sent to the appropriate management applications;

- otherwise, the request is propagated through the use of the proxy relationship defined by the context.

For an **snmpV2-trap**, the contexts and access privileges databases are consulted to determine the parties, if any, to which the trap should be sent. First, the proxy agent looks for any context entries in which:

- **contextProxyDstParty** refers to the originating party; and,

- **contextProxyContext** refers to the context contained in the **SnmpMgmtCom** structure.

For each such context entry, the proxy agent looks for any access policy entries in which:

- `aclResources` refers to the context entry;

- `aclSubject` refers to a party executing locally at the agent; and,

- `aclPrivileges` allows the **snmpV2-trap** operation.

For each such entry, an **snmpV2-trap** is sent from the `aclSubject` party to the `aclTarget` party using the `aclResources` context. The instance of **snmpTrapNumbers** which corresponds to the `aclTarget` party is incremented, and this new value is placed in the **request-id** field. (The **snmpTrapNumbers** object, defined later on page 277, is the number of traps which this entity has sent to a particular party.)

5.4.3   The snmpStats Group

```
snmpStats     OBJECT IDENTIFIER ::= { snmpMIBObjects 1 }
```

Figure 5.8 shows a Case Diagram relating these objects:

snmpStatsPackets: the number of packets received from the transport service;

snmpStats30Something: the number of packets which appeared to be SNMPv1 messages;

snmpStatsEncodingErrors: the number of packets which were improperly encoded;

snmpStatsUnknownDstParties: the number of `SnmpPrivMsg` structures received which identified an unknown local party;

snmpStatsDstPartyMismatches: the number of `SnmpPrivMsg` structures received which contained an `SnmpAuthMsg` identifying a different destination party than the `privDest` field;

snmpStatsUnknownSrcParties: the number of `SnmpAuthMsg` structures received which identified an unknown remote party;

snmpStatsBadAuths: the number of `SnmpAuthMsg` structures received which had incorrect credentials;

snmpStatsNotInLifetimes: the number of `SnmpAuthMsg` structures received outside of message lifetime of the source party;

snmpStatsWrongDigestValues: the number of `SnmpAuthMsg` structures received with an incorrect digest;

snmpStatsUnknownContexts: the number of `SnmpMgmtCom` structures received which identified an unknown context;

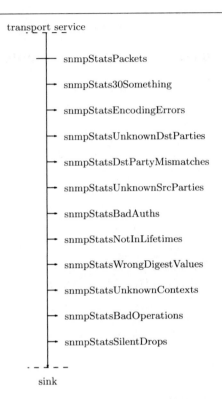

Figure 5.8: Case Diagram for the SNMPv2 Statistics Group

snmpStatsBadOperations: the number of SnmpMgmtCom structures received which were silently dropped because the access policy didn't allow a particular operation; and,

snmpStatsSilentDrops: the number of SnmpMgmtCom structures received which were silently dropped for any other reason.

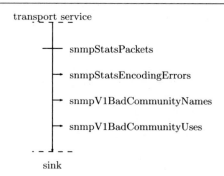

transport service

— snmpStatsPackets

— snmpStatsEncodingErrors

— snmpV1BadCommunityNames

— snmpV1BadCommunityUses

sink

Figure 5.9: Case Diagram for the SNMPv1 Statistics Group

5.4.4   The snmpV1 Group

If the protocol entity implements the original SNMP as well as SNMPv2, then it must implement this group.

```
snmpV1          OBJECT IDENTIFIER ::= { snmpMIBObjects 2 }
```

Figure 5.9 shows a Case Diagram relating these objects:

snmpV1BadCommunityNames: the number of SNMPv1 authentication errors; and,

snmpV1BadCommunityUses: the number of SNMPv1 authorization errors.

along with two in the `snmpStats` group.

5.5 Compliance Statements

Because products which include security technology are subject to export and use controls, there are four compliance statements defined for the `SNMPv2-PARTY-MIB` module:

level	authentication	limited privacy	privacy
unSecurable			
partyNoPrivacy	√		
partyPrivacy	√	√	
fullPrivacy	√	√	√

All compliance levels require implementation of the `noAuth` and `noPriv` protocols. The `unSecurable` level requires nothing else.

The `partyNoPrivacy` level also requires implementation of the

    `v2md5AuthProtocol`

protocol but nothing else.

The `partyPrivacy` and `fullPrivacy` levels require implementation of both the `v2md5AuthProtocol` and the `desPrivProtocol` protocols. Where they differ is in how privacy may be used. The `fullPrivacy` level has no restrictions on the use of privacy, whilst the `partyPrivacy` level allows privacy only for those parties allowed access only to the `SNMPv2-PARTY-MIB` module. In other words, you can use privacy for creating and maintaining parties, but that's it.

So what's the purpose of having these different categories? It is believed that these different categories roughly correspond to the use and export controls exercised by western nations, and that providing this guidance will facilitate the licensing process. The topic of controls `soap...` on the use and export of security technology is perhaps the ultimate conundrum. Nothing has introduced more fear, uncertainty, and doubt, than the introduction of security technology into SNMP. The one thing that seems certain is that this will facilitate the generation of lots of billable hours for legal practitioners. `...soap`

5.6   The Initial Configuration

Finally, when devices are installed, they need to be configured with an initial set of administrative policy information. In order to facilitate this, two **OBJECT IDENTIFIER** prefixes have been assigned for use by each local administration:

```
initialPartyId
            OBJECT IDENTIFIER ::= { partyAdmin 3 }
initialContextId
            OBJECT IDENTIFIER ::= { partyAdmin 4 }
```

These are used in combination with the initial IP address of the device for configuration, e.g., to identify the first party for the device at IP address **a.b.c.d**,

```
initialPartyId.a.b.c.d.1
```

would be used.

Table 5.3 shows the initial configuration for the party database. Six parties are defined:

- a **noAuth**/**noPriv** pair;

- a **v2md5AuthProtocol**/**noPriv** pair; and,

- a **v2md5AuthProtocol**/**desPrivProtocol** pair.

After the initial party secrets have been assigned through an out-of-band means, all party maintenance may be performed using the management protocol.

Table 5.4 on page 238 shows the initial configuration for the context and MIB view databases (in the agent). Two contexts are defined, both referring to MIB views. The first MIB view includes only three small subtree families; in contrast, the second MIB view includes the **internet** subtree, which is likely to be every managed object in the device.

Table 5.5 (also on page 238) shows the initial configuration for the access privileges database. The **noAuth**/**noPriv** party pair are given read-only access to the first context (and thereby the limited

partyIdentity	initialPartyId.a.b.c.d.1	initialPartyId.a.b.c.d.2
partyIndex	1	2
partyTDomain	snmpUDPDomain	snmpUDPDomain
partyTAddress	a.b.c.d, 161	
partyLocal	true	false
partyAuthProtocol	noAuth	noAuth
partyAuthClock	0	0
partyAuthPrivate	"H	"H
partyAuthPublic	"H	"H
partyAuthLifetime	300	300
partyPrivProtocol	noPriv	noPriv
partyPrivPrivate	"H	"H
partyPrivPublic	"H	"H

partyIdentity	initialPartyId.a.b.c.d.3	initialPartyId.a.b.c.d.4
partyIndex	3	4
partyTDomain	snmpUDPDomain	snmpUDPDomain
partyTAddress	a.b.c.d, 161	
partyLocal	true	false
partyAuthProtocol	v2md5AuthProtocol	v2md5AuthProtocol
partyAuthClock	0	0
partyAuthPrivate	(secret)	(secret)
partyAuthPublic	"H	"H
partyAuthLifetime	300	300
partyPrivProtocol	noPriv	noPriv
partyPrivPrivate	"H	"H
partyPrivPublic	"H	"H

partyIdentity	initialPartyId.a.b.c.d.5	initialPartyId.a.b.c.d.6
partyIndex	5	6
partyTDomain	snmpUDPDomain	snmpUDPDomain
partyTAddress	a.b.c.d, 161	
partyLocal	true	false
partyAuthProtocol	v2md5AuthProtocol	v2md5AuthProtocol
partyAuthClock	0	0
partyAuthPrivate	(secret)	(secret)
partyAuthPublic	"H	"H
partyAuthLifetime	300	300
partyPrivProtocol	desPrivProtocol	desPrivProtocol
partyPrivPrivate	(secret)	(secret)
partyPrivPublic	"H	"H

Table 5.3: Initial Configuration for the Party Database

contextIdentity	initialContextId.a.b.c.d.1	initialContextId.a.b.c.d.2
contextIndex	1	2
contextViewIndex	1	2
contextLocalEntity	"H	"H
contextLocalTime	currentTime	currentTime
contextProxyDstParty	0.0	0.0
contextProxySrcParty	0.0	0.0
contextProxyContext	0.0	0.0

viewIndex	1	1	1	2
viewSubtree	system	snmpStats	snmpParties	internet
viewMask	"H	"H	"H	"H
viewType	included	included	included	included

Table 5.4: Initial Configuration for the Context and MIB View Databases

aclTarget	1	2	3	4	5	6
aclSubject	2	1	4	3	6	5
aclResources	1	1	2	2	2	2
aclPrivileges	35	132	43	4	43	4
	get	response	get	response	get	response
	get-next	snmpV2-trap	get-next		get-next	
	get-bulk		set		set	
			get-bulk		get-bulk	

Table 5.5: Initial Configuration for the Access Privileges Database

MIB view). This is necessary in order for the clock synchronization algorithm to function. The remaining party pairs are given read-write access to the second context (and thereby the extensive MIB view).

Observant readers will note that the default configuration gives read-write access to the party, context, access control, and view tables to the two authenticated parties corresponding to a management application. This means that either of these parties can create and re-configure any party with any level of access. In a real configuration, very few parties would be given this level of authorization. Instead, most parties would be given access only to the party table, so that they could maintain their own parameters, but not modify their capabilities. A party with this level of access could also create new parties, or disable existing parties. In response:

- one could categorize this as a denial of service attack, and recall (from page 198) that preventing such attacks isn't a goal of the administrative framework; or,

- one could configure a MIB view which included only those instances in the party table which were associated with a given party.

The first response isn't as *Chamberlain-esque* as might be expected; after all, the management applications are supposed to be cooperating. Further, the second response does have a disadvantage: a separate MIB view is required for each party corresponding to a management application, which leads to a more cumbersome configuration.

Chapter 6

Operational Model

It is now time to examine the role of protocol operations in the management framework. SNMP is an asynchronous request-response protocol based on trap-directed polling. This means that a protocol entity needn't wait for a response after sending a message — it can send other messages or do other activities.

The transport requirements of SNMP are modest: a connectionless-mode transport service, usually the UDP. Although superficially this is consistent with the Fundamental Axiom, there is a more important reason. Network management functions often occur in a trouble-shooting or "firefighting" mode. The management application is in the best position to decide what the reliability constraints are for management traffic. The lowest common denominator is a connectionless-mode transport service, so this is what SNMP prefers to use. This choice allows the management station to determine the appropriate level of retransmission in order to accommodate lossy or congested networks.

Interested readers might wish to consult [59] for a discussion of the relationship between SNMP and the underlying transport service.

Discussion is now divided into three parts:

- protocol interactions;

- transport mappings; and,

- achieving coexistence between the original framework and the SNMPv2 framework.

6.1   Protocol Interactions

In general, an SNMP interaction consists of a request of some kind, followed by a response, e.g.,

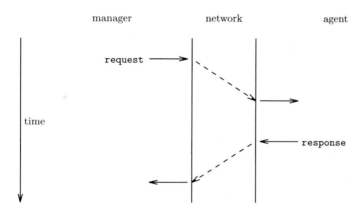

Actually, there are four possible outcomes of an operation:

- a *response* without exception or error;

- a response with one or more *exceptions*;

- a response with an *error*; or,

- a *timeout.*

Before studying the meaning of each of these, it will be helpful to look at the structures which are exchanged by SNMPv2 entities.

The ASN.1 definition of an SNMPv2 PDU is found in Figure 6.1 starting on page 244. The influence of the Fundamental Axiom can be seen in this definition. For example, neither the **error-status** nor the **error-index** fields is used in the **GetRequest-PDU** data type. But, by including them, a single ASN.1 data type can be used for the messages exchanged by all SNMPv2 operations. This means that only two routines need be written to encode and decode these messages for transmission. This approach is contrary to the ASN.1 philosophy of defining specialized, highly-descriptive data types for each message type.

```
PDUs ::=
    CHOICE {
        get−request
            GetRequest−PDU,

        get−next−request
            GetNextRequest−PDU,

        get−bulk−request
            GetBulkRequest−PDU,                          10

        response
            Response−PDU,

        set−request
            SetRequest−PDU,

        inform−request
            InformRequest−PDU,
                                                         20
        trap
            SNMPv2−Trap−PDU
    }

GetRequest−PDU ::=
    [0] IMPLICIT PDU

GetNextRequest−PDU ::=
    [1] IMPLICIT PDU
                                                         30
Response−PDU ::=
    [2] IMPLICIT PDU

SetRequest−PDU ::=
    [3] IMPLICIT PDU

−− [4] is obsolete

GetBulkRequest−PDU ::=
    [5] IMPLICIT BulkPDU                                 40

InformRequest−PDU ::=
    [6] IMPLICIT PDU

SNMPv2−Trap−PDU ::=
    [7] IMPLICIT PDU
```

Figure 6.1: SNMPv2 PDU Format

The fields of the `PDU` data type are now described. Note that by convention, the term *variable binding* refers to the combination of a name and value of an instance of an object.

request-id: an integer-value used by a management application to distinguish among outstanding requests. This allows a management application, if it so desires, to rapidly send several SNMP messages. An incoming reply can then be correlated to the corresponding request. (Agents, of course, are not allowed to modify the `request-id`.)

Further, this provides a simple, but effective, means for the management application to identify messages duplicated by the network (or operations duplicated by retransmissions).

Finally, this also allows a management application to measure the roundtrip time of its traffic.

error-status: if non-zero, this indicates an error occurred when processing the request, and that the `variable-bindings` field should be ignored.

error-index: if non-zero, this indicates which variable in the request was in error.

variable-bindings: a list of variables, each containing a name and value.

The SNMPv2 operations can be categorized as:

retrieval: `get`, `get-next`, and `get-bulk`;

modification: `set`;

trap: `snmpV2-trap`; and,

manager-to-manager: `inform`.

6.1.1 Interactions

Let's first look at the basic style of interaction between two SNMPv2 entities. In subsequent sections, we'll see how this varies in different situations.

To begin, the typical successful interaction goes something like this:

1. The initiating protocol entity issues a request with:

   - a unique `request-id`;

   - a zero-valued `error-status`/`error-index`; and,

   - zero or more variable bindings.

2. If the operation wasn't an `snmpV2-trap`, the responding protocol entity issues a response with:

   - the same `request-id`;

   - a zero-valued `error-status`; and,

   - the same variable bindings.

If a retrieval operation is requested, then in the request, the values associated with the variables have the value `unSpecified`; otherwise, the variable bindings are expected to have values. Similarly, in a response to a retrieval operation, the values are filled in with the appropriate information. If a retrieval operation isn't requested, the variable bindings in the response are identical to those in the request.

Exceptional Interaction

While processing a retrieval request (the `get`, `get-next`, or `get-bulk` operators), the agent might encounter an exception, indicating that a particular variable cannot be processed. There are three kinds of exceptional values, and they occur on a per-variable basis:

noSuchObject: which indicates that the object type corresponding to the variable is not implemented by the agent;

noSuchInstance: which indicates that the particular object instance identified by the variable doesn't exist in the MIB view for the operation; and,

endOfMibView: which, when traversing a collection of management information, indicates that no further information is available in the MIB view for the operation.

Thus, the SNMPv2 interaction involving exceptions goes something like this:

1. The initiating protocol entity issues a retrieval request with:

   - a unique `request-id`;
   - a zero-valued `error-status`/`error-index`; and,
   - zero or more variable bindings.

2. The responding protocol entity issues a response with:

   - the same `request-id`;
   - a zero-valued `error-status`; and,
   - the same variable bindings, but with different values and one or more exceptional values.

Error Interaction

While processing any kind of request, the agent might encounter an error, indicating that the operation cannot be processed. There are several kinds of errors, and, unlike exceptions, they occur on a per-operation basis. Thus, the SNMPv2 interaction involving an error goes something like this:

1. The initiating protocol entity issues a retrieval request with:

   - a unique `request-id`;
   - a zero-valued `error-status/error-index`; and,
   - zero or more variable bindings.

2. The responding protocol entity issues a response with:

   - the same `request-id`;
   - a non-zero `error-status` (the value of `error-index` may be non-zero); and,
   - the exact variable bindings as in the request.

Keeping in mind that errors are never returned in response to a `trap` operation, there are two errors which can be returned in response to any other kind of request:

tooBig: indicates that the response to this request would be too large to send; and,

genErr: a catch-all error, which shouldn't be returned unless no other recourse is available.

The `tooBig` error is special in that the agent truncates the variable bindings in the response before sending it. (This increases the likelihood that the response can be sent.)

While processing a modification request (the `set` operation), there are also several other errors which might be returned. Discussion of these will be postponed until page 265.

Timeout Interaction

The final kind of interaction is one in which a request is sent but a response is never received. There are several possibilities:

- the network dropped the request;

- the agent isn't running;

- the agent dropped the request;

- the network dropped the response; or,

- the timeout was too short.

In order to minimize ambiguity, the `snmpStats` and `snmpV1` groups in the `SNMPv2-MIB` module (introduced earlier starting on page 232) are used to count silent drops which might contribute to the third possibility.

From Interactions to Processing

Now let's look at how the various requests are processed. For each description, the narrative begins after an `SnmpMgmtCom` structure has been approved for execution at the agent. So,

- the `SnmpPrivMsg` structure has been deciphered;

- the `SnmpAuthMsg` structure has been authenticated;

- the `SnmpMgmtCom` structure has been checked against the access policy; and,

- the context for this operation defines a MIB view (and not a proxy relationship).

As a request is processed, its variable bindings are examined. If, for some reason, the request doesn't have an empty `variable-bindings` field (indicating zero variable bindings), then the procedure for each operation collapses to doing nothing more than returning a `noError` response. (Of course, the privacy, authentication, and access control procedures are always performed first.)

6.1.2   Retrieval Requests

Recall from Section 4.1.7 on page 128, that in order to provide an efficient means for traversing the management information, the management framework employs a rather clever method for identifying instances: an OBJECT IDENTIFIER, formed by concatenating the name of the object type with a suffix, is used. By naming instances using OBJECT IDENTIFIERs, a *lexicographic ordering* is enforced over all object instances. This means that, for instance names a and b, one of three conditions consistently holds: either $a < b$, $a = b$, or $a > b$.

With this brief reminder, let's look at the three retrieval requests: the **get**, **get-next**, and **get-bulk** operators.

The Not-So-Wimpy Get Operator

If the management application knows precisely the instances of the management information it wants, then it issues a **get-request**:

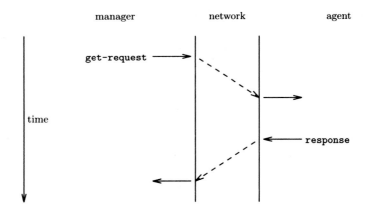

Outside of the catch-all **genErr**, only one other error can be returned, **tooBig**.

Otherwise, for each variable in the request, the named instance is retrieved from the MIB view for this operation:

- if the agent doesn't implement the object type associated with the variable, then a `noSuchObject` exceptional-value is put in the response; otherwise,

- if the instance specified doesn't exist, or if it is outside the MIB view for this operation, then a `noSuchInstance` exceptional-value is put in the response; otherwise,

- the value associated with the instance is put in the response.

The reason why the `get` operator is called the *not-so-wimpy* `get` operator is historical. In the original version of SNMP, exceptional responses did not exist. Instead, an error, `noSuchName`, was returned. This made it impossible for a management application to determine if the agent didn't implement the object or just didn't have the desired instance. From an architectural perspective, there was a certain elegance to this purity of model; but, from an interoperability perspective, this was a constant source of frustration.

The Powerful Get-Next Operator

If the management application knows generally but not specifically the instances of the management information it wants, then it issues a `get-next-request`:

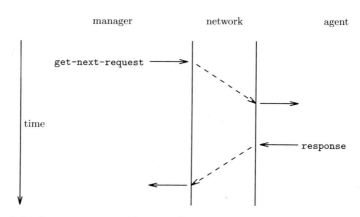

As with the **get** operation, only two errors can be returned: `tooBig` or `genErr`. Otherwise, for each variable in the request, the first named instance which follows the variable is retrieved from the MIB view for this operation:

- if there is no next instance in the MIB view for this variable, then an `endOfMibView` exceptional-value is put in the response; otherwise,

- the variable name is updated to identify the next instance in the MIB view for this variable, and the value associated with the next instance is put in the response.

The **get-next** operator makes good use of the lexicographic ordering of variables. Let's see how:

To begin, observe that an operand of the **get-next** operator needn't identify an instance, it can be *any* OBJECT IDENTIFIER. Hence, the operation

```
get-next ({sysDescr, unSpecified})
```

returns the name and value of the next instance in the MIB view, which we would expect to be

```
sysDescr.0
```

This illustrates an important concept: the `get-next` operator can be used to see if an object is supported by an agent, simply by specifying the name of the object rather than naming the desired instance of that object — historically, this is how one got around the limitations of SNMPv1's wimpy `get` operator.

Similarly, one could imagine that the call

```
get-next ({0.0, unSpecified})
```

would return the name and value of the very first instance in the MIB view for this operation. A traversal is achieved by using the result of the first call to the `get-next` operator as the operand of the second, and so on, until an error is returned.

Further, because of the naming architecture used in the MIB, tables are traversed in column-row order. When traversing a table, each instance of the first column is "walked", then each instance of the second column is "walked", and so on, until the end of the table is reached. At this point, the next object instance, which is arbitrarily distant from the table, lexicographically speaking, is returned. An exception is returned *only* if an operand given to the `get-next` operator is lexicographically greater than or equal to the lexicographically largest instance in the MIB view.

Because the `get-next` operator can be given multiple operands, it is possible to efficiently traverse an entire table. Hence, the call

```
get-next
    ({ipRouteDest,    unSpecified},
     {ipRouteIfIndex, unSpecified},
     {ipRouteNextHop, unSpecified})
```

returns the name and value of these three columns in the first row of the IP routing table. If there was a default route installed in the routing table, we might expect these names to be:

```
ipRouteDest.0.0.0.0
ipRouteIfIndex.0.0.0.0
ipRouteNextHop.0.0.0.0
```

To find the next row in the table, these names are used as operands
to another call to the **get-next** operator:

```
get-next
     ({ipRouteDest.0.0.0.0,     unSpecified},
      {ipRouteIfIndex.0.0.0.0, unSpecified},
      {ipRouteNextHop.0.0.0.0, unSpecified})
```

This process may be continued until the entire table has been traversed. The management application knows that it has reached the
end of the table when a name is returned which no longer shares the
same prefix as the desired object type. Consider this example, in
which only the routing destination object is of interest:

```
get-next ({ipRouteDest,              unSpecified})
         -> ipRouteDest.0.0.0.0

get-next ({ipRouteDest.0.0.0.0,      unSpecified})
         -> ipRouteDest.192.33.4.0

get-next ({ipRouteDest.192.33.4.0, unSpecified})
         -> ipRouteIfIndex.0.0.0.0
```

The third call to the **get-next** operator returned an instance with
a different prefix than the supplied operand. Thus, the management
application knows it has reached the end of that column in the table.

Of course, if one wanted to start the traversal in the middle of the
routing table, only a partial instance-identifier need be used, e.g.,

```
get-next
     ({ipRouteDest.192,     unSpecified},
      {ipRouteIfIndex.192, unSpecified},
      {ipRouteNextHop.192, unSpecified})
```

which will retrieve the first entry in the routing table after the indicated starting point, e.g., for destination IP address `192.33.4.20`.

It should be noted that there is one interesting interaction which
occurs when the **get-next** operator is used with a large number of
operands to sweep an empty table, and the variable following is a large
string. It is possible that a **tooBig** error response might be returned,

instead of returning multiple instances of that next variable. This is a correct protocol interaction since the `get-next` operator could find no instances in the table!

It should be obvious to the reader why this operator is termed the *powerful* `get-next` operator. There is, however, a more subtle meaning. Other management protocols have extremely complicated mechanisms for traversing management information. Usually these involve subtree scoping and attribute filtering. By using a uniform naming scheme, SNMP is able to provide an extremely functional traversal mechanism with little or no additional overhead. Proponents of the management framework always say "the powerful `get-next` operator" to remind proponents of other systems that true power in a well-designed system comes from simplicity in design, not over-wrought complexity. It shouldn't be surprising that this fact is lost on many proponents of the OSI network management framework.

soap...

...soap

The Awesome Get-Bulk Operator

In the original SNMP, the `get-next` operator was used for bulk retrieval, and a number of algorithms were developed to try to minimize the elapsed time when retrieving a large amount of management information, while at the same time trying not to overly burden the agent. For example, [60] describes a "parallel" algorithm which used the pipelining effect of the network together with `get-next` threads running concurrently.

After much thought, a new operator, the `get-bulk` operator was added to SNMPv2:

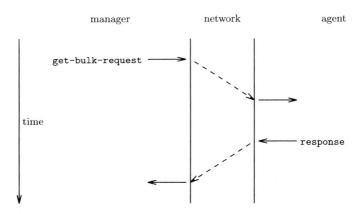

The idea behind this operator was to minimize network interactions, by allowing the agent to return large packets (i.e., the size of the variable bindings in the response could be significantly larger than the size of the variable bindings in the corresponding request). Of course, this scheme still had to work over a connectionless-mode transport service, so that the agent could remain protocol-stateless and the management application would be responsible for controlling each interaction.

It was also observed that most management applications often need a timestamp with each interaction. For example, a management application might ideally want to retrieve one instance of `sysUpTime` and many instances of the columns in the interfaces table. Successive interactions would then allow it to compute various rates such as packets/second, octets/second, and error percentiles for each interface.

```
BulkPDU ::=                        −− MUST be identical in
    SEQUENCE {                     −− structure to PDU
        request−id
            Integer32,

        non−repeaters
            INTEGER (0..max−bindings),

        max−repetitions
            INTEGER (0..max−bindings),                              10

        variable−bindings       −− values are ignored
            VarBindList
    }
```

Figure 6.2: SNMPv2 BulkPDU Format

Figure 6.2 shows the format of the `GetBulkRequest-PDU`, which is actually structurally identical to the format of all the other SNMP operations. (The integer-valued `error-status` and `error-index` fields have merely been renamed and are used for a different purpose.)

The fields in this structure are straightforward:

request-id: the usual;

non-repeaters: the number of variables which should be retrieved at most once;

max-repetitions: the maximum number of times that other variables should be retrieved; and,

variable-bindings: the usual, beginning with the `non-repeater` variables, with the values being ignored.

When an agent receives a `get-bulk`, it calculates the minimum of:

- the sender's maximum message size (`partyMaxMessageSize`); and,

- the agent's own maximum message generation size.

From this it subtracts the sum of two quantities:

- the size of the privacy/authentication wrappers used when generating a reply; and,

- the size of a **response** with no variable bindings.

The difference indicates the maximum amount of space available for variable bindings in the response. If this difference is less than zero, the request is silently dropped (after all, not even an empty response could be sent back). Otherwise, a response is generated, which will have zero or more variable bindings.

The agent then cycles through the first **non-repeaters** variables in the request, using the **get-next** operator on each, appending the new instance and value to the response, and decreasing the amount of free space accordingly. If there isn't enough room, the response is sent before it would overflow.

Then, for up to **max-repetition** times, the agent cycles through any repeating variables in the request (all the variables after the first **non-repeater** variables). For each repetition, the **get-next** operator is used on the results of the previous repetition; the new instance and value are appended to the response, and the amount of free space is decreased accordingly.

Ultimately, either the free space is exhausted or the maximum number of repetitions is performed. It is important to appreciate that the agent may terminate a repetition at any time — before the first variable, after the last variable, or anywhere in between.

Let's look at a brief example. Suppose a management application wants to retrieve all instances of the **ipNetToMediaPhysAddress** and **ipNetToMediaType** columns from the IP address translation table, along with a timestamp. It could issue this request:

```
get-bulk [non-repeaters = 1, max-repetitions = 2]
    ({sysUpTime,                         unSpecified}
     {ipNetToMediaPhysAddress,           unSpecified}
     {ipNetToMediaType,                  unSpecified}) ->
```

The response from the agent might be:

```
response [error-status = 0, error-index = 0]
    ({sysUpTime.0,                          123456},
     {ipNetToMediaPhysAddress.1.9.2.3.4,    "000010543210"},
     {ipNetToMediaType.1.9.2.3.4,           dynamic},
     {ipNetToMediaPhysAddress.1.10.0.0.51,  "000010012345"},
     {ipNetToMediaType.1.10.0.0.51,         static})
```

Because the last variable binding is still in the `ipNetToMediaType`
column, the management station issues another request, again asking
for one instance of a timestamp, and for up to two instances of the
columns (using the last instances retrieved as the starting point):

```
get-bulk [non-repeaters = 1, max-repetitions = 2]
     ({sysUpTime,                              unSpecified}
      {ipNetToMediaPhysAddress.1.10.0.0.51, unSpecified},
      {ipNetToMediaType.1.10.0.0.51,           unSpecified}) ->
```

The response from the agent might be:

```
response [error-status = 0, error-index = 0]
     ({sysUpTime.0,                            123466},
      {ipNetToMediaPhysAddress.2.10.0.0.15, "000010987654"},
      {ipNetToMediaType.2.10.0.0.15,           dynamic},
      {ipNetToMediaNetAddress.1.9.2.3.4,      "9.2.3.4"},
      {ipRoutingDiscards.0,                     2})
```

The management application sees that the last two variable bindings
do not correspond to the information it wanted, so it knows that it
has retrieved all instances of the columns in question — all three
instances.

It turns out that there is one other way in which the **get-bulk**
operation may be prematurely terminated: and that's if an entire
pass through the repeating variables results in the **endOfMibView**
exception being returned. In this case, all future repetitions would
return **endOfMibView** as well and thus are omitted from the response.

Finally, it is important to note that when the agent decides to
process a **get-bulk** request, then only the **genErr** error can be returned — a **tooBig** can never be returned!

Still more on the Awesome Get-Bulk Operator

How could one describe the `get-bulk` operator in one sentence? Perhaps:

> The agent's response to the `get-bulk` operator isn't unlike the concatenation of the agent's responses from up to `max-repetition` number of `get-next` interactions.

(A long sentence, but still a sentence!) In fact, after a little bit of thought, one could see how one could emulate the `get-next` operator using the `get-bulk` operator:

- simply make `non-repeaters` greater than or equal to the number of variables in the request; or,

- simply set `non-repeaters` to zero and `max-repetitions` to one.

(Although, as mentioned earlier, the `get-bulk` operator will never generate a `tooBig` error — unlike the `get-next` operator.)

But, perhaps the best part about the `get-bulk` operator is that it can be implemented in the top-level of an agent rather than in the object-specific routines. In fact, it took the author less than 130 lines of *C* to implement `get-bulk` in his agent; and, when retrieving large tables, the end-to-end throughput was close to an order of magnitude larger than using the `get-next` operator with the parallel algorithm specified in [60].

soap...

Given this amazingly small thrust/payload ratio, it should be obvious to the reader why this operator is termed the *awesome* `get-bulk` operator. As Dr. SNMP says:

> *"That thing's faster than a scalded dog."*

...soap   and the author would have to agree.

6.1.3   Modification Requests

There is one modification request: the **set** operator.

When a management application knows precisely the instances of the management information that it wishes to create or modify, then it issues a **set-request**:

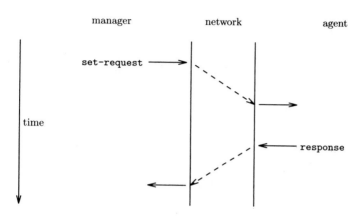

The semantics of the **set** operation are such that the operation succeeds if, and only if, all variables were updated. Further, if the operation succeeds, this implies that the variables were updated "as if simultaneously". In order to explain this, the **set** operation is described using the *two-phase* commit concept. An agent writer is free to use any implementation strategy that's convenient, as long as it provides the semantics of a two-phase commit.

Before starting the two-phase commit, a check is made to ensure that the response won't be too large to send, otherwise, a **tooBig** error occurs. (And, of course, there's always the possibility of a **genErr** being returned.)

Redundantly, a two-phase commit consists of two passes. In the first pass, each variable binding is examined and a check is made to verify that:

- the variable is within the MIB view for this operation;

- if the variable doesn't exist, then the agent is able to create instances of the corresponding object type;

- if the variable does exist, then the agent is able to modify instances of the corresponding object type;

- the new name and value provided are syntactically correct;

- the new value provided is semantically correct; and,

- all resources necessary to make the change are "lockable".

If any of these conditions don't hold for any variable binding, then the appropriate error is returned, and any resources locked are released.

The original SNMP had a *laissez faire* attitude towards modification. If the agent didn't like a particular variable binding, it would simply return `badValue`. Although a paragon of simplicity, the associated ambiguity prevented interoperable behavior. In SNMPv2, nearly a dozen new error codes were introduced in order to increase interoperable behavior (at no additional cost to the agent). As explained by Dr. SNMP, an SNMPv1 agent that doesn't like a `set` says:

> *"No!"*

whilst an SNMPv2 agent says:

> *"No, because. . ."*

Here are the new error codes, and the circumstances in which each is returned (the `error-index` field is updated accordingly in the response):

noAccess: the variable is outside the MIB view for this operation;

noCreation: the variable doesn't exist, and the agent isn't able to create instances of the corresponding object type;

notWritable: the variable does exist, but the agent isn't able to modify instances of the corresponding object type;

wrongType: the new value provided is of the wrong ASN.1 data type;

wrongLength: the new value provided is of the wrong length;

wrongEncoding: the new value provided is incorrectly encoded;

wrongValue: the new value provided is outside the acceptable range of values for the object type;

inconsistentName: the variable doesn't exist, and can't be created because the instance named is inconsistent with the values of other managed objects in the agent;

inconsistentValue: the new value provided is inconsistent with the values of other managed objects in the agent; and,

resourceUnavailable: a required resource cannot be reserved.

The important thing to appreciate about this "laundry list" of error codes is that it allows a management station to determine if the error condition is transient or permanent:

condition	error codes
permanent	`noCreation`
	`notWritable`
eh?	`wrongType`
	`wrongLength`
	`wrongEncoding`
	`wrongValue`
transient	`inconsistentName`
	`inconsistentValue`
	`resourceUnavailable`

The **eh?** condition refers to something which shouldn't happen if the management application and agent have a common understanding of the managed objects in question.

Only if each variable binding was acceptable in the first pass, is a second pass made. In this pass, the change for each variable binding is committed. Implementation experience shows that, despite a good faith implementation, there is a possibility that this second pass will somehow fail. In this case, the agent will try to undo the changes. If this happens, one of two additional errors is returned:

commitFailed: which indicates that somehow there was a failure during the second pass, but that the changes were successfully undone; and,

undoFailed: which indicates that the second pass failed, and that (some of) the changes couldn't be undone.

If either of these two errors are returned, the `error-index` field is set to zero. More importantly, it indicates that there is a severe problem in the agent, and that "all bets are off!" Finally, the existence of these two error codes shouldn't be used as a license for sloppy implementation. Rather, they are present for those rare cases in which, despite good faith efforts, a "can't happen" situation has happened.

Still more on the Set Operator

When a management application uses the **set** operation, there are a few important issues to keep in mind:

- Care should be taken when grouping objects in a single **set** request. For example, if one of the objects to be set has the effect of resetting the agent, then including other objects in that **set** is probably ineffective.

- Recall that the underlying transport service may duplicate requests or deliver successive requests out of order. Consequently, when the operation of one **set** depends upon the success of a previous **set**, the second request must be delayed until it is certain that the packets carrying the first request no longer exist in the network. Before the **TestAndIncr** textual convention existed, the manager had to wait until the **time-to-live** field of the IP datagrams used to carry the first request had expired. Now, it's simpler to include snmpSetSerialNo in the **set** in order to ensure in-order processing of the requests.

- For some objects, a **set** shouldn't be re-transmitted, just because a **response** was not received, without issuing an intervening **get** to test whether the original **set** operation took effect. Although one should include snmpSetSerialNo in the **set** to ensure that the operation is performed at most once, it's still a good idea to issue a **get** to find out what happens when a **response** isn't received.

6.1.4 Manipulating Conceptual Rows

From the protocol perspective, there is no concept of a "row" in SNMP. In particular, there is no relationship between the variables present in a list of variables. Any relationship exists as a characteristic of MIB design, not of protocol operation. That's why, when speaking from the protocol perspective, the term "conceptual row" is always used rather than simply "row".

It turns out that trying to create instances in a conceptual row is quite challenging, given the operational model used by the management framework. Consider:

- the agent may not be able to implement some columns in a conceptual row;

- the agent may require that some columns be created before a conceptual row can be used;

- values for all columns may not fit in a single PDU;

- the management application might want to examine the values of some columns; and,

- cooperating management applications don't want to collide when creating new conceptual rows.

The original SNMP had a *laissez faire* attitude towards conceptual row creation. The management application simply issued a **set** operation which created whatever columns the management application wanted. The agent then got to decide if other instances should be automatically created (if the management application didn't specify all the columns in the conceptual row), or whether the request should be rejected, for any reason whatsoever. As might be expected, from an architectural perspective, there was a certain elegance to this purity of model; but, from an interoperability perspective, this was a constant source of frustration.

In SNMPv2, the **RowStatus** textual convention is used to convey the semantics of manipulating a conceptual row: when a table is defined in a MIB module, a *status* column may be defined as having a **SYNTAX** of **RowStatus**. The significance of a status column variable is that its value indicates the relationship between the device and the conceptual row. With this introduction, let's now see how conceptual rows are manipulated.[1]

A synopsis of the **RowStatus** textual convention is:

```
RowStatus ::= TEXTUAL-CONVENTION
    ...
    SYNTAX    INTEGER {
-- two state/action values, may be read or written
                active(1),
                notInService(2),

-- a state value, may only be read
                notReady(3),

-- three action values, may be only written
                createAndGo(4),
                createAndWait(5),
                destroy(6)
        }
```

So, with this in mind, let's see how to create, modify, and delete a conceptual row.

---

[1]Readers might be interested in knowing why, if conceptual rows are a matter of MIB design and not protocol operation, the discussion of conceptual rows was postponed until the chapter on protocol operations. The reason is simple: the **RowStatus** textual convention makes use of the **get** operator. So you have to understand how the not-so-wimpy **get** operator works before discussing how to manipulate conceptual rows.

Creating a Conceptual Row

The first step in creating a conceptual row is to select an instance-identifier. This is specific to each MIB table:

- the instance-identifier might be semantically significant (e.g., `ipRouteDest` in the IP routing table); or,

- it might be used solely for uniqueness (e.g., `ifIndex` in the interfaces table).

In the latter case, the MIB module may provide an object to help choose an unused instance-identifier. For example, there might be a `nextIndex` object, which when read would return an unused instance-identifier. The trick in implementing such an object is that it not return the same value for "adjacent" retrievals. But, as we shall see, even if two management applications select the same instance-identifier, the `RowStatus` textual convention will provide a means to avoid collision.

The next step is to create the conceptual row. There are two approaches:

- a *one-shot* approach, in which the conceptual row is created and activated for use in the device with a single `set` operation; and,

- a *negotiated* approach, in which the conceptual row is created, and then through a series of protocol interactions, it is initialized and finally activated for use in the device.

From an implementation perspective, it is thought to be difficult for some agents to implement the negotiated approach, as it may require that the agent maintain "shadow" data structures during the process of creation, initialization, and activation.

Regardless of the approach, the management application must still determine for each column:

- which columns the agent requires in order to activate a conceptual row; and,

- which columns the agent won't allow to be created, for one reason or another.

Once a conceptual row has been created, the management application may issue a **get** operation for each column that it knows about, using the instance-identifier that it selected in the first step. It turns out that the response to the not-so-wimpy **get** provides quite a bit of information. For each column requested:

- if a value is returned, the agent is indicating that it implements this column;

- if a **noSuchInstance** exception is returned, the agent is indicating that it implements this column, but that the particular instance doesn't exist; and,

- if a **noSuchObject** exception is returned, the agent is indicating that it doesn't implement the object type corresponding to this column.

With this in mind, let's look at the two different ways to create a conceptual row.

Creating a Conceptual Row – The One-Shot Approach

First, the desired instance-identifier must be selected. Then, the management application may decide to issue a **get** to determine the agent's column requirements. All values returned should be exceptional (otherwise, this indicates that the conceptual row already exists).

The management application now constructs a **set**, which contains values for columns with a **MAX-ACCESS** of **read-create**. In this **set**, the status column is set to **createAndGo**. The **set** is sent to the agent.

When the agent processes the status column in the variable bindings, if the variable already exists, then an **inconsistentValue** error is returned. Otherwise, the agent sees if it has enough information to create and activate the conceptual row. This information comes from both the **set** and any local knowledge that the agent may have.

If there is enough information, then:

- the conceptual row is created;

- a `noError` response is returned;

- the agent assigns default values to those columns in the conceptual row for which no values were specified in the `set`; and,

- the status column is set to `active`.

Otherwise, if there isn't enough information, an `inconsistentValue` error is returned. (So, this error code is ambiguous — it either means "instance already exists" or "not enough information". However, it is easy to disambiguate by issuing a `get` to see if the instance exists.)

It should be noted that all of the required columns may not fit into a single PDU. Also, the response to the `get` indicates those columns that the agent implements may be a superset of the columns which are actually mandatory. As such, in the `set`, the management application need only worry about columns with a `MAX-ACCESS` of `read-create`.

Further, in order for the one-shot approach to work, the version of the MIB module known to the management application must be at least as current as the version known to the agent — because the management application needs to know which columns to ask for when it determines the agent's column requirements.

Creating a Conceptual Row – The Negotiated Approach

As with the one-shot approach, the desired instance-identifier must first be selected.

Then, the management application issues a `set` in which the status column is set to `createAndWait`. (Other columns can also be provided in the `set`, at the discretion of the management application.) The `set` is sent to the agent.

When the agent processes the status column in the variable bindings, if it doesn't support negotiated creation, a `wrongValue` error is returned; or, if the variable already exists, then an `inconsistentValue` error is returned. Otherwise:

- the conceptual row is created;

- a `noError` response is returned;

- the agent may assign default values to those columns in the conceptual row for which no values were specified in the `set`;

- the agent must assign default values to those columns it implements as `read-only`; and,

- the status column is set to either `notInService` or `notReady`, depending on information available to the agent.

The management station can now use a `get` to determine the agent's column requirements. For each `read-create` column requested:

- if a value is returned, the agent is indicating that it implements this column, and, if the management application doesn't like the value, it may decide to issue another `set` to change the value;

- if a `noSuchInstance` exception is returned, the agent is indicating that before the conceptual row can be activated, the management application must issue a `set` to supply a value for this column; and,

- if a `noSuchObject` exception is returned, the agent is indicating that the management application must **not** try to set a value.

When the value of the status column changes to `notInService`, the agent is indicating that the conceptual row is ready to be used in the device, and the management application may set the status column to `active`. (The management application doesn't have to explicitly check; it can simply try to set the status column to `active` and then see what happens.)

Note that it is up to the management application to determine how many `set` operations it wants to use (e.g., it could send several different `sets`, each with one variable at a time, or it could try to minimize the number of operations).

It should be noted that having a row in the `notInService` or `notReady` state introduces a race condition — if the device itself creates or modifies the same conceptual row that's being negotiated between the management application and the agent, then two copies are present, one in the device and one in the agent. Therefore, when the status column is set to `active` in the agent, the conceptual row in the agent will overwrite whatever the device did.

In addition, there is also the possibility that the negotiation process will be interrupted (e.g., by a lossy network or the management application crashing). Thus, the agent must periodically garbage-collect conceptual rows which aren't in the `active` state.

Modifying a Conceptual Row

Some MIB modules require that a conceptual row be taken out of service to be modified. To do this, the management application sets the status column to `notInService`. If the agent doesn't support row suspension, a `wrongValue` error is returned. Otherwise, the conceptual row is made unavailable to the device and a `noError` response is returned.

Suspending a conceptual row is also useful when the modifications won't fit in a single PDU. Of course, until all the modifications are made, the conceptual row will likely be inconsistent. In this case, the agent will set the status column to the `notReady` state.

Deleting a Conceptual Row

Finally, something that's easy: the management application sets the status column to `destroy`. The agent makes the conceptual row unavailable to the device and itself, and then returns a `noError` response.

In Perspective

Table 6.1 presents a state table for the status column. Dr. SNMP reminds us that:

> *"You can't put ten pounds of sugar in a five-pound bag."*

In other words, there are a lot of complicated things going on here and, in order to ensure interoperable behavior, a monstrosity like the `RowStatus` textual convention is needed.

ACTION	STATE			
	A	**B**	**C**	**D**
	status column doesn't exist	status column is notReady	status column is notInService	status column is active
set status column to `createAndGo`	goto **D** or incon...Value	incon...Value	incon...Value	incon...Value
set status column to `createAndWait`	see 1 or wrongValue	incon...Value	incon...Value	incon...Value
set status column to `active`	incon...Value	see 2 or incon...Value	goto **D**	goto **D**
set status column to `notInService`	incon...Value	see 3 or incon...Value	goto **C**	goto **C** or wrongValue
set status column to `destroy`	goto **A**	goto **A**	goto **A**	goto **A**
set any other column to some value	see 4	see 1	goto **C**	goto **D**

1. goto **B** or **C**, depending on information available to the agent.

2. if other variable bindings included in the same PDU, provide values for all columns which are missing but required, then return `noError` and goto **D**.

3. if other variable bindings included in the same PDU, provide values for all columns which are missing but required, then return `noError` and goto **C**.

4. at the discretion of the agent, either `noError` or `inconsistentValue` may be returned. In either case, remain in state **A**.

NOTE: Other processing of the set request may result in a response other than `noError` being returned, e.g., `wrongValue`, `noCreation`, etc.

Table 6.1: State Table for the RowStatus Textual Convention

6.1.5   Trap Interactions

When an agent detects an extraordinary event, an **snmpV2-trap** is generated, and may be sent to one or more management applications:

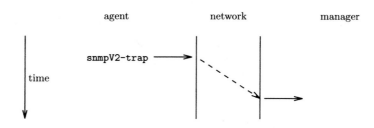

Unlike the trap used in SNMPv1, the **snmpV2-trap** is identical in format to the PDU used for all other requests. The first two variable bindings are special:

sysUpTime.0: the timestamp when the trap was generated; and,

snmpTrapOID.0: the OBJECT IDENTIFIER which identifies the trap.

Recalling the `linkUp` trap defined earlier on page 135, if interface #7 came up 0.06 seconds after the agent started, the variable bindings in the **snmpV2-trap** would be:

```
{sysUpTime.0,   6},
{snmpTrapOID.0, linkUp},
{ifIndex.7,     7}
```

This **snmpTrapOID** object is defined in the **SNMPv2-MIB** module, so let's take a moment and look at that.

The snmpTrap Group

There are four top-level objects in the **snmpTrap** group, three scalar objects and a table. The first object is **snmpTrapOID**, which we've just seen:

```
snmpTrap       OBJECT IDENTIFIER ::= { snmpMIBObjects 4 }

snmpTrapOID OBJECT-TYPE
    SYNTAX      OBJECT IDENTIFIER
    MAX-ACCESS not-accessible
    ...
    ::= { snmpTrap 1 }
```

Note that the **MAX-ACCESS** is **not-accessible** — so that it can't be retrieved or modified, but it can appear in a trap.

The **snmpTrapTable** augments the **partyTable**, and has a single column that keeps track of the number of traps sent by the agent to each party:

```
snmpTrapTable OBJECT-TYPE
    SYNTAX SEQUENCE OF SnmpTrapEntry
    ...
    ::= { snmpTrap 2 }

snmpTrapEntry OBJECT-TYPE
    SYNTAX SnmpTrapEntry
    ...
    AUGMENTS { partyEntry }
    ::= { snmpTrapTable 1 }

SnmpTrapEntry ::=
    SEQUENCE {
        snmpTrapNumbers     Counter32
    }

snmpTrapNumbers
    SYNTAX      Counter32
    ...
```

As for the remaining two objects:

snmpTrapEnterprise: when proxying an SNMPv1 `trap` to an SNMPv2 management application, this object is used to contain SNMPv1-specific information. (We'll look at this later on in Section 6.3.)

snmpV2EnableAuthenTraps: a `TruthValue` indicating whether this agent will generate `authenticationFailure` traps.

Trap Generation

So, when an agent decides to send a trap, how does it determine which management applications should receive the trap? First, the agent looks for any access policy entries in which:

- `aclSubject` refers to a party executing locally at the agent;

- `aclPrivileges` allows the `snmpV2-trap` operation; and,

- `aclResources` refers to a context defining a MIB view (instead of a proxy relationship) which contains the trap's `OBJECT IDENTIFIER` along with the `OBJECT IDENTIFIER` for each object required by the `OBJECTS` clause of the trap definition.

For each such entry, an `snmpV2-trap` is sent from the `aclSubject` party to the `aclTarget` party using the `aclResources` context. The instance of `snmpTrapNumbers` corresponding to the `aclTarget` party is incremented, and this new value is placed in the `request-id` field.

Let's look at an example. Suppose the trap to be sent is the one shown in the earlier example, i.e., the trap's `OBJECT IDENTIFIER` is `linkUp` and there is one variable binding following the timestamp, `ifIndex.7`. Further suppose that the agent is operating as these parties:

$$\alpha\text{-}1,\ \alpha\text{-}3,\ \alpha\text{-}5,\ \beta\text{-}1,\ \beta\text{-}3,\ \gamma\text{-}1,\ \text{and,}\ \gamma\text{-}3$$

and has these contexts (all referring to MIB views):

$$\delta\text{-}1,\ \delta\text{-}2,\ \delta\text{-}3,\ \text{and,}\ \delta\text{-}4$$

If the `aclTable` is:

target	subject	resources	permissions	√
α-1	α-2	δ-1	get, get-next	
α-2	α-1	δ-1	rsp, snmpV2-trap	√
α-3	α-4	δ-2	get, get-next, set	
α-4	α-3	δ-2	rsp, snmpV2-trap	√
α-5	α-6	δ-2	get, get-next, set	
α-6	α-5	δ-2	rsp	
β-1	β-2	δ-3	get, get-next	
β-2	β-1	δ-3	rsp	
β-3	β-4	δ-3	get, get-next, set	
β-4	β-3	δ-3	rsp, snmpV2-trap	√
γ-1	γ-2	δ-4	get, get-next	
γ-2	γ-1	δ-4	rsp, snmpV2-trap	√
γ-3	γ-4	δ-4	get, get-next, set	
γ-4	γ-3	δ-4	rsp	

then the entries in the rightmost column having a √ are the ones satisfying the first two conditions. Now let's look at the `viewTable`:

contextViewIndex	subtree	mask	type
δ-1	system	”H	included
δ-1	snmpParties	”H	included
δ-1	snmpTraps	”H	included
δ-2	internet	”H	included
δ-3	system	”H	included
δ-3	snmpParties	”H	included
δ-3	ifEntry.0.5	'ffa0'H	included
δ-3	snmpTraps	”H	included
δ-4	system	”H	included
δ-4	snmpParties	”H	included
δ-4	ifEntry.0.7	'ffa0'H	included
δ-4	snmpTraps	”H	included

Note that context δ-1 is disqualified, since `ifIndex.7` isn't contained within the MIB view, whilst context δ-2 is qualified. Context δ-3 is disqualified, because row 5 of the interfaces table is held within the MIB view, not row 7:

```
1.3.6.1.2.1.2.2.1.0.5               -- ifEntry.0.5
1 1 1 1 1 1 1 1 0 1 0 0 0 0 0 0 -- viewMask of 'ffa0'H
1.3.6.1.2.1.2.2.1.1.7               -- ifIndex.7
```

In contrast, context δ-4 is qualified, because row 7 of the interfaces table is held within the MIB view:

```
1.3.6.1.2.1.2.2.1.0.7               -- ifEntry.0.7
1 1 1 1 1 1 1 1 0 1 0 0 0 0 0 0 -- viewMask of 'ffa0'H
1.3.6.1.2.1.2.2.1.1.7               -- ifIndex.7
```

So, two traps are sent:

destination party	source party	context
α-4	α-3	δ-2
γ-2	γ-1	δ-4

6.1.6   Manager-to-Manager Interactions

When one management application wishes to inform another management application of some information, it issues an `inform-request`:

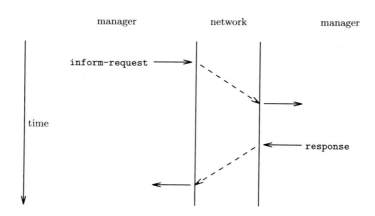

The format of the `InformRequest-PDU` is identical to the PDU used for all other requests. And, as with the `snmpV2-trap`, the first two variable bindings indicate the timestamp of the event and the identity of the event.

As might be expected, only a relatively small number of devices should be empowered to act in a manager role. The reasons for this can be found back on page 68 when the concept of trap-directed polling was introduced. Even so, great care must be taken to minimize the number of `informs` which are generated. To this end, the `SNMPv2-M2M` MIB module contains objects that determine when an event occurs, and which parties should receive the `inform`, along with its retransmission rate (when a `response` isn't received). Great care should be taken in using `inform`, as there is no such thing as a reliable trap. Once again, this implies the use of a trap-directed model: the entity receiving the `informs` must periodically poll the entity which generates the `informs`.

This `SNMPv2-M2M` MIB module contains two groups, which are now examined in turn.

The snmpAlarm Group

Figure 6.3 starting on page 284 shows the `snmpAlarm` group, which consists of one scalar object, a table, and three notification definitions.

The scalar object, `snmpAlarmNextIndex` is used as an aid in creating new instances of conceptual rows in the table. For each context known to the manager, there are zero or more entries, identified by `snmpAlarmIndex`, in the table. The "interesting" objects in the `snmpAlarmTable` are:

snmpAlarmVariable: identifies the object instance that's being sampled;

snmpAlarmInterval: the number of seconds in between sampling;

snmpAlarmSampleType: indicates whether the thresholds are viewed as either absolute values or as deltas;

snmpAlarmValue: the last sampled value that was compared against the thresholds;

snmpAlarmStartupAlarm: indicates the action taken when the first sample exceeds a threshold;

snmpAlarmRisingThreshold: indicates the upper value (absolute or delta) which the sampled value is compared against;

snmpAlarmFallingThreshold: indicates the lower value (absolute or delta) which the sampled value is compared against;

snmpAlarmRisingEventIndex: identifies a row in the `snmpEventTable` which corresponds to the event generated when the sample rises above its rising threshold;

snmpAlarmFallingEventIndex: identifies a row in the `snmpEventTable` which corresponds to the event generated when the sample falls below its falling threshold; and, snmpAlarm   **OBJECT IDENTIFIER** ::= { snmpM2MObjects 1 }

snmpAlarmNextIndex **OBJECT-TYPE**
    SYNTAX   INTEGER (0..65535)
    MAX-ACCESS read−only
    ...
    ::= { snmpAlarm 1 }

snmpAlarmTable **OBJECT-TYPE**   10
    SYNTAX   SEQUENCE OF SnmpAlarmEntry
    ...
    ::= { snmpAlarm 2 }

snmpAlarmEntry **OBJECT-TYPE**
    SYNTAX   SnmpAlarmEntry
    ...
    INDEX   { contextIdentity, snmpAlarmIndex }
    ::= { snmpAlarmTable 1 }
                                                                           20
SnmpAlarmEntry ::=
    SEQUENCE {
        snmpAlarmIndex   **INTEGER**,
        snmpAlarmVariable   InstancePointer,
        snmpAlarmInterval   Integer32,
        snmpAlarmSampleType   **INTEGER**,
        snmpAlarmValue   Integer32,
        snmpAlarmStartupAlarm   **INTEGER**,
        snmpAlarmRisingThreshold   Integer32,
        snmpAlarmFallingThreshold   Integer32,   30
        snmpAlarmRisingEventIndex   **INTEGER**,
        snmpAlarmFallingEventIndex   **INTEGER**,
        snmpAlarmUnavailableEventIndex **INTEGER**,
        snmpAlarmStatus   RowStatus
    }

Figure 6.3: The Manager-to-Manager Alarm Group

snmpAlarmUnavailableEventIndex: identifies a row in the
snmpEventTable which corresponds to the event generated
when the sampling variable is no longer accessible.

snmpAlarmNotifications
        OBJECT IDENTIFIER ::= { snmpAlarm 3 }

snmpRisingAlarm **NOTIFICATION-TYPE**
   OBJECTS { snmpAlarmVariable, snmpAlarmSampleType,
      snmpAlarmValue, snmpAlarmRisingThreshold }
  ...
  ::= { snmpAlarmNotifications 1 }

                                                           10
snmpFallingAlarm **NOTIFICATION-TYPE**
   OBJECTS { snmpAlarmVariable, snmpAlarmSampleType,
      snmpAlarmValue, snmpAlarmFallingThreshold }
  ...
  ::= { snmpAlarmNotifications 2 }

snmpObjectUnavailableAlarm **NOTIFICATION-TYPE**
   OBJECTS { snmpAlarmVariable }
  ...
  ::= { snmpAlarmNotifications 3 }

                                                           20

Figure 6.3: The Manager-to-Manager Alarm Group (cont.)

The snmpEvent Group

Figure 6.4 starting on page 286 shows the **snmpEvent** group, which consists of three scalars and two tables.

The first scalar object, **snmpEventNextIndex** is used as an aid in creating new instances of conceptual rows in the first table. The "interesting" objects in the **snmpEventTable** are:

snmpEventID: identifies the notification to be sent (i.e., the OBJECT IDENTIFIER associated with an invocation of the NOTIFICATION-TYPE macro);

snmpEventDescription: a commentary string describing the event;

snmpEventEvents: the number of times this event has been triggered; and,

snmpEventLastTimeSent: the value of sysUpTime when this event was last triggered.

For **snmpEventID**, a likely value is one of the three notifications defined in Figure 6.3 above.

snmpEvent   **OBJECT IDENTIFIER** ::= { snmpM2MObjects 2 }

snmpEventNextIndex **OBJECT-TYPE**
   SYNTAX   **INTEGER** (0..65535)
   MAX-ACCESS read−only
   ...
   ::= { snmpEvent 1 }

snmpEventTable **OBJECT-TYPE**   10
   SYNTAX   **SEQUENCE OF** SnmpEventEntry
   ...
   ::= { snmpEvent 2 }

snmpEventEntry **OBJECT-TYPE**
   SYNTAX   SnmpEventEntry
   ...
   INDEX   { snmpEventIndex }
   ::= { snmpEventTable 1 }
                                                    20

SnmpEventEntry ::=
   SEQUENCE {
      snmpEventIndex   **INTEGER**,
      snmpEventID   **OBJECT IDENTIFIER**,
      snmpEventDescription   DisplayString,
      snmpEventEvents   Counter32,
      snmpEventLastTimeSent TimeStamp,
      snmpEventStatus   RowStatus
   }

Figure 6.4: The Manager-to-Manager Event Group

snmpEventNotifyMinInterval **OBJECT-TYPE**
    SYNTAX   Integer32
    UNITS   "seconds"
    MAX-ACCESS read−only
    ...
    ::= { snmpEvent 3 }

snmpEventNotifyMaxRetransmissions **OBJECT-TYPE**
    SYNTAX   Integer32
    MAX-ACCESS read−only
    ...
    ::= { snmpEvent 4 }

        10

snmpEventNotifyTable **OBJECT-TYPE**
    SYNTAX   **SEQUENCE OF** SnmpEventNotifyEntry
    ...
    ::= { snmpEvent 5 }

snmpEventNotifyEntry **OBJECT-TYPE**
    SYNTAX   SnmpEventNotifyEntry
    ...
    INDEX   { snmpEventIndex, contextIdentity }
    ::= { snmpEventNotifyTable 1 }

        20

SnmpEventNotifyEntry ::=
    SEQUENCE {
        snmpEventNotifyIntervalRequested   Integer32,
        snmpEventNotifyRetransmissionsRequested Integer32,
        snmpEventNotifyLifetime   Integer32,
        snmpEventNotifyStatus   RowStatus
    }

        30

Figure 6.4: The Manager-to-Manager Event Group (cont.)

The second table identifies which management applications will receive a notification. The "interesting" columns in this table are:

snmpEventNotifyIntervalRequested: the requested number of seconds between retransmissions;

snmpEventNotifyRetransmissionsRequested: the requested number of retransmissions;

snmpEventNotifyLifetime: the number of seconds that this entry will remain active (after which, it is automatically destroyed).

Finally, the other two scalar objects define the minimum retransmission interval along with the maximum number of retransmissions for any notification.

For each entry in the `snmpEventTable`, there are zero or more entries in the `snmpEventNotifyTable`, with each entry identifying a context for the notification. The access policy table is examined to find entries in which:

- `aclSubject` refers to a party executing locally;

- `aclPrivileges` allows the `inform` operation; and,

- `aclResources` refers to the context.

One such entry is chosen, and an `inform` is sent from the `aclSubject` party to the `aclTarget` party using the `aclResources` context. Finally, the instance of **snmpEventEvents** in the entry is incremented. As noted earlier, the first two variable bindings are special:

sysUpTime.0: the timestamp when the event occurred; and,

snmpEventID.i: the event's `OBJECT IDENTIFIER`.

Following this are any variables identified in the `OBJECTS` clause of the instance of the `NOTIFICATION-TYPE` macro which defines the event.

Dual-Role Entities

Recently, there's been a fair bit of interest in so-called *dual-role* entities, devices that contain an agent as well as management applications. These devices collect and process information from *agents* and then make this information available to *managers*.

This all leads to the question:

> *What exactly is a manager, anyway?*

To date, no good definition has been found. But as a rule of thumb, the management framework expects a management application to exhibit management "smarts".

In terms of the SNMPv2 framework, a management application is something that initiates a request-response interaction, i.e.,

who	generates	receives
agent	`response`, `snmpV2-trap`	`get`, `get-next`, `get-bulk`, `set`
manager	`get`, `get-next`, `get-bulk`, `set`, `inform`, `response`	`response`, `snmpV2-trap`, `inform`

6.2   Transport Mappings

SNMP operations are independent of the transport protocol, requiring only a connectionless-mode transport service.

To define a transport mapping, two steps must be specified:

- the rules for taking an `SnmpPrivMsg` structure and serializing it into a string of octets forming a packet; and,

- the rules for sending the packet via the transport service.

There are several transport mappings defined and, at present, each mapping uses the same set of rules for step one. Because all managed objects and SNMP structures are defined using a subset of OSI's Abstract Syntax Notation One (ASN.1), the management framework uses a subset of OSI's Basic Encoding Rules (BER) to turn structures into a string of octets. The BER allows an arbitrary data structure to be encoded as a sequence of octets for sending. When the octets are received, they may be converted back to a data structure with *identical* semantics. Section 6.2.2 beginning on page 295 describes how this is performed. For now, the reader should understand that there is an unambiguous mapping between the ASN.1 data structures defined thus far and a string of octets.

6.2.1 Transport Domains

The pairing of a management protocol with a transport service is termed a *transport domain*. Now let's look at a few of these.

The snmpUDPDomain

When a party's `partyTDomain` object has the value `snmpUDPDomain`, this identifies the use of SNMPv2 over UDP. This is the preferred mapping.

A sending protocol entity serializes an `SnmpPrivMsg` structure and sends it as a single UDP datagram to the transport address of the receiving SNMP entity. The UDP packet format is:

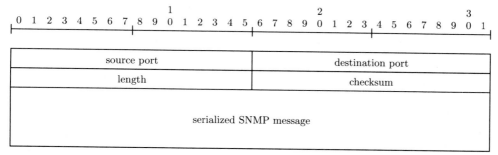

The `partyTAddress` (transport address) object is an octet string of length 6, consisting of an IP address and a UDP port.

octets	contents	encoding
1–4	IP-address	network-byte order
5–6	UDP-port	network-byte order

By convention, SNMP agents listen on UDP port 161, and notifications are sent to UDP port 162. Of course, a party may be configured to use any acceptable UDP port.

The snmpCLNSDomain and snmpCONSDomain

When a party's `partyTDomain` object has the value `snmpCLNSDomain` or `snmpCONSDomain`, this identifies the use of SNMPv2 over the OSI connectionless-mode transport service (CLTS) — `snmpCLNSDomain` is used when the CLTS is running over the OSI connectionless-mode network service (CLNS), whilst `snmpCONSDomain` is used when the CLTS is running over the OSI connection-oriented network service (CONS).

A sending protocol entity serializes a `SnmpPrivMsg` structure and sends it as a single transport service data unit (TSDU) to the transport address of the receiving SNMP entity.

The `partyTAddress` object is an octet string of variable length, consisting of an NSAP (OSI network address) and transport selector:

octets	contents	encoding
1	length of NSAP	"n" (0 or 3..20)
2..(n+1)	NSAP	concrete binary representation
(n+2)..m	transport selector	string of (up to 64) octets

Here are the default transport selectors:

mapping	entity	selector
CLTS over CLNS	agent	`snmp-l`
CLTS over CLNS	notifications	`snmpt-l`
CLTS over CONS	agent	`snmp-o`
CLTS over CONS	notifications	`snmpt-o`

Of course, a party may be configured to use any acceptable transport selector.

The snmpDDPDomain

When a party's `partyTDomain` object has the value `snmpDDPDomain`, this identifies the use of SNMPv2 over AppleTalk®'s DDP.

A sending protocol entity serializes a `SnmpPrivMsg` structure and sends it as a single DDP datagram [61] to the transport address of the receiving SNMP entity.

The `partyTAddress` object is an octet string of variable length, consisting of an object name and a zone name:

octets	contents	encoding
1	length of object	"n" (1..32)
2..(n+1)	object	string of (up to 32) octets
n+2	length of type	"p" (1..32)
(n+3)..(n+2+p)	type	string of (up to 32) octets
n+3+p	length of zone	"q" (1..32)
(n+4+p)..m	zone	string of (up to 32) octets

All SNMP agents listen on NBP type "SNMP Agent" (an ASCII string of 10 characters), and notifications are always sent to NBP type "SNMP Trap Handler" (an ASCII string of 17 characters).

The snmpIPXDomain

When a party's `partyTDomain` object has the value `snmpIPXDomain`, this identifies the use of SNMPv2 over NetWare®'s IPX.

A sending protocol entity serializes a `SnmpPrivMsg` structure and sends it as a single IPX datagram [62] to the transport address of the receiving SNMP entity.

The `partyTAddress` object is an octet string of length twelve, consisting of a network number, a physical address, and a socket number:

octets	contents	encoding
1–4	network-number	network-byte order
5–10	physical-address	network-byte order
11–12	socket-number	network-byte order

By convention, SNMP agents listen on IPX socket 36879 (decimal), and notifications are sent to IPX socket 36880 (decimal). Of course, a party may be configured to use any acceptable IPX socket.

6.2.2 Serialization using the Basic Encoding Rules

It is now time to describe how instances of data types defined using ASN.1 are *serialized* into strings of octets. Just as ASN.1 defines an abstract syntax notation, there is a corresponding *transfer syntax notation* termed the *Basic Encoding Rules* (BER) [63].[2] It is clearly beyond the scope of *The Simple Book* to present a thorough treatment of the BER; the reader should consult [46] for a detailed exposition. Thus, the remainder of this chapter, which is condensed from *The Open Book* [64], will introduce the BER only to the extent that it is used by the management framework.

Although an encoding may be quite complex overall, the actual rules used to produce the encodings are small in number and quite simple to describe. The Basic Encoding Rules are simply a recursive algorithm that can produce a compact octet encoding for any ASN.1 value.

It must be emphasized that the BER is largely a rote topic, as it is a well-understood technology. Whilst it is important to gain an understanding of the issues that the BER addresses, the myriad details are usually implemented by (hopefully well-debugged) programs.

Top-Level

At the top-level, the BER describes how to encode a single ASN.1 type. This may be a simple type such as an **INTEGER**, or an arbitrarily complex type. Conceptually, the key to applying the BER is to understand that the most complex ASN.1 type is nothing more than a number of smaller, less complex ASN.1 types. If this decomposition continues, then ultimately an ASN.1 simple type such as an **INTEGER** is encoded.

---

[2]Not to be confused with *bit error rate*.

Using the BER, each ASN.1 type is encoded as three fields:

- a *tag* field, which indicates the ASN.1 type;

- a *length* field, which indicates the size of the ASN.1 value encoding which follows; and,

- a *value* field, which is the ASN.1 value encoding.

Thus, any ASN.1 type is encoded in three fields:

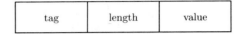

It turns out that each of these fields is of variable length. Because ASN.1 may be used to define arbitrarily complex types, the BER must be able to support arbitrarily complex encodings.

Bit Ordering

Before looking at the details, it is important to appreciate how the BER views octets. Each octet consists of 8 bits — obviously! But, how are the bits numbered? With the BER, the high-order (most significant) bit is called bit 8, whilst the low-order (least significant) bit is called bit 1. This is important to apply consistently because different machine architectures use different ordering rules (some view the high-order bit as being on the left edge of the octet, others view the high-order bit as being on the octet's right edge). Briefly put:

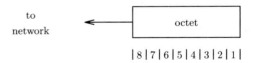

Numeric Representations

Furthermore, a large number of fields encoded by the BER are integer values expressed as binary numbers. There are two ways of representing these numbers, depending on whether negative numbers need to be represented.

To encode an integer that may take on any value (positive, negative, or zero), a *two's-complement* representation is used. In this scheme, a string of bits comprises the number. Bit 8 of the first octet contains the most significant bit, whilst bit 1 of the last octet contains the least significant bit. Although conceptually it is often easier to think of the representation as being octet-aligned, this needn't be the case. For example, the BER may specify that some fields are only 7 bits long. As long as the most significant previously unused bit in the first octet is used as the most significant bit of the string, and the least significant bit unused in the last octet is used as the least significant bit of the string, no ambiguity arises.

Note that a single contents octet can encode an integer value from $-128 \leq x \leq 127$, whilst two contents octets can encode an integer value from $-32768 \leq x \leq 32767$. (In general, with b bits in the string, numbers from $-2^{b-1} \leq x \leq 2^{b-1} - 1$ may be encoded.) In order to ensure that encodings are as compact as possible, the BER doesn't permit the first 9 bits to be zero- or one-filled. (The first octet is redundant in these cases.)

The second representation is used to encode non-negative integer values. This is a simple variation, termed an *unsigned* representation, in which the high-order bit contributes to the counter rather than decrementing from it:

$$x = \left(\sum_{i=1}^{n} bit(i) \times 2^{i-1} \right)$$

for a string of n bits. Because an extra bit is available for representing the magnitude of the integer value, larger numbers may be represented, in the same number of bits, than with a two's-complement encoding. Numbers from $0 \leq x \leq 2^b - 1$ may be encoded. With most applications of the unsigned representation, the BER permits the leading octets to be zero-filled. This is done for compatibility with the 1984 CCITT X.409 Recommendation.

Tag Field

The *tag* field is encoded as one or more *identifier octets*. This encoding must somehow capture the definition of the corresponding ASN.1 type. The BER does this by encoding the ASN.1 tag of the type. Recall that a tag is associated with each type defined using ASN.1.

As noted earlier, there are four classes of tags in ASN.1:

- *universal* tags, for the well-known data types (Table 3.1 on page 83 shows these);

- *application-wide* tags, which are defined within a single ASN.1 module;

- *context-specific* tags, which are used to provide distinguishing information in constructor types; and,

- *private-use* tags, which are used by consenting parties.

In addition to belonging to one of these groups, a tag has associated with it a non-negative integer. Thus, the tag field, officially termed the *identifier octets*, generated by the BER, must encode not only the tag's class but also the tag's number.

In addition, the tag field must encode one other bit of information. As noted earlier, an ASN.1 type might be primitive or it might be constructed. Although we think of it as natural that the value of a primitive type should be encoded as a single collection of octets, it may be more efficient for the sending process to break the value up into smaller, more manageable parts. For example, suppose a facsimile image is being encoded. This is represented in ASN.1 using a BIT STRING. If the image was large, it would probably be convenient to apply the BER to only a part of the image at a time. This may be done using a constructed encoding: after the BER was applied, the resulting octet-aligned encodings would be sent, the next part of the image fetched and then encoded. This would continue until the image had been entirely consumed. If the sender wishes to use this scheme, then it must indicate to the receiving process that it is doing so. Thus, if an ASN.1 type is primitive, it may usually be sent either in a primitive form, or in a constructed form. However, if the ASN.1 type is constructed, then it is always sent in constructed form.

So, encoding the tag field as a sequence of octets is rather simple. The tag field consists of one or more octets. The first octet encodes the tag's class along with an indication as to whether the encoding is constructed. Since there are four classes of tags, the tag's class can be represented in two of the eight bits in the octet.

Finally, the primitive/constructed indication will require a third bit which, for brevity, is termed f and is set for constructed data:

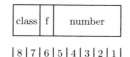

|8|7|6|5|4|3|2|1|

The encoding of the two high-order bits (bits 8 and 7) are:

Class	Bit 8	Bit 7
Universal	0	0
Application-wide	0	1
Context-specific	1	0
Private	1	1

Thus, five bits are left over for encoding the non-negative tag number. These could be used to encode a non-negative integer from 0 to 31. But, this would be rather shortsighted: many more than 32 types are possible! Thus, the BER uses the following rule:

- if the tag's number is less than 31, then it is encoded in the five bits that remain, using the unsigned representation discussed earlier;

- otherwise, bits 5 through 1 are set to all ones, which indicates that the octets that follow contain the tag's number.

So, in many cases (and clearly for all the Universal tags defined thus far), a single octet is sufficient to encode the tag field. In the other cases, one or more octets follow the first octet. The high-order bit (bit 8), if set to zero, indicates that this particular octet is the last octet of the tag field:

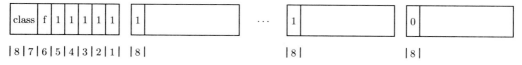

|8|7|6|5|4|3|2|1| |8| |8| |8|

Thus, in the case where the tag's number is greater than or equal to 31, the value is encoded using the unsigned integer representation found by concatenating the 7–bit values in bits 1 through 7 of the tag field octets that follow the initial identifier octet.

Length Field

The *length* field is encoded as one or more *length octets*. This encoding indicates how many of the octets that follow make up the value of the ASN.1 type being encoded.

Observant readers have probably noticed a contradiction in the BER. Earlier, it was noted that it may be useful to encode a primitive type using a constructed encoding if it was difficult to have the entire primitive type available during encoding. If this is the case, then how can the length field be calculated and sent *before* the value? There are two possible solutions to this dilemma, and the BER permits both of them!

The first solution is to provide for a special value for the length field, termed the *indefinite* form. This means that the length of the encoding isn't known ahead of time and that the receiving process should look for a special sequence of octets to detect the end of the value, termed the *end-of-contents*. Obviously, the BER must ensure that no encoding of an ASN.1 type will be able to generate this unique sequence as its value.

The second solution is to note that it is possible, although potentially inefficient, to make two passes through the data: the first to calculate the length, and the second to do the actual encoding.

If the length of the encoding is known, this is termed the *definite* form. In this case, the length field consists of one or more octets encoding the integer-valued length. If the number of octets of the encoding is less than 128, a single octet can be used to encode the length:

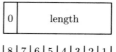

|8|7|6|5|4|3|2|1|

If the length is longer, then more than one octet is used. The first octet has the high-order bit (bit 8) set to one. The remaining seven bits comprise a number saying how many octets follow in the length field (anywhere from 1 to 126 octets).[3] The length is encoded using the unsigned integer representation found by concatenating the octets

---

[3]The value 127 for bits 7–1 is reserved for possible future extension.

that follow the initial length octet. Since all eight bits are used, up to 126×8 or 1008 bits may be used. Since $2^{1008} - 1$ is larger than the address space on any computer likely to be built for quite some time, these are probably enough bits (a polite understatement). Even so, the BER still provides for future extensibility.

If an indefinite form encoding is used, the length field consists of a single octet that has the high-order bit set to one and the remaining bits set to zero. After this octet, the value field is encoded, consisting of zero or more ASN.1 encodings. To mark the end of the encoding, the end-of-contents octets are sent.

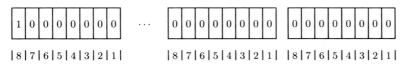

As can be seen, the end-of-contents markers are simply two zero-valued octets. This is equivalent to encoding an ASN.1 type with universal tag value 0 and no length. Since there is no ASN.1 type with this tag, the BER will never produce an ambiguous encoding. Of course, in order to interpret these octets correctly, the BER must know "where to start looking". For this reason, the indefinite length can only be used with constructed encodings. (This will become more clear as the discussion progresses.)

SNMP specifically *disallows* the use of the indefinite length form for messages as well as for the management information carried by those messages. The indefinite length form places a heavy burden on the receiving SNMP entity. Since the definite length form is always needed for primitive encodings, use of the indefinite length form is prohibited.

Value Field

We now consider how the ASN.1 types used in the management framework have their values encoded. The value field is encoded as zero or more *contents octets*.

Simple Types

The simple types provide the fundamental encodings that are used by the BER.

Simple Types – INTEGER

An `INTEGER` value is encoded as one or more contents octets, always in primitive form. The value is encoded using the two's-complement encoding which you will recall prohibits having the first 9 bits as zero- or one-filled, to eliminate redundancy.

For example, the value 100 (decimal) is encoded as:

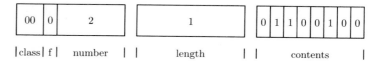

which, ignoring the bits with value zero, is:

$$2^6 + 2^5 + 2^2 = 64 + 32 + 4 = 100$$

Simple Types – BIT STRING

A `BIT STRING` value is encoded as zero or more contents octets, in either primitive or constructed form. (Note that the SMI prohibits using the constructed form.)

A primitive form encoding consists of an initial octet followed by octets encoding the bits in the **BIT STRING**. The initial octet indicates how many bits are unused in the final contents octet (and must take the value 0–7). If no bits are present in the **BIT STRING** value, then a single octet is encoded (the initial octet) with value 0.

First, consider a primitive form encoding for the **BIT STRING** value '101'B:

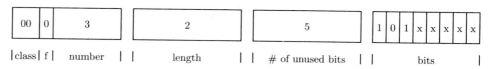

An 'x' in a bit position in a contents octet indicates that the setting is unimportant — that is, the BER doesn't interpret this information.

Note that there is no concept of padding for bitstrings. That is, it isn't possible to prepend non-significant leading zero-valued bits to a value in order to force the significant bits to "line up" on a word boundary.

Simple Types – OCTET STRING

An `OCTET STRING` value is encoded as zero or more contents octets, in either primitive or constructed form. (Note that the SMI prohibits using the constructed form.)

Here is a primitive form encoding for the value "**anon**":

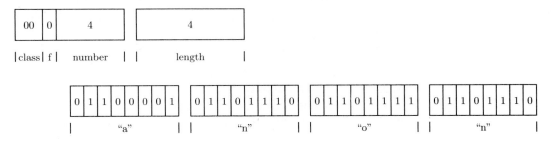

Simple Types – NULL

A `NULL` value is encoded as zero contents octets:

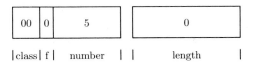

Simple Types – OBJECT IDENTIFIER

An `OBJECT IDENTIFIER` value is encoded as one or more contents octets, always in primitive form.

Recall that an `OBJECT IDENTIFIER` is a sequence of non-negative integer values. The BER places certain restrictions on any `OBJECT IDENTIFIER` it encodes: the first element must take the value 0, 1, or 2; and, the second element must take a value less than 40 if the first element is 0 or 1. (The reason for these limitations is to allow for a slightly optimization in the encoding.) Recall that exactly three subordinates to the root node have been defined, coincidentally having values 0, 1, and 2. Since naming authority for these subordinates resides with ISO and CCITT, they are responsible for ensuring that no immediate subordinates are assigned a number greater than 39.

For the purposes of encoding using the BER:

- the first two elements in the sequence of components form a *sub-identifier* with the value $X \times 40 + Y$, where X is the value of the first element, and Y is the value of the second element; and,

- each element following in the sequence also forms a *sub-identifier* with a value equal to that element's value.

For example,

```
1.0.8571.5.1
```

consists of four sub-identifiers: 40 ($40 \times 1 + 0$), 8571, 5, and 1.

Each sub-identifier is encoded using the unsigned representation in one or more octets. However, the most significant bit of each octet is set to one if another octet follows. Thus, the sub-identifier is represented by concatenating one or more 7–bit values together and treating the resulting string of bits as an unsigned number. In order to ensure a compact encoding, the leading octet may not have bit 8 set to one and all the remaining bits set to zero (i.e., the first seven bits of the encoding must have a non-zero value).

Hence, in order to encode

    `1.0.8571.5.1`

four numbers, 40, 8571, 5, and 1 must be encoded. Three of these can be represented in seven or fewer bits, and, therefore, each can be encoded in a single octet. The other, 8571, requires 14 bits, and hence is encoded using two octets. (If 15 bits had been required to encode the sub-identifier using the unsigned representation, then three octets would be needed for the encoding, as a bit in each octet indicates if another octet is used.)

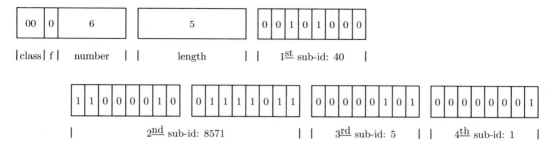

Constructor Types

As the ASN.1 language defined complex types in terms of combining simple types with constructors, so the BER encodes complex types by encoding a constructor whose value portion consists of encodings of simpler types.

The complexity in generating an encoding of the constructor types lies in knowing the proper value to use for the length field. This was one of the key reasons that the notion of an indefinite length was developed — when encoding a constructor type, the sending process generates the tag and length fields (using the indefinite length), generates the encoding for each element of the constructor type, and then generates the end-of-contents octets to "wrap things up". This mechanism allows the sending process to be vastly simplified at the expense of the receiving process, which must now "know how to deal with such things".

Consistent with the Fundamental Axiom, SNMP requires that the definite form be used at all times.

Constructor Types – SEQUENCE

A **SEQUENCE** value is encoded as zero or more contents octets, always in constructed form. Basically, the tag and length fields are generated. Then, for each element present in the **SEQUENCE**, the BER is recursively applied.

The order of the individual encodings must match the order in which they appeared in the definition of the ASN.1 type.

Consider an encoding of:

```
VarBind ::=
    SEQUENCE {
        name
            ObjectName,

        value
            ObjectSyntax
    }
```

Without knowing the definitions of **ObjectName** and **ObjectSyntax**, the encoding for **VarBind** must look something like this:

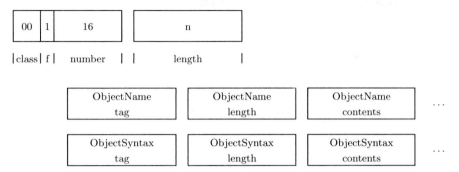

Constructor Types – SEQUENCE OF

A **SEQUENCE OF** value is encoded identically to a **SEQUENCE** value; even the tags are the same. Note that the tags of the elements are truly redundant here. However, they must be encoded to maintain the tag-length-value format.

Tagged Types

A tagged type of the form:

```
SomeType ::=
    [tag]
        IMPLICIT OtherType
```

is encoded using the rules for **OtherType**, the difference being that a new value was used in the tag field intead of the tag value associated with type **OtherType**.

This is straightforward, but leads us to consider how a definition of the form

```
SomeType ::=
    [tag]
        OtherType
```

might be encoded (there is no **IMPLICIT** keyword).

The answer is that a tagged definition of this form is treated as a constructor analogous to:

```
SomeType ::=
    [tag]
        IMPLICIT SEQUENCE {
            OtherType
        }
```

The idea is that the tagging information of **OtherType** is retained intact, being contained within another type that has the new tag. Although the BER doesn't state the encoding rules for tagged types in this fashion, using this conceptualization tends to make the encoding rules appear much more intuitive.

Thus, an encoding of:

```
SomeType ::=
    [APPLICATION 7]
        OtherType
```

always looks something like this:

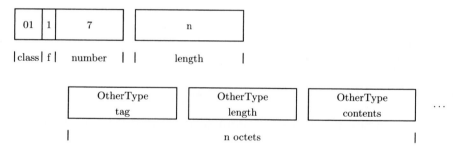

Although neither of the above two examples uses the indefinite length, this is permitted by the BER, as it would be for any type that may be encoded using the constructed form. However, in the interest of simplicity, indefinite length encodings are not allowed by the management framework, so no examples are provided.

The Controversy over TLV encodings

Although the BER generates compact encodings, it isn't particularly efficient in terms of processing. In fact, other encoding mechanisms are often 20 (or more) times faster than using the BER. Whilst these mechanisms are not used to encode ASN.1 data types, they nonetheless exist in highly useful, well-deployed systems.

However, recent work such as [65] suggests that it may be possible to produce efficient coders for the BER, given the characteristics of today's processor caches, and a reasonable mix of string and integer-valued data.

Thus, there has always been some argument as to whether use of the BER (and ASN.1) unnecessarily increases the cost of a managed node. As of this writing, this issue continues to be debated but is largely irrelevant.

An Example

The discussion now turns to an example that shows how the BER may be applied to the ASN.1 data types used in the management framework. Referring back to Figure 6.1 which started on page 244, consider the ASN.1 value (which represents an SNMP **response**):

```
example PDU ::=
    {
        response {
            request-id 17,
            error-status noError,
            error-index 0,
            variable-bindings {
                {
                    name 1.3.6.1.2.1.1.1.0,
                    value {
                        simple {
                            string "unix"
                        }
                    }
                }
            }
        }
    }
```

In generating an encoding using the BER for this value, the first step (conceptually) is to view the value as being composed of ASN.1 simple and constructor types:

```
[2] {
        17,
        0,
        0,
        {
            {
                1.3.6.1.2.1.1.1.0,
                "unix"
            }
        }
    }
```

This gives a more concrete view of the data values to be encoded. The next step is to actually construct the encoding.

An instance of the `PDUs` data type is encoded. Since this is a **CHOICE**, whichever data is specified by the value is encoded instead: in this case, an instance of the `GetResponse-PDU`. This is an **IMPLICIT**ly tagged type, so in turn, a PDU value is encoded, but with a different tag. A PDU data type is a **SEQUENCE**, so it must use the constructed form. We begin by generating the tag and length fields:

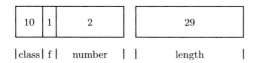

Next, the `request-id`, `error-status`, and `error-index` fields are encoded. All three of these are integers:

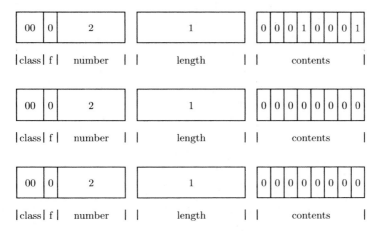

Finally, the variable bindings, a **SEQUENCE OF** value, is encoded. Once again, the tag and length fields are generated:

Each element of the **SEQUENCE OF** value is a `VarBind` value, which is a **SEQUENCE**. Since there is only one element in the **SEQUENCE OF**, only one such value need be encoded. As usual, the tag and length fields are generated:

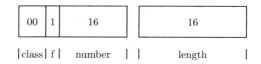

Finally, the components of the `VarBind` value are generated, starting with an `ObjectName` value. This is an `OBJECT IDENTIFIER` with value `1.3.6.1.2.1.1.1.0`, having 8 sub-identifiers:

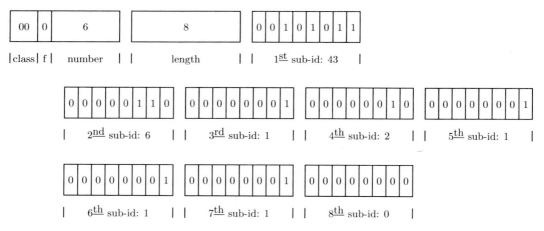

This is followed by an `ObjectValue` value, which is an **OCTET STRING**:

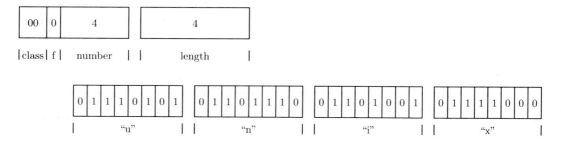

Putting this all together, here are the 31 octets that are generated (in hexadecimal):

```
a2 1d
      02 01 11
      02 01 00
      02 01 00
      30 12
         30 10
                06 08 2b 06 01 02 01 01 01 00
                04 04 75 6e 69 78
```

6.3   Coexistence

> **NOTE:**   Read this section only if you are familiar with the
> original Internet-standard Network Management
> Framework.

The protocol for the original framework is defined in [17].

From a protocol perspective, here are the differences between the
SNMPv1 and SNMPv2:

get-bulk: not present in the original SNMP;

inform: not present in the original SNMP;

traps: a different PDU format was used for `trap`;

exceptions: there are no exceptions (e.g., `noSuchObject`) in the
original SNMP; and,

error codes: in addition to `tooBig` and `genErr`, there are only
three other errors:

    noSuchName: indicates that the agent rejected a variable
name for some reason;

    badValue: indicates that the agent rejected a variable bind-
ing for the `set` operation; and,

    readOnly: should never be generated (due to a bizarre
editing error, this error code was defined, but never
used, by the original specification).

To provide coexistence between SNMPv1 and SNMPv2, two approaches may be used:

- the proxy approach; and,

- the bilingual manager approach.

6.3.1   The Proxy Approach

The proxy approach is implemented through the use of a proxy relationship in which an SNMPv2 agent is configured with a context that defines a proxy relationship instead of a MIB view.

A proxy relationship for SNMPv1 is defined when a context's

```
contextProxyDstParty
```

object identifies a party whose `partyTDomain` (transport domain) object has the value `rfc1157Domain`. The corresponding instances of the `contextProxySrcParty` and `contxtProxyContext` objects are irrelevant.

A party whose transport domain is `rfc1157Domain` uses the original SNMP over UDP. For such a party,

partyTAddress: is an octet string of length 6, consisting of an IP address and a UDP port.

octets	contents	encoding
1–4	IP-address	network-byte order
5–6	UDP-port	network-byte order

partyAuthProtocol: must have the value `rfc1157noAuth`;

partyAuthPrivate: denotes the community used when communicating with the proxy destination;

partyAuthPublic: is irrelevant;

partyAuthClock: is irrelevant; and,

partyAuthLifetime: is irrelevant.

6.3.2   The Bilingual Manager Approach

The bilingual manager approach is implemented at the management station. When a management application needs to contact another protocol entity, it consults a local database to select the correct management protocol to use. If the management protocol is SNMPv1, the management application performs the same mappings as if it were the proxy agent.

6.3.3   The Mapping

When mapping an SNMPv2 request into an SNMPv1 request:

- the `get`, `get-next`, and `set` operations are passed unaltered;

- the `get-bulk` operation is downgraded to a `get-next` operation by changing its PDU tag and setting the `non-repeater` and `max-repetitions` fields to zero; and,

- the `inform` operation is disallowed by the access policy, so an `authorizationError` is returned.

When mapping an SNMPv1 response into an SNMPv2 response:

- on a `tooBig` error, empty the `variable-bindings` field; and,

- always preserve the `error-code` field, even if it is obsolete in SNMPv2.

This latter rule is important because there isn't an unambiguous mapping for the three obsolete error codes

```
noSuchName
badValue
readOnly
```

so the management application must interpret them.

When mapping an SNMPv1 `trap` into an `snmpV2-trap` (Figure 6.5 shows the format of SNMPv1's `trap`):

- set the first variable binding to have `sysUpTime.0` as its name, and the value from the `time-stamp` field of the SNMPv1 `trap` as its value;

- set the second variable binding to `snmpTrapOID.0` and, if the trap is a generic trap, use the corresponding `OBJECT IDENT-IFIER` from the `snmpTraps` group for the value (otherwise, take the `enterprise` field of the SNMPv1 `trap`, and append two sub-identifiers — 0 and the `specific-trap` field);

- copy any variable bindings from the SNMPv1 `trap`; and,

- add a final variable binding of `snmpTrapEnterprise.0` with the value taken from the `enterprise` field of the SNMPv1 `trap`.

```
Trap−PDU ::=
    [4] IMPLICIT SEQUENCE {
        enterprise
            OBJECT IDENTIFIER,

        agent−addr
            NetworkAddress,

        generic−trap
            INTEGER { coldStart(0),                          10
                warmStart(1),
                linkDown(2),
                linkUp(3),
                authenticationFailure(4),
                egpNeighborLoss(5),
                enterpriseSpecific(6)
                },

        specific−trap
            INTEGER,                                         20

        time−stamp
            TimeTicks,

        variable−bindings
            VarBindList
        }

NetworkAddress ::=
    CHOICE {                                                 30
        internet      IpAddress
    }
```

Figure 6.5: SNMPv1 Trap Format

Chapter 7

An Implementation

The Internet-standard Network Management Framework has been implemented on many platforms. Because of this, it is difficult to characterize the nature of these implementations in all but the most general terms.

At a first cut, one can distinguish between agent and manager implementations. At the risk of being too simplistic, agent implementations fall into one of two categories:

- *tightly-integrated*, in which performance is optimized by placing the management instrumentation and protocol into the logical process containing the entities implementing the useful protocols; and,

- *loosely-integrated*, in which flexibility is optimized by separating the implementations of the management protocol and administrative model from the rest of the protocol entities.

The first approach is appropriate for devices such as routers and other special-purpose network entities. The second approach is used for general-purpose computing engines.

Each tightly-integrated implementation is highly tuned and optimized to run on a particular platform.

These implementations are not portable across the product lines of different vendors, and may not even be portable within a single vendor's product line! It should be noted that the benefits of the Fundamental Axiom are most appreciated in these implementations.

319

A loosely-integrated implementation is usually meant to be of general use. Portability is enhanced by structuring the implementation so that it is applicable to a large number of platforms, at the expense of using a generalized, and usually slow, means for interacting with the other protocol entities.

Because of the wide range of needs, all manager implementations tend to be implemented in the same style as loosely-integrated agent systems.

The discussion now turns to consider an implementation of an agent and manager built using this latter style of implementation. The *4BSD/ISODE SNMPv2* package is an implementation of the SNMPv2 framework for Berkeley UNIX® systems. It is layered on top of the *ISO Development Environment* (ISODE), which was developed primarily as a tool for studying the upper-layers of OSI.[1] Although the package contains a full agent implementation, it doesn't contain a large number of management applications. Rather, the manager side of the implementation consists of tools for *rapid prototyping* of network management applications.

The discussion begins by considering common data structures and mechanisms. Following this, the agent and manager software are discussed in turn. ISODE is coded in the *C* programming language and runs on several variants of the UNIX® operating system. Hence, when reading the sections on implementation, it will be helpful to be familiar with the basics of the UNIX® operating system.

For the remainder of this chapter, the reader should keep in mind that an *implementation* of SNMP is being discussed. The data structures and access mechanisms are part of the implementation; they are most certainly not part of the SNMP definition.

---

[1]Ordering information for the 4BSD/ISODE SNMPv2 package can be found on page 401.

7.1 Core

The core of the package consists of a MIB compiler and a supporting run-time library.

7.1.1 MOSY

The *mosy* compiler reads the ASN.1 definitions of a MIB module, and produces a more efficient form used by the run-time library. The name *mosy* stands for the Managed Object Syntax-compiler (YACC-based). The *mosy* compiler supports the definitions used in both the new and the old framework. (It examines the IMPORTS statement and acts accordingly.)

The user runs *mosy* on each MIB module of interest and then concatenates the resulting output files to the file produced by running *mosy* on the SMI module. For example:

```
% mosy snmpV2-smi.my
mosy 7.0 #249 (dbc) of Tue Dec 29 07:56:00 PST 1992
SNMPv2-SMI identifiers: internet directory mgmt
            experimental private enterprises snmpV2
            snmpDomains snmpProxys snmpModules

SNMPv2-SMI types: ObjectName ObjectSyntax SimpleSyntax
            Integer32 ApplicationSyntax IpAddress Counter32
            Gauge32 TimeTicks Opaque NsapAddress Counter64
            UInteger32

% mosy snmpV2-tc.my
...


% mosy mib.my
mosy 7.0 #249 (dbc) of Tue Dec 29 07:56:00 PST 1992
RFC1213-MIB identifiers: mib-2 system interfaces at
            ip icmp tcp udp egp transmission snmp

RFC1213-MIB objects: sysDescr sysObjectID sysUpTime
            sysContact sysName sysLocation sysServices
            ifNumber ifTable ifEntry
...


% cat snmpV2-*.defs mib.defs > objects.defs
```

might be used to create a file containing definitions for MIB-II. This file is then installed in a system area and is read by the run-time library when a management application (or agent) initializes itself.

The syntax of the file is largely unimportant as it is read only by the run-time library. It is essentially a "flat" representation of the information defined in the OBJECT-TYPE macro. There are actually three different formats that can be used by the run-time library. This "flat" representation, termed the *basic* format, is the most portable and can be edited by hand. Unfortunately, it introduces a somewhat high cost when the run-time library initializes itself. In contrast, the *C-source compiled* format, which is a compiled form of the *C* data structures corresponding to the objects, is least portable but loads the fastest.

7.1.2 Run-time Library

The run-time library consists of routines to keep track of the managed objects in the configuration file. This is divided into three areas: syntax, objects, and instances.

The library is initialized by calling the routine loadobjects, e.g.,

```
#include <isode/snmp/objects.h>

char    *defs = (char *) 0;
...

if (loadobjects (defs) == NOTOK)
    error ("readobjects: %s", PY_pepy);
```

If the parameter defs is non-empty, then it indicates the name of a compiled MIB file in the basic format to be read. Otherwise, the compiled data structures loaded with the program are used.

Object Syntax

The *C* structure used to model an object's syntax is:

```
typedef struct object_syntax {
    char    *os_name;           /* syntax name */

    IFP     os_encode;          /* data -> PE */
    IFP     os_decode;          /* PE -> data */
    IFP     os_free;            /* free data */

    IFP     os_parse;           /* str -> data */
    IFP     os_print;           /* data -> tty */


    ...

}               object_syntax, *OS;
#define NULLOS  ((OS) 0)
```

where IFP is a pointer to a function returning an integer value, and PE is an internal form used to represent data values already encoded for network transmission.

The run-time library contains definitions for all of the syntaxes defined in the SMI:

syntax	C structure
Integer32	integer
BIT STRING	struct PElement *
OCTET STRING	struct qbuf *
OBJECT IDENTIFIER	struct OIDentifier *
IpAddress	struct sockaddr_in *
Counter32	u_long
Counter64	counter64
Gauge32	u_long
TimeTicks	u_long
UInteger32	u_long
NsapAddress	struct sockaddr_iso *

These are all simple data structures defined in the run-time library.

Object Syntax – integer

This is used for this syntax:

```
Integer32
```

The definition on most systems is:

```
typedef long integer;
```

Object Syntax – u_long

This is used for these syntaxes:

```
Counter32
Gauge32
TimeTicks
UInteger32
```

The definition on most systems is:

```
typedef unsigned long u_long;
```

Object Syntax – counter64

This is used for this syntax:

```
Counter64
```

The definition is:

```
typedef struct counter64 {
    u_long      hiword;
    u_long      loword;
}       counter64;
```

Object Syntax – struct PElement

This is used for this syntax:

```
BIT STRING
```

The definition is rather obscure, so we'll skip it in favor of looking at the manipulation routines.

To turn a bit on, use

```
int    bit_on (pe, i)
struct PElement *pe;
int    i;
```

Similarly, a bit can be turned off with

```
int    bit_off (pe, i)
struct PElement *pe;
int    i;
```

These routines both extend the internal structure as necessary when setting the value of non-existent bits.

Finally, the routine

```
int    bit_test (pe, i)
struct PElement *pe;
int    i;
```

can be used to test the truth-value (and existence) of a particular bit.

Object Syntax – struct qbuf

This is used for this syntax:

```
OCTET STRING
```

The definition is:

```
struct qbuf {
    struct qbuf *qb_forw; /* doubly-linked list */
    struct qbuf *qb_back; /*    .. */

    int     qb_len;       /* length of data */
    char    *qb_data;     /* current pointer into data */
    char    qb_base[1];   /* extensible... */
};
```

(If the string was encoded using the constructed form, there are multiple qbufs in the ring.)

The macro QBFREE is used to traverse the qb_forw field to free all qbufs in the ring:

```
QBFREE (qb)
struct qbuf *qb;
```

To allocate a new string from a ring of qbufs, use

```
char *qb2str (q)
struct qbuf *q;
```

The resulting string is terminated with a null character. Note, however, that the repertoire for the string needn't be ASCII.

To allocate a new qbuf which contains a given string, use

```
struct qbuf *str2qb (s, len, 1)
char    *s;
int     len;
```

and to free an allocated qbuf, use qb_free which calls QBFREE and then free on its argument.

Object Syntax – struct OIDentifier

This is used for this syntax:

```
OBJECT IDENTIFIER
```

The definition is:

```
typedef struct OIDentifier {
    int     oid_nelem;  /* number of sub-identifiers */

    unsigned int *oid_elements;
                /* the (ordered) list of sub-identifiers */
}                       OIDentifier, *OID;
#define NULLOID ((OID) 0)
```

To compare two OIDs, use

```
int     oid_cmp (p, q)
OID     p,
        q;
```

which returns -1 if $p < q$, 1 if $p > q$, and 0 otherwise.

To allocate a new OID and copy it from another, use

```
OID     oid_cpy (p)
OID     p;
```

and to free an allocated OID, use `oid_free`.

To take an OID and produce a string in numeric form use

```
char    *sprintoid (oid)
OID     oid;
```

The result is returned in a static area, so subsequent calls will over-write this value. The inverse routine is:

```
OID     str2oid (s)
char    *s;
```

which returns an OID from a static area.

Object Syntax – struct sockaddr_in

This is used for this syntax:

```
IpAddress
```

The definition of this structure is well-known to anyone familiar with Berkeley UNIX® [66].

Object Syntax – struct sockaddr_iso

This is used for this syntax:

```
NsapAddress
```

which is similar in form to a `struct sockaddr_in`.

Defining a new Syntax

New syntaxes are added by defining a new *C* structure and then five routines which manipulate the structure. Consider Figure 7.1 which shows how the `Integer32` syntax is realized.

The only structure not defined thus far is a PE or *presentation element*. This is a *C* data structure which is an intermediary form between the structures used by the programmer and the encoding used on the network. (It is also used to represent `BIT STRING` values.)

From a high-level perspective, a PE is nothing more than a modestly complex *C* structure that represents an ASN.1 value as either a string of octets or bits (primitive types) or as a linked list of other presentation elements (constructor types). Layered on top of this are numerous routines that convert between PEs and the data structures used by a target architecture. These routines are usually accessed by code generated by the mechanisms described in Section 7.2.5 on page 354.

Obviously, use of presentation elements introduces an inherent inefficiency: at some point two (or perhaps three) copies of data reside in the system. Further, the current implementation of presentation elements is memory-resident. This means that large ASN.1 structures, when converted to and from PEs, must remain entirely in memory. However, the generality is substantial; by using a common internal form, many tools can be built that manipulate them. This encourages reuse and rapid prototyping. By having one set of well-debugged routines that manipulate PEs, developers focus their time on other, higher level issues.

```
integer_encode (x, pe)
integer *x;
PE     *pe;
{
   return ((*pe = int2prim (*x)) == NULLPE ? NOTOK : OK);
}

integer_decode (x, pe)
integer **x;
PE      pe;
{
   integer   i = prim2num (pe);

   if ((i == NOTOK && pe -> pe_errno != PE_ERR_NONE)
            || (*x = (integer *) malloc (sizeof **x)) == NULL)
        return NOTOK;
   **x = i;

   return OK;
}

integer_free (x) integer *x; { free ((char *) x); }

integer_parse (x, s)
integer **x;
char    *s;
{
   long   l;

   if (sscanf (s, "%ld", &l) != 1
            || (*x = (integer *) malloc (sizeof **x)) == NULL)
        return NOTOK;
   **x = (integer) l;

   return OK;
}

integer_print (x, os) integer *x; OS os; { printf ("%d", *x); }

...

add_syntax ("Integer32", integer_encode, integer_decode, integer_free, integer_parse, integer_print);
```

Figure 7.1: Realizing the Integer32 Syntax

Object Types

The C structure used to model an object type is:

```
typedef struct object_type {
    char    *ot_text;       /* descriptor */
    OID      ot_name;       /* identifier */

    OS       ot_syntax;     /* SYNTAX */

    int      ot_access;     /* ACCESS */
#define OT_NONE         0x00
#define OT_RDONLY       0x01
#define OT_WRONLY       0x02  /* for compatibility */
#define OT_RDWRITE      0x03
#define OT_RDCREAT      0x04

    int      ot_status;     /* STATUS */
#define OT_OBSOLETE     0x00
#define OT_CURRENT      0x01
#define OT_OPTIONAL     0x02  /* for compatibility */
#define OT_DEPRECATED   0x03

    IFP      ot_getfnx;     /* agent pointer */
    IFP      ot_setfnx;     /*    .. */
    caddr_t  ot_info;       /*    .. for object */
    caddr_t  ot_save;       /* for set method */

    ...
}                   object_type, *OT;
#define NULLOT  ((OT) 0)
```

The library provides several routines to find the MIB objects which have been read in from configuration files.

The routine **name2obj** takes an **OBJECT IDENTIFIER** and returns the corresponding *prototype*. What this means is that if an object is exactly named, or an instance of that object is named, the structure corresponding to that object is returned. Thus (taking a few liberties with the C language), a call to

```
name2obj ( OID { ipNextHop.0.0.0.0 } )
```

returns the object type for `ipNextHop`.

The routine `text2obj` takes a string and returns the exact object type, e.g.,

```
text2obj ("ipNextHop")
```

will succeed, but

```
text2obj ("ipNextHop.0.0.0.0")
```

will fail.

The routine `text2oid` takes a string and returns the name (i.e., **OBJECT IDENTIFIER**) associated with the corresponding object. The string can be numeric, symbolic, or combined, so all three of these calls

```
text2oid ("1.3.6.1");

text2oid ("internet");

text2oid ("iso.3.6.1");
```

return the same **OID**.

Finally, the routine `oid2ode` takes an **OID** and returns a string suitable for pretty-printing, in symbolic form (whenever possible).

Object Instances

The *C* structure used to model an object instance is:

```
typedef struct object_instance {
    OID     oi_name;      /* instance OID */
    OT      oi_type;      /* prototype */
}               object_instance, *OI;
#define NULLOI  ((OI) 0)
```

There are three routines to manipulate MIB instances.

The routine **name2inst** takes a variable name and returns the corresponding instance, e.g.,

```
name2inst ( OID { ipNextHop.0.0.0.0 } )
```

will return an **OI** with the **oi_name** field set to its argument and **oi_type** set to the object type for **ipNextHop**.

The routine **next2inst** finds the closest object type before the variable name and returns an OI corresponding to that object type. This is used by an agent with a two-level algorithm (discussed later on) implementing the **get-next** operator.

Finally, the routine

```
OI      text2inst (text)
char    *text;
```

calls **text2oid** to get the **OID** corresponding to the argument, then calls **name2obj** to get the object type associated with that **OID**, and copies the information into a static area.

7.1.3 Party Database

The package uses the UNIX® filesystem as stable-storage for SNMPv2 party information. A party database, named **prefix**, consists of four or five ASCII files, named:

```
prefix.public
prefix.private
prefix.context
prefix.access
prefix.view
```

The first two files contain information about the parties known in the party database, whilst the last file is present only if the party database is for an agent.

A UNIX® shell script is provided to generate the default administrative policy for the agent. After the agent initializes itself for the first time, it is solely responsible for maintaining its party database. Any changes to the database should be made using SNMPv2; in case of a catastrophe, the agent can be halted and the database edited manually (it is stored in a simple ASCII format).

The routine `init_party` is used to read a party database, e.g.,

```
if (init_party (pParty, AGENT, rflag, &pParty) == NOTOK)
    adios (NULLCP, "%s", PY_pepy);
```

and the routine `sync_party` is used to synchronize the in-core version with the copy on disk, e.g.,

```
if (sync_party (pParty, AGENT, 0) == NOTOK)
    error ("stable storage suspect: %s", PY_pepy);
```

The first parameter to each identifies the name of the party database, whilst the second parameter indicates whether the party database is being held by an agent or manager entity. In the case of `init_party`, there are routines to find parties and contexts by either **OBJECT IDENT-IFIER** or integer index, e.g.,

```
struct snmp_party *p = find_party_index (3, AGENT);
OID id = text2oid ("initialContextId.192.103.140.1.2");
struct snmp_context *c = find_context (id);
```

will find the party whose internal index is 3, and the context whose identity is

```
initialContextId.192.103.140.1.2
```

The routine `authenticate_incoming` is used to authenticate an incoming message.

```
int authenticate_incoming (privmsg, authmsg, srcParty,
                           dstParty, reason)
```

The parameters are:

privmsg: the internal representation of an `SnmpPrivMsg` structure that has been received;

authmsg: the internal representation of an `SnmpAuthMsg` structure which was extracted after applying the destination
party's privacy protocol;

srcParty: the local database information corresponding to the
source party identified in the `SnmpMgmtCom` structure contained within the `SnmpAuthMsg` structure;

dstParty: the local database information corresponding to the
destination party identified in the `SnmpMgmtCom` structure
contained within the `SnmpAuthMsg` structure; and,

reason: a pointer to an integer-valued location which is updated
if the `SnmpAuthMsg` structure is deemed to be unauthentic,
with one of the following values:

- the destination party identified in the `SnmpPrivMsg`
  structure did not match the destination party identified in the `SnmpMgmtCom` structure contained within
  the `SnmpAuthMsg` structure;

- inappropriate credentials for the source party were
  present in the `SnmpMgmtCom` structure contained within
  the `SnmpAuthMsg` structure;

- the message was received outside of its lifetime; or,

- the computed digest did not match the value found in
  the `SnmpAuthMsg` structure.

Similarly, the routine `generate_outgoing_auth` constructs an `OCTET`
`STRING` value suitable for inclusion in an `SnmpPrivMsg` structure.

```
struct qbuf *generate_outgoing_auth (msg, srcParty,
                                        dstParty, watch)
```

The `watch` parameter is used to indicate whether logging information
should be generated.

7.2   Agent Implementation

Since the protocol entities in Berkeley UNIX® reside in the kernel, user-processes, such as the SNMP agent, *snmpd*, must go to special lengths in order to carry out the directives of the management protocol. However, as a user-process, *snmpd* is permitted more freedom than a kernel-resident entity when additional configuration information is required. Further, a failure in *snmpd* shouldn't result in either UNIX® or the protocol entities failing. On balance, the performance loss and extra machinations required are acceptable.

7.2.1   Initialization

In its initialization phase, the agent:

1. Examines its command line arguments for directives from the user. This allows for debugging and special configurations to be accomplished. For example, it may be useful to run a test version of the agent on a different UDP port from the normal SNMP service. This can be accomplished by telling the agent to use an alternate party database.

2. If invoked during system start-up, the program then detaches and performs the usual daemon-initialization functions.

3. The run-time library for managed objects is initialized.

4. Next, the MIB subsystem in the agent is initialized. For each object supported by the agent, the corresponding object type is fetched from the library and the `ot_getfnx` and `ot_setfnx` fields are initialized to the addresses of procedures which will access instances of the object.

5. The party database is read.

6. Next, the agent configuration file is read.

7. The agent then starts listening on each transport address for which it is responsible. These are determined by examining the parties in the party database which are configured for local

execution. Normally, such parties will listen on UDP port 161 on the local host. However, this is a matter of convention only. The party database indicates which transport mappings and transport addresses should be used.

The agent will listen only for those parties which use SNMPv2. UDP is the only transport mapping available in the current release; however, mappings onto other transports have been done in the past.

8. Finally, a `coldStart` trap is sent according to the access privileges database to the appropriate management applications.

Not all of the information defined in the MIB can be found in the UNIX® kernel. Thus, *snmpd* needs some help from the system administrator. A configuration file is used for this purpose.

As shown in Figure 7.2, each line of the file contains a directive and one or more arguments:

variable *name***:** which sets the value of a leaf object.

variable interface: which sets the value of those columns in the interfaces table which are not instrumented by the Berkeley UNIX® kernel. The arguments are:

- a kernel-level name; and,

- one or more attribute-value pairs.

For example, the kernel doesn't store information indicating what kind of hardware is associated with a particular interface. The system administrator, who presumably is cognizant of such things, can supply this information to the agent.

logging: which tailors the logging package used by the agent.

```
variable      sysContact \
   "Marshall Rose (+1 415 968 1052) <mrose@dbc.mtview.ca.us>"
variable      sysLocation      "upstairs machine room"

variable      interface lo0    ifType=24        ifSpeed=0
variable      interface le0    ifType=6
variable      interface du0    ifType=23        ifSpeed=19200

logging       file=snmpd.log   size=50
logging       slevel=fatal     slevel=exceptions       slevel=notice
logging       sflags=close     sflags=create           sflags=zero
```

Figure 7.2: Example Agent Configuration File

7.2.2 Main Loop

The main-loop of *snmpd* is straightforward: the agent waits for an incoming datagram. Upon receiving one:

1. It reads the datagram and notes the transport address of the sending entity. **snmpStatsPackets** is incremented.

2. It de-serializes the datagram into an ASN.1 structure. If an error occurs, **snmpStatsEncodingErrors** is incremented, and the packet is discarded.

   If the packet appears to be an SNMPv1 packet, it is expected to be a response in a proxy relationship. It is dealt with accordingly, and the agent then returns to waiting for the next datagram.

   Otherwise, the ASN.1 structure is then translated into the appropriate instance of an **SnmpPrivMsg** structure. If an error occurs, **snmpStatsEncodingErrors** is incremented, and the packet is discarded.

3. The destination party identified in the **SnmpPrivMsg** structure is looked up in the party database. If the party isn't present in the database, **snmpStatsUnknownDstParties** is incremented, and the packet is discarded.

4. The privacy algorithm associated with the destination party is applied to the data contained within the `SnmpPrivMsg` structure and translated into an `SnmpAuthMsg` structure. If an error occurs, `snmpStatsEncodingErrors` is incremented, and the packet is discarded.

   Otherwise, the `SnmpMgmtCom` structure contained within the `SnmpAuthMsg` structure is extracted.

5. The source party identified in the `SnmpMgmtCom` structure is looked up in the party database. If the party isn't present in the database, `snmpStatsUnknownSrcParties` is incremented, and the packet is discarded.

   Otherwise, `authenticate_incoming` is called to authenticate the `SnmpAuthMsg` structure based on the authentication algorithm associated with the source party. If the `SnmpAuthMsg` structure is deemed unauthentic, the appropriate counter is incremented, `authorizationFailure` traps may be generated, and the packet is discarded.

6. The context identified in the `SnmpMgmtCom` structure is looked up in the party database. If the context isn't present in the database, `snmpStatsUnknownContexts` is incremented, and the packet is discarded.

7. The access policy is checked to see if the operation contained within the `SnmpMgmtCom` structure may be performed. If not, `snmpBadOperations` is incremented and, if the operation is neither a `response` nor a `trap`, then an `authorizationError` `response` is returned.

8. A special integer-value variable, `quantum`, is incremented. This keeps track of the logical request-id being processed by the agent.

9. The context is examined to see if it relates to a MIB view or a proxy relationship.

   If the latter, then control proceeds, based on the kind of operation:

response: the corresponding request is identified, and the appropriate response sent to the original requestor;

trap: the access policies in the party database are consulted to determine the managers to which the trap should be sent;

otherwise: information about the request (e.g., the parties and contexts identified, the originating transport address, and the `request-id`) is stored in the agent so that it may later be answered; a message is sent to the appropriate device, and control then returns to waiting for the next datagram.

10. If the context relates to a MIB view, then if the operation is an `inform`, `response`, or `trap`, it is rejected as if it were denied by the access policy.

11. Otherwise, the agent loops through the list of variables in the request.

    The agent finds the prototype by calling `name2inst`. If there is no prototype, then:

    - for the `get` operation, the value of the variable is set to the `noSuchObject` exception, and control loops to the next variable;

    - for the `set` operation, a `noCreation` error occurs, and the loop terminates; and,

    - for the `get-next` operation, the routine `next2inst` is called to find the next prototype.

    Once a prototype is found, if the operation is either `get` or `set`, the variable is checked against the MIB view. If the variable isn't in the view, then:

    - for the `get` operation, the value of the variable is set to the `noSuchInstance` exception, and control loops to the next variable; and,

    - for the `set` operation, a `noAccess` error occurs, and the loop terminates.

Otherwise, the agent invokes an access method to perform the desired operation. For a retrieval operation, the access method tries to locate the appropriate information; for a `set` operation, the access method analyzes the proposed value and then reserves any required resources, without actually performing the set. When the access method returns:

- If an error occurs, no further processing is done; instead, a `response` with the appropriate error is returned and the packet is discarded.

- If an exception occurs, control loops to the next variable.

- If the access method for the `get-next` operator was invoked and a value was returned, the new variable is checked against the MIB view. If this new variable isn't in the view, the access method is called again to retrieve the next instance.

  Otherwise, it is possible that there are no instances of this object type which are lexicographically greater than the variable given (e.g., the end of a table has been reached). In this case, a special value is returned by the access method. The agent then calls `next2inst` to find the next object type supported by the agent, and the access method associated with that object is invoked. If `next2inst` knows of no later objects, the value of the variable is set to the `endOfMibView` exception, and control loops to the next variable.

In the case of the `get` and `get-next` operator, after exhausting the list of variables in the first pass, the agent returns a `response` and discards the packet.

12. Otherwise, in the case of the `set` operation, if the first pass completed without error, then a second pass, called the `commit` pass is made. This invokes the access methods associated with the list of variables in the request a second time, and tells them to commit the change.

    Instead, if the first pass encountered an error, then a second pass, called the `rollback` pass is made. This invokes the access methods associated with the list of variables in the request, and tells them to discard any information about changes they were prepared to make.

Note that for the **get-next** operator, the MIB view is checked after the access method returns. Because the MIB view can have instance-level granularity, the access method must be called again, as the next instance returned by the access method might not be contained within the view. Needless to say, this can impose a significant performance penalty on the agent. To minimize this, when the agent calculates its MIB views, it keeps track of whether or not instance-level granularity is requested. If not, then instead of calling the same access method again, the next prototype is found, and its access method is invoked.

Observant readers are likely wondering why the discussion above didn't include the **get-bulk** operator. The answer is that it is initially treated as a **get-next** operator: control loops through the entire list of variables (repeaters and non-repeaters). If the result is too large, then it is trimmed accordingly. Otherwise, the agent creates a pointer to the answers associated with the repeater variables. It then loops through this new list again, and appends the answer to the **response**. The pointer is then set to the answers just received. This algorithm continues to iterate until either:

- the **max-repetitions** field from the request is achieved;

- an **endOfMibView** is returned for each repeating variable; or,

- the combined **response** is too large.

In the latter case, the **response** is trimmed accordingly.

7.2.3   Get Methods

Earlier it was noted that the *C* structure used to model an object type has two fields, `ot_getfnx` and `ot_setfnx`, which point to access methods that can be used to perform the SNMP `get`, `get-next`, or `set` operations on a variable. It was also noted that, during agent startup, these fields are initialized for each variable supported by the agent. The routine is free to use the `ot_info` field in order to handle several MIB objects. For example, the routine `o_ip` handles all the non-tabular objects in the IP group. Linkage between the agent and the access method might be accomplished like this:

```
#define ipForwarding     0
...
extern  int     o_ip ();


...


OT     ot;

if (ot = text2obj ("ipForwarding")) {
    ot -> ot_getfnx = o_ip;
    ot -> ot_setfnx = s_ip;
    ot -> ot_info = (caddr_t) ipForwarding;
}
...
```

It is now time to see how these access methods are implemented. Operations are invoked in the same way:

```
int     result = (*ot -> ot_getfnx) (oi, v, offset)
OI      oi;
struct type_SNMP_VarBind *v;
int     offset;
```

where:

- the `oi` parameter contains the name of the variable along with a pointer to the prototype object structure;

- the `v` parameter also contains the name of the variable, and a field in which to store the value:

```
struct type_SNMP_VarBind {
    OID     name;

    PE      value;
};
```

and,

- the `offset` parameter identifies which operation is to be performed, either `get` or `get-next`.

It turns out that these access methods are written in one of two ways, depending on whether the routine is used to access a scalar or tabular variable. Each case is now considered in turn.

Non-tabular variables

Figure 7.3 starting on page 345 sketches how the `o_ip` routine is implemented. The first action is to determine which leaf object is being referenced. The corresponding symbolic constant is placed in the variable `ifvar`. Then a switch is made, based on the operation:

- For the `get` operation, all instances are identified by the object type followed by `.0` (e.g., `ipForwarding.0`).

  The code checks to see if the `OID` associated with the object instance is exactly one longer than the `OID` associated with the object type, and that the extra sub-identifier has the value `0`.

  If the instance doesn't match, then a `noSuchName` error is returned. This error, a throwback to the days of SNMPv1, is treated as a `noSuchInstance` exception by the calling routine. (This is an example of how an SNMPv1 method routine can be used, unaltered, in an SNMPv2 agent!)

- For the `get-next` operation, there are really two cases, depending on whether some instance-identifier is present.

  If an instance is present, then for a non-tabular leaf object, the next variable *must* belong to some other object type, so the access method simply returns the value `NOTOK`, and the calling routine in the agent will find the next object, as described earlier.

Otherwise, if no instance is identified, a new OID is constructed and initialized. The old OID is freed and the new one inserted in its place.

Now that the correct instance has been identified, a check is made to see if the UNIX® kernel should be consulted. (The agent will read a kernel data structure *at most* once for each SNMP message it processes.) Finally, the instance value is encoded and the access method returns.

The agent contains several routines to encode instance values for the standard syntaxes. For example,

```
int     o_number (oi, v, number)
OI      oi;
struct type_SNMP_VarBind *v;
integer number;
```

is used to stuff a numeric value into a variable. First, the prototype and object syntax corresponding to the instance are extracted. Then, the os_encode routine is called to create a presentation element corresponding to the number. If a value is already present in the variable, it is freed. Regardless, the variable's value is then set to the newly-created presentation element. If an error occurs in processing, then the appropriate SNMP error is returned.

```
static int     lastq = −1;

static int     ipforwarding;
#define FORW_GATEWAY 1
#define FORW_HOST      2

static struct ipstat ipstat;


int       o_ip (oi, v, offset)                                            10
OI     oi;
register struct type_SNMP_VarBind *v;
int      offset;
{
    int     ifvar;
    register struct ipstat *ips = &ipstat;
    register OID    oid = oi −> oi_name;
    register OT     ot = oi −> oi_type;

    ifvar = (int) ot −> ot_info;                                          20
    switch (offset) {
        case type_SNMP_PDUs_get_request:
            if (oid −> oid_nelem != ot −> ot_name −> oid_nelem + 1
                    || oid −> oid_elements[oid −> oid_nelem − 1] != 0)
                return int_SNMP_error_status_noSuchName;
            break;

        case type_SNMP_PDUs_get_next_request:
            if (oid −> oid_nelem == ot −> ot_name −> oid_nelem) {
                OID    new;                                               30

                if ((new = oid_extend (oid, 1)) == NULLOID)
                    return int_SNMP_error_status_genErr;
                new −> oid_elements[new −> oid_nelem − 1] = 0;

                if (v −> name)
                    free_SNMP_ObjectName (v −> name);
                v −> name = new;
            }
            else                                                         40
                return NOTOK;
            break;

        default:
            return int_SNMP_error_status_genErr;
    }
}
```

Figure 7.3: Get and Get-Next of Non-Tabular Objects

```
    if (quantum != lastq) {
        lastq = quantum;

        if (getkmem (nl + N_IPFORWARDING, (caddr_t) &ipforwarding,
                    sizeof ipforwarding) == NOTOK
            || getkmem (nl + N_IPSTAT, (caddr_t) ips, sizeof *ips)
                    == NOTOK)
            return int_SNMP_error_status_genErr;
    }
                                                                            10
    switch (ifvar) {
        case ipForwarding:
            return o_integer (oi, v, ipforwarding ? FORW_GATEWAY : FORW_HOST);

...

        default:
            return int_SNMP_error_status_noSuchName;
    }
}
                                                                            20
```

Figure 7.3: Get and Get-Next of Non-Tabular Objects (cont.)

Tabular variables

Figure 7.4 starting on page 348 sketches how the `o_ip_route` routine is implemented. This routine is used to realize the IP routing table.

The first action is to call a routine called `get_routes`. This checks to see if the routing tables should be copied from the kernel. If so, a data structure is created containing this information.

The next action is to determine which leaf object is being referenced. The corresponding symbolic constant is placed in the variable `ifvar`. Then, a switch is made based on the operation. Because these are tabular objects, the instance refers to a row in the table (and the leaf object refers to a column in the table, of course).

- For the `get` operation, all instances are identified by the object type followed by the destination IP address for the route (e.g., `ipRouteNextHop.192.33.4.21`).

  The code checks to see if the `OID` associated with the object instance is of the right length (at least four sub-identifiers longer than the `OID` associated with the object type).

  If so, the `get_rtent` routine is called to retrieve this entry from the data structure built by a previous call to `get_routes`. Otherwise, a `noSuchName` error is returned, which the calling routine treats as a `noSuchInstance` exception.

- For the `get-next` operation, the first action is to "normalize" the instance-identifier. At least four octets are expected, so if an instance-identifier is present, but isn't four octets, a normalized name is constructed.

  Next, there are really two cases, depending on whether some instance-identifier is present.

  If no instance is identified, a new `OID` is constructed and initialized for the first row of the table. The prior call to `get_routes` put the routing entry corresponding to the lexicographically smallest instance-identifier in the variable `rts_inet`. The old `OID` is freed and the new one inserted in its place.

  Otherwise, if some instance-identifier is present, the `get_rtent` routine is called to find the routing entry corresponding to the row whose instance-identifier is larger than, but closest to, the indicated instance-identifier.

  If no such row is found, the next variable belongs to some other object type, so the access method simply returns the value `NOTOK`, and the calling routine in the agent will find the next object, as described earlier.

Now that the correct routing entry has been identified, the instance value is encoded and the access method returns.

The problem with this approach is the overhead in reading the routing table from the UNIX® kernel. To combat this, `get_routes` will retrieve the entire routing table *at most* once for each SNMP message. This means that if a request is for many routing variables, accurate answers can be returned from this one *kernel dive*, and the only overhead incurred is when the *first* routing variable in a request is referenced. A reference to any other routing variable can be satisfied by the cache built by `get_routes`.

Unfortunately, the amount of interaction between a user-process and the kernel in order to retrieve the *entire* routing table is substantial; typically three system calls must be made for *each* route.

```
int       o_ip_route (oi, v, offset)
OI        oi;
register struct type_SNMP_VarBind *v;
int       offset;
{
    int       ifvar;
    register int    i,
                        j;
    register unsigned int *ip,
                            *jp;                                                  10
    register struct rtetab *rt;
    register OID    oid = oi -> oi_name;
    OID       new;
    register OT       ot = oi -> oi_type;

    if (get_routes (offset) == NOTOK)
        return int_SNMP_error_status_genErr;

    ifvar = (int) ot -> ot_info;
    switch (offset) {                                                            20
        case type_SNMP_PDUs_get_request:
            if (oid -> oid_nelem < ot -> ot_name -> oid_nelem + IFN_SIZE)
                return int_SNMP_error_status_noSuchName;
            if ((rt = get_rtent (oid -> oid_elements
                                    + ot -> ot_name -> oid_nelem,
                                oid -> oid_nelem
                                    - ot -> ot_name -> oid_nelem,
                                rts_inet, 0))
                        == NULL)
                return int_SNMP_error_status_noSuchName;                          30
            break;

        case type_SNMP_PDUs_get_next_request:
            if ((i = oid -> oid_nelem - ot -> ot_name -> oid_nelem) != 0 && i < IFN_SIZE) {
                for (jp = (ip = oid -> oid_elements + ot -> ot_name -> oid_nelem - 1) + i;
                        jp > ip;
                        jp--)
                    if (*jp != 0)
                        break;
                if (jp == ip)                                                     40
                    oid -> oid_nelem = ot -> ot_name -> oid_nelem;
                else {
                    if ((new = oid_normalize (oid, IFN_SIZE - i, 256)) == NULLOID)
                        return int_SNMP_error_status_genErr;
                    if (v -> name)
                        free_SNMP_ObjectName (v -> name);
                    v -> name = oid = new;
                }
            }
```

Figure 7.4: Get and Get-Next of Tabular Objects

```
        if (oid −> oid_nelem == ot −> ot_name −> oid_nelem) {
            if ((rt = rts_inet) == NULL)
                return NOTOK;

            if ((new = oid_extend (oid, rt −> rt_insize)) == NULLOID)
                return int_SNMP_error_status_genErr;
            ip = new −> oid_elements + new −> oid_nelem − rt −> rt_insize;
            jp = rt −> rt_instance;
            for (i = rt −> rt_insize; i > 0; i−−)
                *ip++ = *jp++;                                                10

            if (v −> name)
                free_SNMP_ObjectName (v −> name);
            v −> name = new;
        }
        else {
            if ((rt = get_rtent (ip = oid −> oid_elements + ot −> ot_name −> oid_nelem,
                                  j = oid −> oid_nelem − ot −> ot_name −> oid_nelem,
                                  rts_inet, 1)) == NULL)
                return NOTOK;                                                 20

            if ((i = j − rt −> rt_insize) < 0) {
                if ((new = oid_extend (oid, −i)) == NULLOID)
                    return int_SNMP_error_status_genErr;
                if (v −> name)
                    free_SNMP_ObjectName (v −> name);
                v −> name = new;

                oid = new;
            }                                                                30
            else
                if (i > 0)
                    oid −> oid_nelem −= i;

            ip = oid −> oid_elements + ot −> ot_name −> oid_nelem;
            jp = rt −> rt_instance;
            for (i = rt −> rt_insize; i > 0; i−−)
                *ip++ = *jp++;
        }
        break;                                                               40

    default:
        return int_SNMP_error_status_genErr;
}
```

Figure 7.4: Get and Get-Next of Tabular Objects (cont.)

```
switch (ifvar) {
    case ipNextHop:
        return o_ipaddr (oi, v, (struct sockaddr_in *) &rt -> rt_gateway);

...


    default:
        return int_SNMP_error_status_noSuchName;
}
}
```
10

Figure 7.4: Get and Get-Next of Tabular Objects (cont.)

On systems with a large routing table, the overhead is notable. In the latest version of Berkeley UNIX®, a new interface to the kernel was introduced to reduce this problem. Even so, the agent currently uses a simplistic caching algorithm optimized for traversing the entire routing table using the `get-next` operator.

7.2.4   Set Methods

Figure 7.5 starting on page 351 sketches how the `s_ip` routine is implemented.

The first action is to determine which pass is being made. Next, the object syntax associated with the leaf object is extracted. Next, a determination is made as to which leaf object is being referenced. If the instance doesn't exist, then a `noSuchName` error is returned. This error, a throwback to the days of SNMPv1, is treated as a `noCreation` error by the calling routine. (Again, this is an example of how an SNMPv1 method routine can be used, with minimal alteration, in an SNMPv2 agent!)

The corresponding symbolic constant is placed in the variable `ifvar`. (The example shows only the code for the `ipForwarding` object.) A switch is then made, based on the pass:

- For the first pass, a check is made to see if the scratchpad storage associated with this object is already in use. If so, this would indicate that the variable is being set more than once in a single operation. As the result of such an operation is undefined, the

```
int      s_ip (oi, v, offset)
OI     oi;
register struct type_SNMP_VarBind *v;
int     offset;
{
   int     ifvar;
   register OID    oid = oi −> oi_name;
   register OT     ot = oi −> oi_type;
   register OS     os = ot −> ot_syntax;

   switch (offset) {
      case type_SNMP_PDUs_set_request:
      case type_SNMP_PDUs_commit:
      case type_SNMP_PDUs_rollback:
         if (oid −> oid_nelem != ot −> ot_name −> oid_nelem + 1
               || oid −> oid_elements[oid −> oid_nelem − 1] != 0)
            return int_SNMP_error_status_noSuchName;
         break;

      default:
         return int_SNMP_error_status_genErr;
   }

   if (os == NULLOS) {
      advise (LLOG_EXCEPTIONS, NULLCP,
            "no syntax defined for object \"%s\"", ot −> ot_text);

      return int_SNMP_error_status_genErr;
   }
```

Figure 7.5: Set of Non-Tabular Objects

```
switch (ifvar = (int) ot −> ot_info) {
    case ipForwarding:
        switch (offset) {
            case type_SNMP_PDUs_set_request:
                if (ot −> ot_save)
                    (*os −> os_free) (ot −> ot_save), ot −> ot_save = NULL;
                if ((*os −> os_decode) (&ot −> ot_save, v −> value)
                        == NOTOK)
                    return v −> value −> pe_errno;
                switch (*((integer *) ot −> ot_save)) {                        10
                    case FORW_GATEWAY:
                    case FORW_HOST:
                        ipforwarding = *((integer *) ot −> ot_save)
                                        == FORW_GATEWAY;
                        break;

                    default:
                        return int_SNMP_error_status_wrongValue;
                }
                break;                                                          20

            case type_SNMP_PDUs_commit:
                if (setkmem (nl + N_IPFORWARDING, (caddr_t) &ipforwarding,
                        sizeof ipforwarding) == NOTOK)
                    return int_SNMP_error_status_genErr;
                /* and fall */

            case type_SNMP_PDUs_rollback:
                if (ot −> ot_save)
                    (*os −> os_free) (ot −> ot_save), ot −> ot_save = NULL;     30
                break;
        }
        break;

    ...

    default:
        return int_SNMP_error_status_noSuchname;
    }
                                                                               40
    return int_SNMP_error_status_noError;
}
```

Figure 7.5: Set of Non-Tabular Objects (cont.)

access method simply gets rid of the proposed value from a previous variable binding.

Next, the proposed value is decoded and checked to make sure that it is within bounds. If the value is acceptable, the static variable ipforwarding is updated. Otherwise, the wrongValue error is returned.

- For a commit pass, the kernel is told about the new value, and the object-specific scratchpad storage is released.

- For a rollback pass, the object-specific scratchpad storage is released.

One could imagine that a similar access method could be written for tabular objects.

However, it must be emphasized that this example is trivial, e.g., some MIB objects, when being set, may require that they can only be modified in combination with other MIB objects in the same request (e.g., as discussed earlier on page 201, an instance of the partyAuthClock object can be reset only when the corresponding instance of the partyAuthPrivate object is changed). In this case, there is a requirement for interaction between the functions implementing sets for different MIB objects.

To accommodate this, when a set method doing the first pass decides that there is an inter-object dependency, it allocates a small data structure called a checklist:

```
struct checklist {
    IFP     ck_fnx;     /* routine to call */
    caddr_t ck_info;    /* pointer to data structure
                           containing dependency */

    int     ck_idx;     /* for error-index */

    struct checklist *ck_next;
};
```

and appends it onto a linked list. If the first pass is successful, then prior to making the commit pass, each checklist is invoked to verify

that the inter-object dependency was satisfied. If not, the appropriate
error code is recorded, and a rollback pass is made instead.

7.2.5   Encoding and Decoding SNMP Structures

The last topic to be discussed is how the `SnmpPrivMsg` structure is
encoded into a string of octets for transmission and decoded into a
C structure upon reception. The routines which perform these tasks
were automatically generated!

ISODE contains a series of compilers which read ASN.1 modules
and produce equivalent C structures. In addition, these compilers generate C routines to translate between presentation elements and the C
structures. Finally, the run-time library in ISODE contains routines
to encode and decode presentation elements for network transmission
and reception.

Thus, the applications programmer deals exclusively in C structures. All of the infrastructure required to send and receive these
structures on the network is automatically processed. (Section 8.4 of
The Open Book [64] discusses these concepts more fully.)

For now, it is important to realize that sending is a two-step
process:

- a routine is called to convert the C structure to a presentation
  element; then,

- a routine is called to serialize the presentation element onto a
  transport service, such as TCP or UDP.

The receiving process is inverted.

The advantage of this approach is that it is flexible, predictable,
and doesn't require any thought from the applications programmer.
The disadvantage is that it makes a second copy of the data (the
presentation element) during the transmission or reception process.

There are, of course, many other approaches. The use of ASN.1 in
the management framework is specifically focused on allowing efficient
hand-coded routines to be written. These can achieve significant
performance improvements over the ISODE approach, at the risk of
substantially reduced functionality.

7.3 Manager Implementation

The 4BSD/ISODE SNMPv2 package doesn't contain a large number of management applications. Rather, it consists of tools for the rapid prototyping of network management applications.

At the simplest level, an SNMP initiator program *snmpi*, is available which makes each SNMP operation (except **trap**) available to the user. For example,

```
% snmpi get sysUpTime.0
sysUpTime.0=45366736 (5 days, 6 hours, 1 minutes, 7.36 seconds)
```

retrieves the one and only instance of **sysUpTime**. In addition to implementing each SNMP operation, *snmpi* performs a few other functions:

adjustclock: executes the clock-synchronization algorithm;

agent/manager/context: sets the agent party, manager party, or management context;

audit: examines a logfile of traps and displays the information contained therein;

compile: generates a C-source format-compiled MIB file;

dump: retrieves all variables subordinate to the named object (e.g., **dump system** will retrieve all the variables in the **system** group);

retries: sets the maximum number of retransmissions for retrieval operations;

secrets: changes the authentication (and privacy) secrets for a party;

sync: forces the in-core party database to be written to stable-storage (normally this is performed only when *snmpi* terminates);

timeout: sets the retransmission timer; and,

tune: updates non-secret information about an agent's party by making authenticated retrieval requests.

snmpi is useful for debugging, but that's about it. However, *snmpi* does give us the opportunity to show how a proxy relationship might work — Figure 7.6 shows a proxy to SNMPv1. Note that, although *snmpi* knows about the context which identifies the proxy relationship, it doesn't have any knowledge about the ultimate destination party.

7.3.1   SNMP-capable gawk

Rather than supplying management applications, a language for building new applications is defined. This is done by modifying one of the common UNIX® commands used for rapid prototyping, the *awk* program. In particular, the GNU version of *awk*, named *gawk*, was selected. The result is called "SNMP-capable gawk."

The *gawk* program is a pattern scanning and processing language used to interpret "scripts" that contain

```
pattern     { action }
```

pairs. For each line of input, *gawk* checks to see if the input matches the pattern; if so, the action, which is written in a language very much like *C*, is executed. In addition, there are two special patterns,

```
BEGIN     { actions }
```

and

```
END       { actions }
```

which are executed at the beginning and end, respectively, of the input.

This structure allows a programmer to test out ideas with very fast turnaround. Once an idea is proven, it can then be recoded entirely in *C* to achieve a performance boost. Of course, many programmers never bother with the second step: many *awk* scripts perform quite adequately in a production environment.

SNMP-capable *gawk* reads a compiled MIB file, and recognizes the leaf objects (both tabular and non-tabular) as special variables. The

```
% snmpi
snmpi> pp
No.   Identity                              Authentication        Privacy
  1*A initialPartyId.192.103.140.1.1        noAuth                noPriv
      residing at 192.103.140.1/161
  2*M initialPartyId.192.103.140.1.2        noAuth                noPriv
  3 A initialPartyId.192.103.140.1.3        v2md5AuthProtocol     noPriv
      residing at 192.103.140.1/161
  4 M initialPartyId.192.103.140.1.4        v2md5AuthProtocol     noPriv
  5 A initialPartyId.192.103.140.1.5        v2md5AuthProtocol     desPrivProtocol
      residing at 192.103.140.1/161
  6 M initialPartyId.192.103.140.1.6        v2md5AuthProtocol     desPrivProtocol

snmpi> context
No.   Identity                              Information
  1*  initialContextId.192.103.140.1.1      view  1
  2   initialContextId.192.103.140.1.2      view  2
  3   initialContextId.192.103.140.1.3      proxy initialPartyId.192.103.140.1.7
      src 0.0 ctx 0.0

Psnmpi> status
  1*A initialPartyId.192.103.140.1.1        noAuth                noPriv
      residing at 192.103.140.1/161
  2*M initialPartyId.192.103.140.1.2        noAuth                noPriv
  1*C initialContextId.192.103.140.1.1      view  1

snmpi> dump system
sysDescr.0="4BSD/ISODE SNMPv2"
sysObjectID.0=fourBSDisodeAgent
sysUpTime.0=18 hours, 55 minutes, 34.49 seconds (6813449 timeticks)
sysContact.0="Marshall Rose (+1 415 968 1052) <mrose@dbc.mtview.ca.us>"
sysName.0="dbc.mtview.ca.us"
sysLocation.0="upstairs machine room"
sysServices.0=0x48<transport,application>

snmpi> context 3

snmpi> status
  1*A initialPartyId.192.103.140.1.1        noAuth                noPriv
      residing at 192.103.140.1/161
  2*M initialPartyId.192.103.140.1.2        noAuth                noPriv
  3*C initialContextId.192.103.140.1.3      proxy initialPartyId.192.103.140.1.7
      src 0.0 ctx 0.0

snmpi> dump system
sysDescr.0="unixd"
sysObjectID.0=fourBSDunixdPeer
sysUpTime.0=18 hours, 54 minutes, 12.46 seconds (6805246 timeticks)
sysName.0="dbc.mtview.ca.us"
sysServices.0=0x40<application>
```

Figure 7.6: Demonstrating a Proxy Relationship with snmpi

current implementation allows both reading and writing of variables in a MIB available via SNMPv2. This means that MIB variables can occur either as *rvalues* or *lvalues* in an expression.

Non-tabular variables

To retrieve an object which doesn't occur inside a table, the name of the object is used, and the instance-identifier is automatically calculated, e.g.,

```
% gawk 'BEGIN { print sysDescr; }'
```

Instead, if you want to supply a special instance-identifier, then reference the variable as an array. Hence, an equivalent command is:

```
% gawk 'BEGIN { print sysDescr[0]; }'
```

This is less intuitive, but it's your choice. Both statements invoke the SNMP operation

```
get (sysDescr.0)
```

and print the value returned by the agent.

Since an SNMP operation might fail, there are two special variables that may be examined:

- **DIAGNOSTIC**, which returns a textual description of any problem which occurred with the last SNMP operation; and,

- **ERROR**, which contains the **error-status** returned by the last SNMP operation.

Hence:

```
% gawk 'BEGIN { print "sysDescr: ", sysDescr, DIAGNOSTIC; }'
```

prints either the system description of the agent, or a diagnostic, depending on what happened with the SNMP interaction.

Tabular variables

A value of an object occurring in a table can be retrieved in one of two ways.

First, the instance-identifier can be written as an array reference, e.g.,

```
ifDescr[1]
```

which is equivalent to a **get** operation on the variable

```
ifDescr.1
```

or

```
ipRouteNextHop["10.0.0.0"]
```

which is equivalent to a **get** operation on the variable

```
ipRouteNextHop.10.0.0.0
```

This is called the "subscript notation".

Second, the table can be traversed. This is done with the *gawk* **for-in** construct, e.g.,

```
for (i in ipRouteDest) {
    printf "route to %s via %s\n",
        ipRouteDest, ipRouteNextHop;
}
```

which says to traverse the table containing the object `ipRouteDest`. The for-loop body will be executed once for each row of the table; for each iteration, the control variable will be assigned the value of the instance-identifier for that row (**not** the value of the column in that row). This allows other parts of the MIB to be referenced using the same instance-identifier, e.g.,

```
for (i in ipRouteDest) {
    printf "route to %s via %s (flags %s)\n",
        ipRouteDest, ipRouteNextHop, unixIpRouteFlags[i];
}
```

which iterates through MIB-II's IP routing table, and also fetches a value from a column in a corresponding table in an "enterprise-specific" MIB module.

The **for-in** construct retrieves a row of a table using a single **get-next** operation. If a particular column isn't returned by the agent, then referencing the corresponding variable will return the empty string. Note that within the for-loop body, repeated references to a column of a table won't result in additional SNMP operations. If, for some reason, it is desirable to refresh a variable's value, the subscript notation is used, e.g.,

```
for (i in ipRouteDest) {
    printf "route to %s via %s\n",
        ipRouteDest, ipRouteNextHop[i];
}
```

which causes each iteration to use the **get-next** operator to bind values to each column in the **ipRoutingTable**, while the corresponding instance-identifier is assigned to i. Then, when the **printf** statement is executed, a separate **get** operation will be used to supply a (possibly) new value for **ipRouteNextHop**. Usually, the subscript notation is used when it is necessary to look at a variable in another table, e.g.,

```
for (i in ipRouteDest) {
    printf "route to %s via %s on %s (interface #%d)\n",
        ipRouteDest, ipRouteNextHop,;
        ifDescr[ipRouteIfIndex], ipRouteIfIndex;
}
```

which causes each iteration to use the **get-next** operator to bind values to each column in the **ipRoutingTable**, while the corresponding instance-identifier is assigned to i. Then, when the **printf** statement is executed, a separate **get** operation will be used to supply the corresponding value of **ifDescr**.

Of course, there's always the question of dealing with agents which may not support the table or when an error occurs. Usually, the following code fragment is sufficient:

```
didone = 0;
for (i in tabularVariable) {
    didone = 1;

#    handle each row of the table here...
}
if (didone == 0) {
    if (DIAGNOSTIC) {
#        handle table error here...
    }
    else {
#        handle empty table here...
    }
}
else
    if (DIAGNOSTIC) {
#        handle partial table here...
    }
```

Finding an empty or partial table is often unimportant, so the boilerplate usually is:

```
didone = 0;
for (i in tabularVariable) {
    didone = 1;

#    handle each row of the table here...
}
if (!didone && DIAGNOSTIC)
    printf "table: %s\n", DIAGNOSTIC;
```

Unless the subscript notation is used, it is illegal to reference a tabular variable outside of a **for-in** loop. This causes a fatal error in a *gawk* script.

Further, referencing non-leaf variables (e.g., **ifTable**) will cause a fatal error in a *gawk* script.

Non-tabular variables (revisited)

If a script is accessing a lot of non-tabular variables sharing a common
parent (e.g., within the `system` group), the `for-in` construct can be
used to traverse this degenerate tree, e.g.,

```
for (i in sysDescr) {
#    this for-loop is executed at most once...
}
```

will cause all the non-tabular variables having the same immediate
parent as `sysDescr` to be retrieved in a single `get-next` operation,
while the corresponding instance-identifier (i.e., `0`) is assigned to `i`.

This syntax is used primarily for optimization of network traffic.

Assigning values to variables

The current implementation supports this in a sub-optimal fashion.
Each assignment operation results in a single `set` operation. Hence,
a compound assignment, e.g.,

```
ipForwarding = clnpForwarding = 1;
```

results in two `set` operations, each with one operand.[2] The optimal
approach would be to have a single `set` operation, with two operands.

---

[2]Actually, it's even worse than this: in the current implementation, a `get`
operation is performed prior to each `set` operation on a variable!

Data typing

The *gawk* program has two kinds of data types: numbers and strings. When mapping MIB objects to these data types, the following conventions are used:

Syntax	Type	Format
INTEGER	number	
BIT STRING	string	`"10101010101"`
OCTET STRING (binary)	string	`"%02x: ... : %02x"`
OCTET STRING (ascii)	string	
OBJECT IDENTIFIER	string	`"%u. ... .%u"`
IpAddress	string	`"a.b.c.d"`
Counter32	number	
Counter64	number	
Gauge32	number	
TimeTicks	number	
UInteger32	number	
NsapAddress	string	`"%02x: ... : %02x"`

New Variables

There are a few built-in, read-write variables available in SNMP-capable *gawk*:

AGENT	string	agent party identity
MANAGER	string	manager party identity
CONTEXT	string	management context
DIAGNOSTIC	string	last thing that went wrong
ERROR	number	last SNMPv2 error status
RETRIES	number	times to retry SNMPv2 operation (default 3)
TIMEOUT	number	seconds between retries (default 10)

The **AGENT**, **MANAGER**, and **CONTEXT** variables are initialized from the party database. By default, *gawk* will use the first **noAuth/noPriv** agent and manager parties it can find.

The **DIAGNOSTIC** and **ERROR** variables are set after each SNMP operation. If no error occurs, the **DIAGNOSTIC** variable is set to the empty string, and the **ERROR** variable is set to zero.

New Functions

There are a few new built-in functions available in SNMP-capable *gawk*:

- The `bitwise_and(i,j)` function returns the bit-wise AND of the two unsigned long quantities, `i` and `j`.

- The `bitwise_or(i,j)` function returns the bit-wise OR of the two unsigned long quantities, `i` and `j`.

An Example

In order to put everything in perspective, consider Figure 7.7. This prints out information about each interface on a managed node, e.g.,

```
% gawk -f mib.interfaces
Name Mtu   Net/Dest    Address      Ipkts     Ierrs Opkts    Oerrs
le0  1500  192.33.4.0  192.33.4.21  1460533   122   1309675  0
lo0  1536  127.0.0.0   127.0.0.1    48599     0     48599    0
```

The interesting part in this script is how the IP address for each interface is determined. A nested `for-in` construct is used to traverse the IP address table. Once the desired address is found, the **break** statement is used to terminate the loop early.

```
BEGIN {
    printf "%-4s %-4s %-14s %-15s %-7s %-5s %-7s %-5s\n",
            "Name", "Mtu", "Net/Dest", "Address", "Ipkts", "Ierrs",
            "Opkts", "Oerrs";

    didone = 0;
    for (i in ifIndex) {
        didone = 1;

        dest = "";
        addr = "";
        for (j in ipAdEntAddr) {
            if (ipAdEntIfIndex == ifIndex) {
                split(addr = ipAdEntAddr, a, ".");
                split(ipAdEntNetMask, b, ".");
                dest = bit_and(a[1],b[1]) "." \
                        bit_and(a[2],b[2]) "." \
                        bit_and(a[3],b[3]) "." \
                        bit_and(a[4],b[4]);
                break;
            }
        }

        printf (length(ifDescr) <= 4 ? "%-4s " : "%s\n        "),
            ifDescr;
        printf "%-4d %-14s %-15s %-7d %-5d %-7d %-5d %-4d %-5d\n",
            ifMtu, dest, addr, ifInUcastPkts+ifInNUcastPkts,
            ifInErrors, ifOutUcastPkts+ifOutNUcastPkts,
            ifOutErrors;
    }
    if (!didone && DIAGNOSTIC)
        printf "ifTable: %s\n", DIAGNOSTIC;
}
```

Figure 7.7: Example Script for SNMP-capable gawk

7.3.2   SNMP-based TCL

It should be noted that SNMP-capable *gawk* is only one of many possible programming paradigms for the management framework. Let's briefly look at another.   The Tool Command Language, *tcl*, is a language used for building tools [67]. The basic data structures in *tcl* are strings and lists. Among the features found in *tcl* are extensibility and inter-process communication. Hence, when a family of programs is built using *tcl*, users are able to consistently modify the behavior of the programs, both locally and remotely.

As a part of the *tcl* package an X Window System toolkit, *tk*, is available [68]. This allows the application programmer considerable flexibility in developing programs with customizable and extensible graphical user interfaces. For example, *snmptcl* is a program written partially in both *C* and *tcl*. The *C* portion manages the *tcl* interpreter and exports several SNMP-related commands and variables. The *tk* toolkit is invoked from *snmptcl* to manage the user interface. When invoking *snmptcl*, a user can specify a *tcl* command-file, containing one or more management applications. By using the *tcl* language, these applications make use of the *tk* toolkit for their interface to the user, along with the SNMP-related commands and variables for their interface to the agents.

It is far beyond the scope of *The Simple Book* to discuss *tcl* or *tk* in detail. Instead, let's look at one of the TCL-based procedures, which is loaded when *snmptcl* starts. The definition of the `getInstances` procedure is shown in Figure 7.8 starting on page 368. This procedure is invoked when an application has a list of objects and wants to retrieve every instance of those objects using the `get-bulk` operator. The procedure is invoked with two parameters: an integer (`size`) indicating a guess as to how many instances there might be (e.g., the value of `ifNumber.0` might be used if retrieving instances of the interfaces table); and, a list of object names (`vs`). An optional third parameter, `oops`, may also be present.

The procedure begins by adjusting the `size` parameter to a "reasonable" default (if no value is provided), or by incrementing it by one (to aid in determining when all instances have been retrieved). Next, the return value, a list of variable bindings (`vbs`) is initialized to the empty list. A `get-bulk` operation is then iteratively built into `query`, by appending each of the object names from the `vs` parameter. (The command `snmp` is defined using *C* and then exported into *tcl* when *snmptcl* initializes the interpreter.) Finally, `lvs` is set to the number of objects contained in the input list. Control now enters an endless loop.

First, the `get-bulk` operation is executed. The `snmp` command returns a list. The first element of that list reports the error status of the operation. If there was an error, a dialog-box is presented to the user, and the procedure returns whatever variable bindings it had collected. Otherwise, each variable binding (`vb`) returned is examined. The instance (`name`) is retrieved, along with the expected object (`expect`). If an exception was associated with this binding, then `skips` is incremented and control loops to the next variable binding. Next, a determination is made if the variable returned is an instance of the expected object. If not:

- if this has been the case for each object in the input list, then the endless loop is terminated; otherwise,

- control loops to the next variable binding.

If the variable returned is an instance of the expected object, then the instance-identifier is extracted (`suffix`). If this instance-identifer differs from the instance-identifer seen with previous variables, it is remembered. Regardless, the variable binding is appended onto the result being built.

Once each variable binding has been examined, a check is made to see if this pass did any work. If not, then the procedure returns whatever variable bindings it had collected (if no variable bindings had ever been collected, then a dialog-box might be presented to the user just prior to the return). If some work was done, then a determination must be made as to the next `get-bulk` operation to be issued. To do this, an instance-identifier must be selected which will be appended onto each object in the input list. To make this determiniation a check is made to see if at least one instance of each object was potentially retrieved. If not, then the results from the operation are used as the operands; otherwise, the last instance-identifier which was seen for all objects is used.

```
proc     getInstances                    {size vs {oops ""}} {
   if {$size <= 0} { set size 12 } else { incr size }

   set           vbs            ""
   set           query          "snmp op bulk 0 $size"
   foreach       v       $vs {  append    query " " $v }

   set           lvs            [llength $vs]
   while {1} {
         set     query          [eval $query]                                    10

      if {[lindex $query 0] != "noError:"} {
         mkDialog      .err       "-text \"$query\""
         return        $vbs
      }

      set     didone         0
      set     skips          0
      set     i              0
      set     inst1          ""                                                   20
      set     inst2          ""
      set     inst3          ""
      foreach vb        [lrange $query 1 end] {
         set            name     [lindex $vb 0]
         set            expect   [lindex $vs $i]
         if {[incr i 1] >= $lvs} { set i 0 }

         if {[string last : $name] >= 0} { incr skips; continue }

         set            prefix   [string range $name 0 \                          30
                                 [set index [expr [string first . $name]-1]]]
         if {$expect != $prefix} {
               if {[incr skips] >= $lvs} {              break }
            continue
         }

         set            suffix   [string range $name [expr $index+1] end]
         if {[string compare $inst1 $suffix]} {
               set      inst2    $inst1
               set      inst1    $suffix                                          40
         }

         lappend        vbs      $vb
         if {$i == 0} {                   set inst3 $suffix }
         set            didone   1
         set            skips    0
   }
```

Figure 7.8: The TCL-based procedure getInstances

```
      if {!$didone || ($lvs <= $skips)} {
          if {([llength $vbs] == 0) && ($oops != "")} {
              mkDialog \
                       .err      "-text \"$oops\""
          }
          return $vbs
      }

      if {[set lq [llength $query]] <= $lvs} {
          if {($lq <= 1) && ([llength $vbs] == 0)} {                          10
              mkDialog \
                       .err      "-text \"awesome get-bulk returned nothing!\""

              return $vbs
          }

          set          qwery    "snmp op bulk 0 $size"

          foreach vb   [lrange $query 1 end] {
              append   qwery    " " [lindex $vb 0]                            20
          }

          set          query    $qwery
      } else {
          if {$inst1 == $inst3} {
              set      inst2     $inst1
          }

          set          query    "snmp op bulk 0 $size"
          foreach      v         $vs {                                        30
              append   query     " " $v$inst2
          }
      }
  }
}
```

Figure 7.8: The TCL-based procedure getInstances (cont.)

Chapter 8

The Future

In closing *The Simple Book*, let's look at the problems which face us and speculate as to where things might be going. Since this chapter is entirely opinion and conjecture, it is enclosed within a soapbox. `soap...`

Cost of Entry

Perhaps the greatest lesson of the SNMP experience has been that technology must be *tractable* if it is to be successful. Certainly, the widespread adoption of SNMPv1 proved this with a vengeance. This may come as a surprise to people who still believe in OSI, but the cost of entry has an inverse relationship to the rate of adoption. (Of course, a lot of people view OSI as more of an embarrassment than a solution these days.)

From a design perspective, SNMP:

- makes minimal use of abstractions and choices;

- makes minimal requirements from the transport service, the communications stack, and agent resources; and,

- this results in a minimal impact on managed nodes, the cost of entry is thereby minimized, and the rate of adoption — in the market — is maximized.

With SNMPv2, the cost of entry was significantly increased (e.g., from three documents totaling less than 150 pages, to 12 documents totaling over 400 pages). In addition, SNMPv2 delves into the murky realm of security technology, whilst SNMPv1 did not. Fortunately, very little of these changes resulted in an increase on the "bits on the wire"!

However, despite this nearly three-fold increase in documentation, the upgrade process is surprisingly straightforward and relatively inexpensive. No doubt, some of this is due to the fact that much of the additional documentation doesn't require additional coding. More importantly, however, those parts of the documentation which do require additional coding are zealously faithful to the original SNMP ideals. Further, tremendous emphasis was placed on coexistence with SNMPv1.

Consider that when security technology was developed for SNMP, these changes were carefully scrutinized for their impact on effective management. Although tediously painful to the designers, this intellectual investment was necessary to produce secure technology that would still be able to manage networks in the real world. Fortunately, the design team responsible for most of SNMPv2 were also implementors, and iterated between design, specification, and implementation. This leads to a soapbox within a soapbox, a publishing first!

soap...

The procedure used to develop SNMPv2 was somewhat different from what is customary in the Internet community. In March of 1992, the Internet Engineering Steering Group issued a call for proposals to evolve the Internet-standard Network Management Framework. Contributors were invited to submit proposals for an evolutionary technology based on the original SNMP.

Three months later, a design team announced a proposal termed the *Simple Management Protocol (SMP) and Framework*, along with four independent, interoperable implementations. The members of the self-selecting design team, consisting of Jeffrey D. Case, Keith McCloghrie, Marshall T. Rose, and Steven L. Waldbusser, were all implementors of SNMP technology (either commercially or openly available), and had participated extensively in the development of several SNMP-related standards (e.g., Jeffrey D. Case, perhaps best known as "Dr. SNMP," was one of the original authors of SNMP). The simultaneous release of complete specifications and reference implementations was quite intentional — it provided a platform for interested parties to immediately study and experiment with the new proposal.

At the following meeting of the IETF, a decision was made to declare a deadline for further proposals, and to form a working group to evaluate all submissions, select one as the initial specification for SNMPv2, and then finish working on the specification — changing it accordingly. Because the community was very concerned about the impact of two transitions, the recently completed work on SNMP security (a four-year design and development effort) was re-opened, and its working group tasked to align with the newly-formed working group. The result would be a single, consistent set of documents defining the new Internet-standard Network Management Framework.

The deadline came and went and no other proposals were forthcoming. The working group began its discussions via electronic mail and held two physical meetings. The quality of the SMP documents, now termed SNMPv2, was improved, and the two working groups completed their business by early 1993. Superficially, the effort was a successful interaction between design teams and working groups. However, this wasn't the entire story.

On the mailing list, there were several heated and prolonged arguments regarding additional features. The chair of the working group, Robert L. Stewart, was scrupulously neutral in his handling of the issues. But even so, this did not prevent surreptitious mumblings of "rubber-stamping" the proposal by the so-called *gang of four*. At the chair's request, one of the originators acted as editor of the SNMPv2 document series, making changes as directed by the chair when the working group achieved consensus on the issues. (Recall from page 16 that working groups in the IETF operate by rough consensus, not by voting.)

Independent of this, the author of *The Simple Book* was also one of the more vocal participants in the working group. Regrettably, the author's participation was mostly to provide "adult supervision". In brief, the problem was that the contributions from many members of the working group weren't very well thought out. Perhaps this was to be expected. Consider this analogy: in the film *Of Unknown Origin*, a man renovating a house is plagued by a large, ferocious rat of preternatural instinct and abilities. The man (played by the notable

Peter Weller, who is perhaps best known for his portrayal of the title role in the film *The Adventures of Buckaroo Banzai*), has tried several different approaches to get the rat — all to no avail. He then consults with an expert, who chastises him:

> *"You spend what, five, maybe 10% of your time thinking about that rat? That rat spends 100% of his time thinking about you. After all, it's a rat, what else does it have to do?"*

The point here is that the rat is **always** going to win because it thinks longer and harder about the situation.[1]

So it is with design teams and working groups. Each member of the design team has devoted every spare hour to intensive discussion, design, specification, and implementation of the proposal. Each member of the design team has done this for several months. Is it any wonder, then, when a working group member cobbles together a contribution, that it is often easily discredited by a member of the design team? Of course not. Now, this shouldn't imply that any of the members of the design team were against changing the proposal as it became the SNMPv2 specification. Quite the contrary. But, with the change must come an overall improvement. Furthermore, the change must not cause damage to another part of the specification. And herein is where the controversy arose: People with an architectural perspective often don't consider engineering issues, and people with a research perspective often don't consider issues of practicality. Of course, some people just want to make their mark on the emerging standard, and as such they'll fight to the death trying to get their change adopted. But then again, any member of the design team, each immersed in all aspects of the specification, could easily evaluate the worth of each new contribution and then "do the right thing".

As noted in the soapbox ending back on page 71, a few topics have achieved *problematic* status. In polite company, it is considered bad manners or, at the very least, provincial behavior to raise a *problematic* topic. Naturally, such a topic was destined to find its way

---

[1]At the end of the film, the man finally gets the rat. But this is to be expected, since most films have a "storybook" ending rather than a "the real world is a hard place" ending.

into the working group's discussions, eliciting what might be viewed as extremely poor table manners on the part of the contributors. The particular issue was that of "atomic" row manipulation, and it was accompanied by the usual (wrong) solution, namely, the introduction of two new protocol operations, used to create and delete instances in conceptual rows. As explained back in section 6.1.4, the issues of conceptual row creation and deletion are thorny ones and you simply can't solve them by adding a couple of new operators. But, this didn't stop the contributors and long-time supporters of such a poorly thought-out solution. After much argument, and with the help of several members of the working group, the proposal deservedly went down in flames. The good news is that as a result of the discussion, some improvements were made to the specification's original approach. The bad news is that it took a lot of energy to educate the supporters as to their lack of understanding of the real issues involved, and why their solution simply wouldn't work. The author wouldn't mind this so much, except for the fact that the next time this *problematic* topic arises, we'll go through the whole pointless exercise again, and again.

It is important to appreciate that working groups legitimize the efforts of a design team by taking ownership of a proposal and turning it into a specification for the community. It is equally important to acknowledge that everyone is entitled to an opinion. However, what often goes unsaid is that no one is entitled to have a "correct" opinion, nor are all opinions created equally. Thus, when a contribution spectacularly goes down in flames, it might be asked whether it was a good idea for the contributor to start the presentation with:

> *"I had this idea as I was reading the documents (for the first time) on the plane over to this meeting."*

The author will refrain from continuing on this subject, despite the fact he has a lot more venom that he could spit at the guilty. Instead, to end this inner-soapbox on a happy note, it should be emphasized that despite these problems, the quality of the specification was improved. The author just wishes, in order to get those improvements, that the thrust/payload ratio wasn't so frustratingly poor.

`...soap`

MIB Madness

Looking back to Table 4.2 on page 140, it is clear that a large number of MIB modules have been specified and are edging their way along the standards track. Although the table might look impressive, it really masks three problems.

First, the MIB modules are useful primarily for "managing wires". That is, they deal largely with different kinds of media. Although this is an important part of internet management, there is still a lot more ground to be covered. Fortunately, by late 1992, there were a few inklings that this might change:

- a MIB module for the Domain Name System was nearing completion;

- a Host Resources MIB, for determining the resources and components available on an end-system, was also nearing completion; and,

- work was just beginning on a MIB for electronic mail management.

Still, there are a lot of applications that need management, and our collective understanding of applications management is hardly mature.

Second, quite a few of the MIB modules shown in the table entered the standards track in mid-1991 and they remain proposed standards. That is, there has been insufficient pull from the market to motivate the community to advance these documents along the standards track. Part of this may be due to several of these MIB modules being focused on specific segments of the market. Perhaps a more significant reason is that it was easier for people to form a working group to produce the document than for them to go out and put the resulting technology into products. Fortunately, the Internet standardization process has a remedy for this: things don't go forward (and eventually are sidetracked) if there isn't market pull. Perhaps, though, the third problem provides an insight into understanding the lack of market pull.

Third, the MIB modules are all geared towards instrumentation rather than problem solving. For example, look at the routing table in MIB-II or in the IP Forwarding Table MIB. Both provide a lot of information about the routes known to a device. But neither tells the implementor of a management station the kinds of problems that can be solved using this information, nor does either tell the implementor what algorithms to implement in order to solve those problems. So, the MIB module can be implemented in agent products, but the implementors of management stations are given little help in making use of this information. This may perhaps explain why most of today's management applications are either of the "browser" or the "flashing", but not the "thinking" variety. The author has long speculated that perhaps we need to re-focus MIB definition on identifying problems, selecting algorithms, and then defining objects. This sounds like an interesting area to be pursued, but whether such an approach would lead to standardized MIB modules is doubtful.

The Comprehensive Perspective

Although SNMP is a solution to many problems, it isn't the solution to the entire problem of internet management — nor was it ever intended to be. Having said that, it is clear that SNMP provides a framework for the exchange of management information within an administrative jurisdiction. How that information is used (as noted just moments ago, a topic outside the current scope of standardization), and how the processes that use that information fit into an organization, remain open questions.

Despite this, the SNMP experience teaches us that taking a simple, extensible approach often yields surprisingly useful results in the face of an overwhelming problem. It has often been noted that:

> *"Eighty percent of success is just showing up."*

Early experience with SNMP showed that simply being able to monitor information was amazingly helpful in managing networks, even though additional control features would have helped even more. The point being that once operators were able to remotely monitor devices, they were much better equipped to deal with the problems they faced.

How does this apply towards solving the entire problem? Other than instilling a basic philosophy towards problem-solving, I don't

know. What I do know is that there isn't any panacea. I know
that because the market hungers for a solution, it occasionally finds
itself supporting solutions which exist less as products than as view-
graphs — solutions which exist more as wishful thinking than as the
result of hard architectural choices and solid engineering discipline.
And perhaps this is why the "rough consensus and running code"
principle has served the Internet community so well.

In Conclusion

Regardless of the "spin" one places on the problems we face, it is clear
that internets *require* network management. It is also clear that the
original Internet-standard Network Management Framework and its
Fundamental Axiom have produced a useful and, more importantly,
a workable, system for internet management.

As of this writing, SNMPv2 seems poised to be the worthy successor to the original SNMP. However, the only true measure of success
is implementation and wide deployment. Thus, regardless of the
author's enthusiasm for its engineering excellence, SNMPv2 can only
be judged a success in terms of its market adoption. And, on this
⎡...soap⎤ note, *The Simple Book* ends.

Appendix A

Relevant Internet Documents

The *Request for Comments* (RFC) document series provides for the dissemination of information about the Internet suite of protocols. Not all RFCs are standards; quite the reverse: relatively few RFCs enjoy any level of standardization. Rather, the majority of RFCs are research notes intended for discussion.

RFCs are available in both printed and electronic form. The printed copies are available for a modest fee from the DDN Network Information Center:

Postal:	DDN Network Information Center
	14200 Park Meadow Drive
	Suite 200
	Chantilly, VA 22021
	US
Phone:	+1 800–365–3642
	+1 703–802–4535
Mail:	nic@nic.ddn.mil

In electronic form, users may use "anonymous" FTP to the host `nic.ddn.mil` (residing at [192.112.36.5]) and retrieve files from the directory "`rfc/`", e.g.,

```
% ftp nic.ddn.mil
Connected to nic.ddn.mil
220-*****Welcome to the Network Information Center*****
     *****Login with username "anonymous" and password "guest"
     *****You may change directories to the following:
       ddn-news          - DDN Management Bulletins
       domain            - Root Domain Zone Files
       ien               - Internet Engineering Notes
       iesg              - IETF Steering Group
       ietf              - Internet Engineering Task Force
       internet-drafts   - Internet Drafts
       netinfo           - NIC Information Files
       netprog           - Guest Software (ex. whois.c)
       protocols         - TCP-IP & OSI Documents
       rfc               - RFC Repository
       scc               - DDN Security Bulletins
220 And more.
Name (nic.ddn.mil:mrose): anonymous
331 Guest login ok, send "guest" as password.
Password (nic.ddn.mil:anonymous): guest
230 Guest login ok, access restrictions apply.
ftp> cd rfc
250 CWD command successful.
ftp> ascii
220 Type A ok.
ftp>
```

Certainly the first RFC to retrieve is the Index of RFCs:

```
ftp> get rfc-index.txt
200 PORT command successful.
150 Opening ASCII mode data connection for rfc-index.txt.
226 Transfer complete.
167512 bytes received in 1.1e+02 seconds (1.4 Kbytes/s)
ftp> quit
%
```

Other sites also maintain copies of RFCs, e.g.,

> ftp.nisc.sri.com
> venera.isi.edu
> wuarchive.wustl.edu
> ftp.concert.net
> nis.nsf.net
> nisc.jvnc.net
> src.doc.ic.ac.uk

Of course, this list might change, but it's a good place to start.

If your site doesn't have IP-connectivity to the Internet community, but does have electronic mail access, you can send an electronic mail message to the electronic mail address

> `mail-server@nisc.sri.com`

and in the subject field indicate the RFC number, e.g.,

> `Subject: SEND rfcs/rfc1130.txt`

A reply to your electronic mail message will contain the desired RFC.

If your site has electronic mail access to the Internet community, and you desire notification when new RFCs are published, send a note to the electronic mail address

> `rfc-request@nic.ddn.mil`

and ask to be added to the RFC notification list.

Internet Drafts

Internet Drafts, which document the work in progress of the IETF, are available only in electronic form. (Recall that Internet Drafts have no standardization status whatsoever.) Use "anonymous" FTP to the host **nnsc.nsf.net** (residing at **[192.31.103.6]**) and retrieve files from the directory **internet-drafts/**, e.g.,

```
% ftp nnsc.nsf.net
Name (nnsc.nsf.net:mrose): anonymous
Password (nnsc.nsf.net:anonymous): guest
230 Guest login ok, access restrictions apply.
ftp> cd internet-drafts
ftp> ascii
```

Other sites also maintain copies of Internet Drafts, e.g.,

```
munnari.oz.au
ftp.nisc.sri.com
nic.nordu.net
nic.ddn.mil
```

Of course, this list might change, but it's a good place to start.

If your site doesn't have IP-connectivity to the Internet community, but does have electronic mail access, you can send an electronic mail message to the electronic mail address

```
mail-server@nisc.sri.com
```

and in the subject field indicate the name of the draft, e.g.,

```
Subject: SEND internet-drafts/draft-ietf-foo-bar-00.txt
```

A reply to your electronic mail message will contain the desired draft.

If your site has electronic mail access to the Internet community, and you desire notification when new Internet Drafts are published, send a note to the electronic mail address

```
ietf-request@venera.isi.edu
```

and ask to be added to the **ietf** list. Note that other IETF administrative announcements are also posted to this list.

A.1 Administrative RFCs

The key administrative RFCs are:

RFC	Name	Status
1410	IAB Official Protocol Standards	Required
1340	Assigned Numbers	Required
1122	Host Requirements — Communications	Required
1123	Host Requirements — Applications	Required
1009	Gateway Requirements	Required

Note that these RFCs are periodically updated. As with the rest of the RFC series, the most recent document always takes precedence. In particular, note that the Official Protocols Standards document (in theory) is updated quarterly.

The information which follows is taken from the Official Standards RFC [23], published in March, 1993. By the time of this reading, a new version of this RFC will no doubt have been published.

A.2   Core Protocol RFCs

The RFCs pertaining to the core of the Internet suite of protocols are:

RFC	Name	Status
791	Internet Protocol	Required
950	Subnet Extension	Required
919	Broadcast Datagrams	Required
922	Broadcast Datagrams with Subnets	Required
792	Internet Control Message Protocol	Required
1112	Host extensions for IP multicasting	Recommended
768	User Datagram Protocol	Recommended
793	Transmission Control Protocol	Recommended
854	TELNET Protocol	Recommended
855	TELNET Options	Recommended
959	File Transfer Protocol	Recommended
821	Simple Mail Transfer Protocol	Recommended
822	Format of Electronic Mail Messages	Recommended
1049	Content-type header field	Recommended
1119	Network Time Protocol (v2)	Recommended
1034	Domain Name System Concepts and Facilities	Recommended
1035	Domain Name System Implementation and Specification	Recommended
974	Mail Routing and the Domain Name System	Recommended
904	Exterior Gateway Protocol	Recommended
862	Echo Protocol	Recommended

There are also many other Internet standards of a less critical nature:

RFC	Name	Status
1001	NetBIOS over TCP Concepts and Methods	Elective
1002	NetBIOS over TCP Detailed Specifications	Elective
863	Discard Protocol	Elective
864	Character Generator Protocol	Elective
865	Quote of the Day Protocol	Elective
866	Active Users Protocol	Elective
867	Daytime Protocol	Elective
868	Time Protocol	Elective
1350	TFTP Protocol (revision 2)	Elective
1058	Routing Information Protocol	Elective
1006	ISO Transport Services on top of the TCP	Elective

There are also many Internet standards pertaining to transmission of
the IP over various media:

RFC	Name	Standard
826	Address Resolution Protocol	Full
891	DC Networks	Full
894	Ethernet Networks	Full
895	Experimental Ethernet Networks	Full
903	Reverse Address Resolution Protocol	Full
907	Wideband Network	Full
1042	IEEE802 Networks	Full
1044	Hyperchannel	Full
1051	ARCNET	Full
1055	Serial Links	Full
1088	NetBIOS	Full
1132	IEEE802 over IPX Networks	Full
1149	Avian Networks	Informational
1201	ARCNET	Proposed
1209	SMDS	Proposed
1294	Frame Relay	Proposed
1356	X.25 and ISDN	Proposed
1374	HIPPI	Proposed
1390	FDDI	Full

Note that, although the status of these standards is *elective*, if a device
elects to transmit IP datagrams over one of the media above, then it
is *required* to use the procedures defined in the relevant RFC(s).

A.3 Network Management RFCs

A.3.1 The Original Framework

The original *Internet-standard Network Management Framework* is defined in these four documents:

RFC	Name	Status
1155	Structure of Management Information	Recommended
1212	Concise MIB Definitions	Recommended
1157	Simple Network Management Protocol	Recommended
1213	Management Information Base II	Recommended

All of these documents are full standards.

In addition, these three documents define transport mappings for SNMPv1 for different protocol suites:

RFC	Name	Status
1418	SNMP over OSI	Recommended
1419	SNMP over AppleTalk	Recommended
1420	SNMP over IPX	Recommended

As of this writing, these three documents are proposed standards.

A.3.2   The SNMPv2 Framework

The new framework is defined in these twelve documents:

RFC	Name	Status
1441	Introduction to SNMPv2	Recommended
1442	SMI for SNMPv2	Recommended
1443	Textual Conventions for SNMPv2	Recommended
1444	Conformance Statements for SNMPv2	Recommended
1445	Administrative Model for SNMPv2	Recommended
1446	Security Protocols for SNMPv2	Recommended
1447	Party MIB for SNMPv2	Recommended
1448	Protocol Operations for SNMPv2	Recommended
1449	Transport Mappings for SNMPv2	Recommended
1450	MIB for SNMPv2	Recommended
1451	Manager-to-Manager MIB	Recommended
1452	Coexistence between SNMPv1 and SNMPv2	Recommended

As of this writing, all of these documents are proposed standards. Once they achieve full standard status, the documents comprising the original framework will be obsoleted.

A.3.3 MIB Modules

There are several RFCs which define MIB modules for particular environments:

RFC	Name	Standard
1229	Extensions to the generic-interface MIB	Proposed
1231	IEEE 802.5 Token Ring Interface Type MIB	Proposed
1239	Reassignment of Experimental MIBs to Standard MIBs	Proposed
1243	AppleTalk® MIB	Proposed
1253	OSPF version 2 MIB	Proposed
1269	BGP version 3 MIB	Proposed
1271	Remote LAN Monitoring MIB	Proposed
1285	FDDI Interface Type MIB	Proposed
1286	Bridge MIB	Proposed
1289	DECnet Phase IV MIB	Proposed
1304	SMDS Interface Protocol (SIP) Interface Type MIB	Proposed
1315	Frame Relay DTE Interface Type MIB	Proposed
1316	Character Device MIB	Proposed
1317	RS-232 Interface Type MIB	Proposed
1318	Parallel Printer Interface Type MIB	Proposed
1354	SNMP IP Forwarding Table MIB	Proposed
1368	IEEE 802.3 Repeater MIB	Proposed
1381	X.25 LAPB MIB	Proposed
1382	X.25 PLP MIB	Proposed
1389	RIP version 2 MIB	Proposed
1398	Ether-Like Interface Type MIB	Draft
1406	DS1 Interface Type MIB	Proposed
1407	DS3 Interface Type MIB	Proposed
1414	Identification MIB	Proposed

All of these documents have a status of "recommended". At present, these MIB modules can be used with either SNMPv1 or SNMPv2.

However, during their advancement, they will likely be translated to use SNMPv2's SMI.

A.3.4   Miscellaneous RFCs

There are several RFCs which are either informational or experimental in nature:

RFC	Name	Status
1147	A Network Management Tool Catalog	Informational
1187	Bulk Table Retrieval with the SNMP	Experimental
1215	A Convention for Defining Traps for Use with the SNMP	Informational
1224	Techniques for Managing Asynchronously Generated Alerts	Experimental
1227	SNMP MUX protocol and MIB	Experimental
1228	SNMP Distributed Program Interface (SNMP-DPI)	Experimental
1238	CLNS MIB	Experimental
1270	SNMP Communication Services	Informational
1303	A Convention for Describing SNMP-based Agents	Informational
1321	MD5 Message-Digest Algorithm	Informational

Many of these have been obsoleted by the work on SNMPv2, i.e., RFCs 1187, 1215, 1224, and 1303 apply only to SNMPv1.

A.3.5   Historic RFCs

Over time, some RFCs have been superseded. If you run across any of these documents, be aware that you are reading "yesterday's news".

RFC	Name	See RFC
1156	Management Information Base I	1213
1161	SNMP over OSI	1418
1230	IEEE 802.4 Token Bus Interface Type MIB	
1232	DS1 Interface Type MIB	1406
1233	DS3 Interface Type MIB	1407
1283	SNMP over OSI	1418
1284	Ether-Like Interface Type MIB	1398
1298	SNMP over IPX	1420
1351	SNMP Administrative Model	1445
1352	SNMP Security Protocols	1446
1353	SNMP Party MIB	1447

A.4   Network Management Assignments

The Assigned Numbers document contains the registry of all subtrees assigned for network management:

Subtree	Prefix
directory	1.3.6.1.1
mgmt	1.3.6.1.2
mib-2	1.3.6.1.2.1
transmission	1.3.6.1.2.1.10
experimental	1.3.6.1.3
enterprises	1.3.6.1.4.1

The list of enterprise assignments is also available via "anonymous" FTP:

```
host   venera.isi.edu
area   mib
file   snmp-vendors-contacts
mode   ascii
```

As of this writing, over 500 assignments had been made!

A.4.1   Getting an Experimental Assignment

To register a new experiment, one must first coordinate with the *Area Director for Network Management* in the Internet Engineering Steering Group. (The Internet Assigned Numbers Authority can provide this contact information.) The Area Director will coordinate with the IANA to request an experimental number.

Once contact is made with the Area Director, a working group of the IETF will be formed (if appropriate) to oversee the experiment. In particular, the working group must author an Internet Draft, defining the experimental MIB. This draft will be made available for public review.

A.4.2 Getting an Enterprise Assignment

Contact the IANA and ask for one.

Some enterprise-specific MIB modules are available for FTP on the host `venera.isi.edu`. Use "anonymous" FTP and retrieve the files from the directory "`mib/`".

The IANA also maintains a public repository of enterprise-specific MIB modules. Note that MIB modules in the repository are not "registered" in any sense — they are simply available for public inspection (unlike experimental MIB modules which are registered as Internet Drafts).

To submit an enterprise-specific MIB module for publication, mail a copy to:

`mib-checker@isi.edu`

Your MIB module will be automatically run through a MIB compiler and any errors will be reported back to you. Once your module has passed the compiler, the IANA will place it in the repository.

Here is the access information for the public repository:

```
host   venera.isi.edu
area   mib
```

A.5   Contact Information

The RFC Editor can be reached at:

> Postal: Jonathan B. Postel
> RFC Editor
> USC/Information Sciences Institute
> 4676 Admiralty Way
> Marina del Rey, CA 90292-6695
> US

> Phone: +1 310–822–1511

> Mail: postel@isi.edu

The Internet Assigned Numbers Authority can be reached at:

> Postal: Joyce K. Reynolds
> Internet Assigned Numbers Authority
> USC/Information Sciences Institute
> 4676 Admiralty Way
> Marina del Rey, CA 90292-6695
> US

> Phone: +1 310–822–1511

> Mail: iana@isi.edu

Appendix B

Other Resources

If you're interested in learning more, there are several other resources available!

B.1   The Simple Times

The Simple Times is an openly-available publication devoted to the promotion of the Simple Network Management Protocol. In each issue, *The Simple Times* presents: a refereed technical article, an industry comment, and several featured columns:

- Applications and Directions

- Ask Dr. SNMP

- Security and Protocols

- Standards

- Working Group Synopses

In addition, some issues include brief announcements, summaries of recent publications, and an activities calendar.

Past technical articles have included:

- A New View on Bulk Retrieval with SNMP

- Sets are Fun: Introducing the SMDS Subscription MIB Module

- An Implementation of SNMP Security

- Customer Network Management of the InterSpan Frame Relay Service

- Accomplishing Performance Management with SNMP

- An Introduction to SNMP MIB Compilers

The Simple Times is openly-available. You are free to copy, distribute, or cite its contents. However, any use must credit both the contributor and *The Simple Times*. Further, this publication is distributed on an "as is" basis, without warranty. Neither the publisher nor any contributor shall have any liability to any person or entity with respect to any liability, loss, or damage caused or alleged to be caused, directly or indirectly, by the information contained in *The Simple Times*.

Subscription Information

The Simple Times is available via electronic mail in three editions: *PostScript*, *MIME* (the multi-media 822 mail format), and *richtext* (a simple page description language). For more information, send a message to

    st-subscriptions@simple-times.org

with a `Subject` line of

    Subject: help

In addition, *The Simple Times* has numerous hard-copy distribution outlets. Contact your favorite SNMP vendor and see if they carry it. If not, contact the publisher and ask for a list:

Postal:	*The Simple Times*
	c/o Dover Beach Consulting, Inc.
	420 Whisman Court
	Mountain View, CA 94043–2186
Tel:	+1 415–968–1052
Fax:	+1 415–968–2510
E-mail:	st-editorial@simple-times.org
ISSN:	1060–6068

Submission Information

The Simple Times solicits high-quality articles of technology and comment. Technical articles are refereed to ensure that the content is marketing-free. By definition, commentaries reflect opinion and, as such, are reviewed only to the extent required to ensure commonly-accepted publication norms.

The Simple Times also solicits announcements of products and services, publications, and events. These contributions are reviewed only to the extent required to ensure commonly-accepted publication norms.

Submissions are accepted only in electronic form. A submission consists of ASCII text. (Technical articles are also allowed to reference encapsulated PostScript figures.) Submissions may be sent to the contact address above, either via electronic mail or via magnetic media (using either 8-mm `tar` tape, $\frac{1}{4}$-in `tar` cartridge-tape, or $3\frac{1}{2}$-in MS-DOS floppy-diskette).

Each submission must include the author's full name, title, affiliation, postal and electronic mail addresses, telephone, and fax numbers. Note that by initiating this process, the submitting party agrees to place the contribution into the public domain.

B.2 How to Write a MIB Module

David T. Perkins has an article discussing how to write a MIB module. It is entitled:

Understanding SNMP MIBs

To get a copy, send an electronic mail message to:

`dperkins@synoptics.com`

B.3   Implementations

There are two openly-available implementations of SNMPv2: the
CMU package and the 4BSD/ISODE SNMPv2 package. The announcements for each package are reproduced below:

B.3.1   CMU SNMP/SNMPv2

The CMU SNMP/SNMPv2 package is a portable development platform for SNMP and SNMPv2 as well as a collection of network management tools. This package was developed by Carnegie Mellon University for its own use and to help spread SNMP technology into the
marketplace.

The package includes source code for:

- a portable SNMP/SNMPv2 library;

- a portable SNMP/SNMPv2 (bilingual) agent suitable for general-
  purpose or embedded-system platforms;

- a portable mid-level agent for manager-to-manager applications;

- an SNMP/SNMPv2 API for bi-lingual applications;

- an interface to the Tcl/Tk application programming language;
  and,

- a collection of network management applications.

This package continues to enjoy major support from CMU as well
as the community. The SNMP Security implementation had major
support from Lexcel. Other contributors to the code include TGV,
BBN, and Shiva. Portions of the code were derived from the RSA
Data Security, Inc. MD5 Message-Digest Algorithm.

This package is freely-available, but is not in the public-domain.
This code may be used for any purpose, for-profit or otherwise, without fee. Derivative works may provide further restrictions or charge
fees, but must leave the original copyrights intact and must give credit
to the contributors in supporting documentation.

This package is available via anonymous FTP:

host	`lancaster.andrew.cmu.edu`
area	`pub/snmp-dist`
file	`README`
mode	`ascii`

The `README` file contains instructions as to the current version and file name of the latest release. Any *tar* file included in this directory must be retrieved in binary mode.

B.3.2 4BSD/ISODE SNMPv2

I am pleased to announce that there is now a SNMPv2 implementation available for the ISODE 8.0 release. The release of the

4BSD/ISODE SNMPv2 package

implements version 2 of the Simple Network Management Protocol (SNMPv2).

Features

The 4BSD/ISODE SNMPv2 package is a relatively complete implementation of SNMPv2, with these exceptions:

administrative model: The administrative model is completely implemented, with the exception that no privacy functions are included. Note that if you specify view entries which provide instance-level access control, then this has a big performance impact on the agent.

structure of management information: Although all macros are fully recognized, only invocations of the `OBJECT-TYPE` macro receive extensive scrutiny.

textual conventions: Although the `TEXTUAL-CONVENTION` macro is fully recognized, the `DISPLAY-HINTS` clause is used only for textual (non-numeric) syntaxes.

conformance statements: Although all macros are fully recognized, very little semantic scrutiny is made.

transport mappings: The `snmpUDPdomain` is the only transport mapping provided.

managed objects: Although all SNMPv2 MIB objects are implemented, since the agent doesn't support dynamically-configurable object resources, the `snmpORTable` is always empty. (You should use a proxy relationship instead.)

protocol operations: The agent implements all operations; however, responses to the bulk operation are not always as large as they could be.

manager-to-manager: The manager doesn't implement any of these objects.

coexistence (proxy): The agent supports proxy operations for both the `rfc1157Domain` and `snmpUDPdomain` transport domains. This allows the SNMPv2 agent to act as a front-end for these other devices, termed *proxy-targets*. In addition, if you want to export a MIB module, you do this by writing your own proxy-target program, and then defining the appropriate proxy relationships. A future release of the package will support a bilingual API for management applications.

Acknowledgements

Originally, this work was partially supported by the US Defense Advanced Research Projects Agency and the US Air Force Systems Command under contract number F30602–88–C–0016. Marshall T. Rose wrote the original (insecure) 4BSD/ISODE SNMP package.

David L. Partain of the Department of Computer and Information Science at Linköping University, Sweden, added most of the administrative facilities as a part of his Masters work at the University of Tennessee, Knoxville. Dr. Jeffrey D. Case of SNMP Research supervised his work, and Keith McCloghrie of Hughes LAN Systems provided implementation guidance.

The MD5 implementation used in this package is taken from RFC-1321, and is hereby identified as "derived from the RSA Data Security, Inc. MD5 Message-Digest Algorithm".

NOTICE

This package is openly available but is NOT in the public domain. You are allowed and encouraged to take this software and use it for any lawful purpose. However, as a condition of use, you are required to hold harmless all contributors.

Permission to use, copy, modify, and distribute this software and its documentation for any lawful purpose and without fee is hereby granted, provided that this notice be retained unaltered, and that the name of any contributors shall not be used in advertising or publicity pertaining to distribution of the software without specific written prior permission. No contributor makes any representations about the suitability of this software for any purpose. It is provided "as is" without express or implied warranty.

ALL CONTRIBUTORS DISCLAIM ALL WARRANTIES WITH REGARD TO THIS SOFTWARE, INCLUDING ALL IMPLIED WARRANTIES OF MERCHANTABILITY AND FITNESS FOR THE PARTICULAR PURPOSE, TITLE, AND NON-INFRINGEMENT.

IN NO EVENT SHALL ANY CONTRIBUTOR BE LIABLE FOR ANY SPECIAL, INDIRECT OR CONSEQUENTIAL DAMAGES, WHETHER IN CONTRACT, TORT, OR OTHER ACTION, ARISING OUT OF OR IN CONNECTION WITH, THE USE OR PERFORMANCE OF THIS SOFTWARE.

Availability

The software is available ONLY via anonymous FTP. If you don't have
FTP-access to the Internet, you are out of luck — NO EXCEPTIONS.

host	`ftp.ics.uci.edu`
area	`mrose/isode-snmpV2/`
file	`isode-snmpV2.tar.Z`
mode	`binary`

Questions on the package may be addressed to:

`ISODE-SNMPv2@ida.liu.se`

All correspondence must be via electronic mail. Further, under no
circumstances will any messages be answered if they relate to legal
issues.

B.4 MIB Compilers

There are two openly-available MIB compilers: *mosy* and *smic*.

B.4.1 mosy

The *mosy* compiler is a part of the 4BSD/ISODE SNMPv2 package, which is described above starting on page 401. If you just want to syntax-check a MIB module, and really don't care about having the source (or binary) to the *mosy* compiler, then send an electronic mail message containing your MIB module to:

    mosy@dbc.mtview.ca.us

Your MIB module will be automatically run through a MIB compiler and any errors will be reported back to you.

B.4.2 smic

This package is available via anonymous FTP:

host	`ftp.synoptics.com`
area	`eng/mibcompiler`
file	`README`
mode	`ascii`

The `README` file contains information about the components of the package.

The package will run on MS-DOS and many versions of UNIX®, and includes source code for a MIB compiler and a MIB stripper, along with "corrected" versions of MIB modules from various RFCs. Compiler features include:

- multiple input files;

- concise MIB format (RFC 1212);

- concise trap format (RFC 1215);

- multiple MIB modules;

- items in IMPORTS;

- textual conventions;

- alias assignments for modules and object names;

- selective checking of MIB constructs;

- extensive MIB syntax checking and continuation of syntax checking after syntax errors;

- extensive checking of MIB consistency;

- multiple output options (including `mosy` compatible output); and,

- environment variable to locate "included" files.

The *smic* package is "freely-available" but it is not public domain. The following is the copyright and rights to use message for *smic*:

For further information, contact:

`dperkins@synoptics.com`

Appendix C

Network Management is Simple: you just need the "right" framework!*

Following is a reprint of an invited paper [69] presented at 1990 IFIP International Symposium on Integrated Network Management, held in Washington, D.C., from April 1–5. The paper is reprinted by permission.

From a historical perspective, readers should appreciate that this paper was written at a time when the term Internet-standard Network Management Framework referred to the original three documents (the fourth, RFC 1212, had not yet been included in the set).

---

*From "Network Management is Simple", by Marshall T. Rose in *INTEGRATED NETWORK MANAGEMENT II* (1991), Elsevier Science Publishers B.V., pp. 9-25.

C.1   Introduction

Readers of these proceedings should be well-versed in the need for solutions that provide vendor-independent, interoperable network management. Indeed, as open systems (embodied by either the Internet or OSI suite of protocols) have risen to the forefront of networking, so has the need to manage networks which use these technologies. In the interest of brevity, this introduction omits any discussion of the history of networking, open systems, or the protocol suites which compose open systems. Instead, we merely note that just as today's enterprises need networking technology which is vendor-independent and fully-interoperable across product and vendor lines, so do today's enterprises need network management capabilities which exhibit the same properties.

Readers of these proceedings are likely well-versed in the politics of open systems and in particular of network management within open systems. Indeed, some pundits have gone so far as to publish amusing treatises outlining the deficiencies of the standardization process. This paper is also critical of the process, but in a serious tone, as the author feels that the standardization process for OSI network management has made a tragic mis-step.

In this paper, we present an alternate perspective on network management, one which has proven successful in the market, namely the *Internet-standard Network Management Framework*. Throughout the presentation a comparison is made to the OSI approach to network management, and several myths about network management are hopefully "debunked". In the concluding remarks, a plea is made for a drastic change in the course being taken by OSI network management.

C.2   Models and Architectures

Models and architectures are like "motherhood and apple pie", but not nearly as respectable. Every system has them, and, in a highly-political and market-crazed industry, there are few objective criteria which can be used to distinguish good design from poor design. Nonetheless, let us ask ourselves what singular property should be promoted by a network management technology and proceed from there.

Clearly, network management must be *ubiquitous* if it is to be truly useful. That is, each and every network node must be capable of being a *managed* node. However, there are two mediating concerns:

- network nodes exhibit great differences: some are super-computers or workstations or terminal servers, others are routers, and still others are media devices, such as a bridge or modem; and,

- users purchase network nodes, not for the purposes of management, but for other purposes (e.g., a super-computer is purchased for "number crunching", not because it can run a network management protocol).

These concerns provide a tremendous focus, which can be summarized as the *Fundamental Axiom*:

> *The impact of adding network management to managed nodes must be minimal, reflecting a lowest common denominator.*

Thus, if we are to achieve ubiquitous management capabilities, then we must design our management technology so that it can be realized on the least "capable" devices in the network. Consistent with this, when the technology is realized on a network node, it should not adversely affect the performance of that node. In brief, the Fundamental Axiom argues for a technology which can be implemented and executed efficiently on a managed node.

Further, since there will be many more managed nodes in the network than management stations, economy of scale argues for placing the computational and network burden on the stations rather than the managed nodes. Thus, for each design decision in which functionality must be split between the management stations and the managed nodes, the decision will be made in favor of reducing the functionality required of the managed nodes.

Of course, the easiest way to achieve efficiency is through *simplicity*: if we can develop a simple design, capable of meeting the basic needs of network management, then efficiency is a likely outcome. Further, by emphasizing simplicity, we also hope to achieve the scalability in deployment which is our chief goal.

C.2.1   The Internet-standard Network Management Framework

Although the time-frame in which OSI will achieve dominance is widely debated, it is clear that the *Internet Suite of Protocols*, commonly referred to as TCP/IP, has achieved the promise of open systems as today's *de facto* standard for open networking.

It has only been since mid-1987 that work began towards standardized management capabilities for the Internet suite. Further, despite both knowledge of, and participation in, the International standardization process, the community working on the Internet-standard Network Management Framework produced a system quite different from the OSI framework. The differences in the two network management approaches can be viewed as a micro-example of the distinctions between the Internet and OSI protocol suites: the Internet approach is tightly focused, the problem area is well-defined and the technical approach is geared towards that problem.

The key advantage of such an approach is that it produces *tractable technology*, which is the fundamental building block for a mature market. Consider:

- an important characteristic of a mature market is the competition of robust products;

- in order to develop robust products, it is necessary to deploy the technology in a large number of operational environments and subsequently "harden" it; and,

- in order to deploy technology, it is necessary to be able to implement that technology within a reasonable time-frame.

Although anything can be viewed as "a simple matter of coding," experience has shown that simpler technologies are more tractable, and in being so exhibit a greater likelihood of being implemented in a timely fashion. Clearly, the technology comprising the Internet suite of protocols is much more tractable than the corresponding OSI technology; and, just as clearly, the Internet suite has been widely-implemented, deployed in numerous operational environments, and has a tremendous number of mature products in market competition.

Thus, whilst the OSI approach to management has been to develop an all-encompassing model and respective service in an effort to architect a "complete" solution, the Internet-standard Network Management Framework has been specified, agreed upon, widely-implemented, and is already delivering useful service in the market.

The current framework is based on three documents:

- the Internet-standard *Structure of Management Information* (SMI) [54];

- the Internet-standard *Management Information Base* (MIB) [51]; and,

- the *Simple Network Management Protocol* (SNMP) [17].

Readers of these proceedings should be well-versed in the terms SMI and MIB as used in the OSI framework. However, the use and scope of these terms in the Internet-standard framework is somewhat different.

C.2.2   Structure of Management Information

The OSI framework views the network management problem as solved with an *object-oriented* paradigm. Objects defined in this framework have *attributes*, generate *events*, and perform *actions*. Further, objects are scoped by numerous hierarchies, e.g., for the purposes of inheritance or containment. Towards this end, ASN.1 is used as an object-oriented specification language to define these characteristics, along with a set of *Guidelines for the Definition of Managed Objects* (the ISO GDMO).

In contrast, the Internet-standard framework views managed objects as little more than simple (scalar) variables residing in a virtual store. The SMI is used as the schema for this database, and provides a naming relationship between managed objects (to provide for efficient traversal of the MIB), along with the syntax for the object, and a default access level. Towards this end, a subset of ASN.1 is used, as a notation to provide concise information to implementors.

In examining this difference in perspective, it should be observed that the Internet-standard approach is simply a formalized restating of the *remote-debugging* paradigm commonly used in earlier management technology. Although the panacea of object-oriented programming is quite attractive to some, others argue that both past and present experience shows little to recommend it. If the basic needs of network management can be met without this seemingly large investment, then there is little reason to require all managed nodes to implement it. In brief, "neat" architectures are, by themselves, unimpressive; in contrast, useful architectures are needed to solve real problems in real networks. Argumentative readers should consult the Appendix on page 427 for further exposition.

C.2.3   Management Information Base

As might be expected, definitions of managed objects often differ greatly between the two approaches. The most marked difference, however, is the minimalist perspective taken by the Internet-standard approach. For example, the Internet-standard MIB defines a scant 111 objects for the core aspects of the Internet suite of protocols, divided into 8 groups.

To provide for future growth, the Internet-standard SMI provides three extensibility mechanisms:

1. addition of new standard objects through definitions of new versions of the Internet-standard MIB;

2. addition of widely-available, but non-standard, objects through an "experimental" subtree; and,

3. addition of private objects through an "enterprises" subtree.

All three of these mechanisms have received use:

1. the successor to the Internet-standard MIB, MIB-II [70], was produced some two years later and contains 170 objects;

2. as of this writing there are some 20 experimental MIB modules under development (for management of everything from the CLNS, to FDDI, to SMDS); and,

3. numerous vendors have developed their own extensive private MIB modules which are specific to their product line. This is inevitable, and in fact, quite necessary: until such time as network devices are sold generically — in white boxes with blue lettering (e.g., "Router") — there will always be vendor-specific objects that are unique to each product.

In 1990, an interesting development has been the use of the experimental forum for "de-osifying" MIB modules defined by ANSI and the IEEE. That is, the essence of a given MIB module is restated using the language of the Internet-standard SMI. In comparing MIB modules written using the two frameworks, several key differences can be found.

First, a MIB module conforming to the Internet-standard SMI has **no** optional objects. Instead, related objects are grouped, and these groups form the basic unit of conformance. For example, in the Internet-standard MIB, there is a TCP group: implementation of *all* the objects in that group is mandatory for *all* managed nodes which implement TCP.[1]

The rationale for this is straightforward: if there is a large number of optional managed objects, then there is likely to be a decrease in the overlap between the objects supported by managed node implementations and manager implementations, and interoperability suffers.

Second, experience with the Internet-standard Network Management Framework has shown that it is better to define a core MIB

---

[1] However, as a consequence of the Fundamental Axiom, a management station must be prepared to interact with managed nodes that implement only a subset of the desired managed objects.

module first, containing only essential objects; later, if experience demands, other objects can be added.

The rationale for this is also straightforward: it helps implementors to focus on core issues. By stressing the basics first, a relatively large number of implementations can be produced from different sources. As management of real networks takes place, practical experience, and not the mercurial whims of a committee, is the best judge as to what additional objects are needed.

Finally, *traps* (roughly equivalent to "events" in the OSI framework) are used sparingly. Discussion of this is postponed until the next section, when an overall philosophy for using traps is presented for the Internet-standard Network Management Framework.

C.3   Protocols and Mechanisms

Having now taken the top-level view of the Internet-standard Network Management Framework, it is time to see how the Fundamental Axiom affects the design of the underlying technology.

C.3.1   Transport Mappings

SNMP assumes only a basic CL-mode transport service, whilst the OSI Common Management Information Protocol (CMIP) uses a connection-oriented model as a part of an application-layer entity.

The OSI approach is general, in that network management uses the same framework as all the other OSI applications. However, network management is unlike "normal" applications and requires special mechanisms. For example, with either the CO-mode transport or network services, sophisticated algorithms are used to ensure reliability of the transmission. Unfortunately, these mechanisms, which are designed to hide problems in the network, are intended for applications like file transfer and electronic mail. When the network is collapsing, this behavior is most likely inappropriate when trying to manage the network! CL-mode access means that there are no handshaking packets required before management can occur, and that each management application controls the level of retransmission. This allows for different retransmission schemes based on the requirement of each management application.

Further, implementation of a full OSI stack in addition to management instrumentation is simply *problematic* on smaller networks nodes. The likelihood, or even desirability, of a full OSI implementation on a MAC-level bridge is quite small: the additional resource cost (processor, memory, and programming) poses a large burden in a market segment which is highly competitive. Users want network management capabilities, but they certainly aren't going to be happy if it substantively increases price or decreases performance.

One response might be to suggest either an abbreviated stack (e.g., layering CMIP directly on top of the LLC), or use of a proxy. However, neither approach is satisfying: the former approach lacks generality in that network management cannot occur beyond each LAN segment;

and, the latter approach may lose information if the proxy protocol is sufficiently different from the OSI framework.

In contrast, observe that by combining a simple protocol with minimal requirements on the underlying stack (a CL-mode transport service), a complete management stack can be easily implemented in virtually any network node. For example, experience has shown that the burden of adding a CL-mode network and transport protocol along with SNMP to a MAC-level bridge is quite small.

Finally, from a theoretical perspective, considering that the basic unit of commerce in a network is the datagram, it should be easy to grasp that the management protocol must have a direct mapping onto an underlying datagram service.

C.3.2   Operations

SNMP performs operations on scalar variables; in contrast, CMIP performs operations on collections of objects. In terms of functionality it should be noted that both SNMP and CMIP use request-reply interactions, and that the object-oriented operations of CMIP can be modeled using the few operations of SNMP (e.g., the CMIP `action`, `create`, and `delete` operations can be performed by the SNMP `set` operation).

However, by imposing a "scalar view" on the managed nodes, instrumentation for, and implementation of, SNMP is much simpler. As such, management stations can layer whatever "high-powered" approach they want for management, but managed nodes need only implement the simplest paradigm, that of remote-debugging.

In practice, use of a CL-mode transport service does not impose undue complexity upon well-designed management stations: even use of a CO-mode service is not a complete guarantee of reliability. The well-known (but often little understood) *end-to-end argument* [33] shows that ultimate responsibility for reliability resides with each application. As such, mapping operations onto a CO-mode service achieves little benefit in a robust management station.

Finally, although CMIP offers linked replies (for so-called *incremental reading* of large results), this still places a significant implementational burden on the managed node. The SNMP approach, in which management stations can dynamically adapt to the abilities of the managed node (through a well-defined error response), is less invasive.

C.3.3   Data Representation

Only a subset of both ASN.1 and the BER are used by SNMP, in contrast to the full generality allowed by CMIP.

In particular, a scalar object ultimately resolves to either an INTEGER, OCTET STRING, or OBJECT IDENTIFIER. Further, the rows of a conceptual table contain only scalars. Experience has shown that this limitation is not a serious restriction as the basic data structures of computing are numbers, byte strings, and structures. Hence, one can easily emulate the semantics of the remaining ASN.1 data types. For example, a BOOLEAN can be represented by an INTEGER taking the value zero (for false) and non-zero (for true). Similarly, a BIT STRING can be represented by an OCTET STRING in which some of the bits in the last octet might be marked as "reserved" if the string of bits is not a multiple of eight in length.

By omitting support for arbitrarily complex data types, substantive savings can be achieved — in terms of program development, code size, and execution time.

Finally, SNMP mandates the use of the definite-length form encoding with the BER, and, whenever possible, primitive encodings are used rather than constructed encodings (e.g., for OCTET STRINGs). Again, the restrictions here are intended to simplify the option space to allow for faster systems with greater interoperability.

C.3.4   Identifying Management Information

SNMP employs a novel mechanism for identifying management information. At the coarsest level, managed objects are of two kinds: *columnar* objects, which exist in conceptual tabular structures; and, non-columnar objects. Each conceptual table contains zero or more rows, and each row may contain one or more scalar objects — termed columnar objects. It must be emphasized that, at the protocol level, relationships among columnar objects in the same row are a matter of convention, not of protocol: instances of columnar objects which appear as operands in SNMP are treated separately.

An ASN.1 `OBJECT IDENTIFIER` identifies each object instance. An instance of a non-columnar object is identified by appending a zero-valued sub-identifier to the object name. For example, the one and only instance of the `sysDescr` object (as defined in the Internet-standard MIB) which resides in a managed node is identified by:

    sysDescr.0

or, more concretely:

    1.3.6.1.2.1.1.1.0

For each columnar object, there is an associated definition which describes how the instance-identifier is formed. This collection of one or more sub-identifiers is appended to the name of the columnar object. For example, in the Internet-standard MIB, instances of the columns of the interfaces table are identified by using the value of the `ifIndex` column. So, the instance of `ifDescr` associated with the first interface is identified by:

    ifDescr.1

or, more concretely:

    1.3.6.1.2.1.2.2.1.2.1

There is an important observation on naming in SNMP: by naming instances using `OBJECT IDENTIFIER`s, a *lexicographic ordering* is enforced between all object instances: for instance names a and b, one of three conditions uniformly holds: either $a < b$, $a = b$, or $a > b$. This is the *only* retrieval methodology which a managed node must support and is in stark contrast to the CMIP approach, which introduces complex scoping and filtering mechanisms to identify object instances.

As a first comparison, recall that since SNMP treats operands separately, it is straightforward for a single management operation to reference two objects in different parts of the information tree. With CMIP, additional management traffic is often required, as a single scope may contain too many irrelevant objects.

However, in order to appreciate the true power of the SNMP approach to naming, we must examine how traversal is performed. SNMP provides a powerful `get-next` operator, which takes one or more operands, and, for each, returns the name and value of the object instance immediately following. Since each operand is simply an `OBJECT IDENTIFIER`, and needn't correspond to an existing instance, management stations may exploit the naming scheme to the fullest.

There are several traversal strategies which can be realized using this single retrieval methodology:

- To see if a particular non-columnar object exists, a management station uses the `get-next` operator on the object name (not the instance name), e.g.,

  ```
  get-next (sysDescr)
  ```

  If the instance for the desired object is returned, the management station has the desired information; otherwise, if some other instance is returned, then the management station has determined that the object is not supported by the managed node. This is particularly useful when retrieving a collection of non-columnar objects in a single operation.

- Since the result returned by the `get-next` operator is an instance name and corresponding value, a management station can use the result of one invocation as the operand to subsequent invocation of the `get-next` operator.

  In the simplest case, to examine all objects supported by the managed node, a managed station could simply start with

  ```
  get-next (0.0)
  ```

  and traverse the entire space of object instances until the last instance is returned. The `get-next` operator, when provided with an operand that is lexicographically greater than all instances in the managed node, will return a well-defined error response.

A more useful example of traversal is to consider how columnar objects are examined:

- At first cut, a tabular sweep can be started by invoking the `get-next` operator with the names of the columnar objects of interest, e.g.,

    ```
    get-next (ipRouteDest, ipRouteIfIndex,ipRouteNextHop)
    ```

    which will return the instances of these objects that correspond to the "first" row in the corresponding conceptual table. To find the next row in the table, these instance names can be used as operands for the next invocation, e.g.,

    ```
    get-next (ipRouteDest.0.0.0.0,
             ipRouteIfIndex.0.0.0.0,
             ipRouteNextHop.0.0.0.0)
    ```

    The sweep might continue until an instance of a different object type is returned, e.g.,

    ```
    get-next (ipRouteDest.192.33.4.0) ->
                                ipRouteIfIndex.0.0.0.0
    ```

    An important side effect of this strategy is that the instance-identifiers are, by and large, opaque handles — the management station needn't interpret them as they are simply strings passed back and forth through SNMP. (Historically, such a strategy has proven particularly successful for "stateless" applications which utilize a CL-mode transport service.)

- Of course, given an appropriate definition of instance-identification, a sophisticated manager might sweep only a portion of a table, e.g.,

    ```
    get-next (ipRouteDest.192,
             ipRouteIfIndex.192,
             ipRouteNextHop.192)
    ```

    can be used to start a sweep in the IP routing table looking for those destinations with IP addresses that start with 192. When a result is returned which does not have this prefix, the sweep terminates.

Again, it must be emphasized that managed nodes need implement only a single retrieval methodology based on lexicographic ordering. The management station can layer whatever strategy it wishes on top of this. In contrast, a node being managed with CMIP must be prepared to accept arbitrary scoping and filtering directives. As such, it is not possible to bound the complexity involved in processing a single CMIP operation, whilst each SNMP operation is of fixed (and almost certainly smaller) complexity.

Of course, there are occasional arguments about "efficiency" when conceptual tables are retrieved in bulk using SNMP. Unfortunately, these arguments are often put forward without much exploration of possible implementation strategies. For example, the author and his colleagues have developed a parallel algorithm for bulk retrieval using SNMP[60]. The algorithm works in two phases:

- In the first phase, all instances of a single columnar object are retrieved.

  This is achieved by issuing several invocations of the `get-next` operator, each with several operands. The naming space is divided up by generating sub-identifier suffixes. For example, the first request might appear as:

  ```
  get-next (ipRouteNextHop,
            ipRouteNextHop.63,
            ipRouteNextHop.127,
            ipRouteNextHop.159,
            ipRouteNextHop.192)
  ```

  The algorithm keeps track of the invocations that are outstanding, along with the **OBJECT IDENTIFIER** bounds that are active in each. For each result returned in an invocation: if the result is outside its assigned bounds, that result is removed; otherwise, the name and value of that instance is stored, and possibly the bounds is split into two (depending on the observed performance of the managed node and the network).

  When all of the bounds have been removed, all instances of the single columnar object have been retrieved and the second phase begins.

- In the second phase, instances of any other desired columnar objects (in the same conceptual table) are retrieved.

  This is achieved by use of the SNMP `get` operation. The instance-identifiers are taken from the results determined in the first phase.

The algorithm uses an adaptive retransmission strategy in order to maximize throughput whilst avoiding overunning the agent. It should be noted that the transmission strategy is one in which ordering of invocations is, by and large, unimportant. Thus, intermittent network lossage results in retransmission only of lost traffic; traffic corresponding to other parts of the table is neither retransmitted nor delayed.

Initial implementation of the algorithm in a prototype environment shows a speed-up of roughly an order of magnitude over the serial retrieval approach.

C.3.5 Traps

SNMP uses *trap-directed polling* to report extraordinary events, and as noted earlier, a CL-mode transport service is used for transfer. The management station is then responsible for initiating further interactions with the managed node in order to determine the nature and extent of the problem. Of course, since traps are sent unreliably, low-frequency polling is performed by the management station. Many feel that this choice has proven to be an effective compromise between trap-based and polling-based approaches.

Trap-based approaches suffer from requiring substantive resources on the part of managed nodes, management stations, and the network:

- It requires resources to generate the trap. If the trap must contain a lot of information, the managed node may be spending too much time on the trap and not enough time on its primary task (e.g., routing packets for the user).

- If the trap requires some sort of acknowledgement from the manager, this places further requirements on the resources of the managed node. With CMIP, in which a CO-mode transport service is used, either a connection is maintained between the management station and the managed node (which has serious implications as to how many managed nodes a station can manage), or a connection must be established immediately prior to sending the trap.

- Of course, use of a CO-mode transport service is no guarantee as to the reliability of traps — network failures can *always* prevent traps from getting through.

- Further, if several extraordinary events occur, a lot of network bandwidth is tied up containing traps, which is hardly desirable if the report is about network congestion. A managed node might use *thresholds*: traps are generated only when the occurrence of an event exceeds some threshold.

  Unfortunately, this means that the managed node must usually spend substantial time determining if an event should generate a trap, and these cycles are usually spent during the *critical path* (e.g., during the forwarding loop for a router). In contrast, the management station could make this decision in deciding whether a trap should generate an alert for the operator. That is, the same functionality is present in the management system, except that the management station, and not the managed node, has the burden of implementation.

In any event, the managed node has only a very limited view of the network, so it is arguable as to whether it can provide "the big picture" on the problem by using traps. For all these reasons, traps are used sparingly in the Internet-standard Network Management Framework.

With trap-directed polling, the impact on managed nodes remains small; the impact on network bandwidth is minimized; problems can be dealt with in a timely fashion; and, the management station is in control as it determines what "the big picture" really is.

C.4   Conclusions

Given these criticisms of the OSI approach to network management, is it any wonder that some network management wags often use the catch-phase:

> *If the answer is OSI network management, then the question must have been mis-stated!*

As the discussion has shown, from both a theoretical and practical perspective, it would appear that the OSI approach may be tragically detached from reality.

Why is this so? Perhaps the fundamental reason can be seen from the seemingly harmless introductory statement:

> ... just as today's enterprises need networking technology which is vendor-independent and fully-interoperable across product and vendor lines, so do today's enterprises need network management capabilities which exhibit the same properties.

The problem is that, although open network management is needed, the model, architecture and design of such technology needn't be identical to that of the other applications in the protocol suite. Network management is unlike other applications:

- network management is often time-critical;

- network management must continue to work during catastrophic network failure, even when all other applications fail; and,

- network management should be deployed on each and every network node, if it is to be truly useful.

These characteristics all argue for a paradigm different than that of the other applications which provide file service, message handling, directory service, and the like.

C.4.1   The Problems of the Real World

It must be emphasized that

> *The problems of the real world are remarkably resilient towards administrative fiat.*

Thus, citing "successful" implementation agreements for OSI management, well-intentioned government mandates for OSI, and other bits of "excellent progress", are largely unimpressive: users probably want a robust market with competing mature products that solve their problems. Users may be willing to put up with the standardization process, but *only* if it is a means towards the end of a robust market. Standards, per se, are probably of no interest to users without robust products which implement those standards.

Over the last four years, there has been some experience with the OSI framework in the Internet, involving considerable support from both vendors and the US Federal government. However, products have been sadly lacking. In contrast, the Internet-standard Network Management Framework has been solving problems quite handily and has developed an enthusiastic following amongst network managers throughout the International community using the Internet suite. With the introduction of SNMP over OSI-based transports[71], some are beginning to suspect that the OSI networks of tomorrow will be managed with SNMP and not CMIP.

This has lead to the so-called "soft-pillow" defense for the OSI approach: namely that SNMP will manage network nodes, and perhaps CMIP will be used for communication between management stations. However, the market may be unwilling to accept a dual protocol approach: it may be more attractive to use SNMP for all management tasks — simply to avoid the loss-of-leverage inherent with the dual approach.

C.4.2   A Plea for Sanity

Perhaps it is time to re-think the OSI approach to network management and take a more pragmatic, workable solution? Much can be learned from successful systems, and good things often come from copying these successes. Perhaps the International standards community can profit by adopting the Fundamental Axiom and using the Internet-standard Network Management Framework as the basis for OSI network management.

Acknowledgements

In presenting this paper, the author is acting as an interpretive historian: the Fundamental Axiom of the Internet-standard Network Management Framework, and the philosophy which embodies it, is the work of many others, most notably Case, Davin, Fedor, and Schoffstall, who present an elegant argument for the Fundamental Axiom in [43]. The author's presentation has been to focus on these issues and present a concise, albeit painful, criticism of the OSI approach to network management.

Keith McCloghrie of Hughes LAN Systems provided substantive comments, and his contributions are greatly appreciated. Ole J. Jacobsen of Interop Company provided a thorough proof-reading of a manuscript, and his help is greatly appreciated. Finally, the author apologizes for shamelessly using a colloquialism in the first sentence of Section C.2.

Appendix: A Cautionary Tale

The story which follows is unattributed, as reported by Manny Farber to the author. Any individual who can prove authorship of the story is entitled to a particularly *fine dinner* at the expense of the author!

> Once upon a time, in a kingdom not far from here, a king summoned two of his advisors for a test. He showed them both a shiny metal box with two slots in the top, a control knob, and a lever. "What do you think this is?"
>
> One advisor, an engineer, answered first. "It is a toaster." he said. The king asked, "How would you design an embedded computer for it?" The engineer replied, "Using a four-bit microcontroller, I would write a simple program that reads the darkness knob and quantizes its position to one of 16 shades of darkness, from snow white to coal black. The program would use that darkness level as the index to a 16-element table of initial timer values. Then it would turn on the heating elements and start the timer with the initial value selected from the table. At the end of the time delay, it would turn off the heat and pop up the toast. Come back next week, and I'll show you a working prototype."
>
> The second advisor, a computer scientist, immediately recognized the danger of such short-sighted thinking. He said, "Toasters don't just turn bread into toast, they are also used to warm frozen waffles. What you see before you is really a breakfast food cooker. As the subjects of your kingdom become more sophisticated, they will demand more capabilities. They will need a breakfast food cooker that can also cook sausage, fry bacon, and make scrambled eggs. A toaster that only makes toast will soon be obsolete. If we don't look to the future, we'll have to completely redesign the toaster in just a few years.
>
> "With this in mind, we can formulate a more intelligent solution to the problem. First, create a class of breakfast foods. Specialize this class into subclasses: grains, pork, and poultry. The specialization process should be repeated with grains divided into toast, muffins, pancakes, and waffles; pork divided into sausage, links, and bacon; and poultry divided into scrambled

eggs, hard-boiled eggs, poached eggs, fried eggs, and various omelet classes.

"The ham and cheese omelet class is worth special attention because it must inherit characteristics from the pork, dairy, and poultry classes. Thus, we see that the problem cannot be properly solved without multiple inheritance. At run time, the program must create the proper object and send a message to the object that says, 'Cook yourself.' The semantics of this message depend, of course, on the kind of object, so they have a different meaning to a piece of toast than to scrambled eggs.

"Reviewing the process so far, we see that the analysis phase has revealed that the primary requirement is to cook any kind of breakfast food. In the design phase, we have discovered some derived requirements. Specifically, we need an object-oriented language with multiple inheritance. Of course, users don't want the eggs to get cold while the bacon is frying, so concurrent processing is required, too.

"We must not forget the user interface. The lever that lowers the food lacks versatility, and the darkness knob is confusing. Users won't buy the product unless it has a user-friendly, graphical interface. When the breakfast cooker is plugged in, users should see a cowboy boot on the screen. Users click on it, and the message 'Booting UNIX® v. 8.3' appears on the screen. (UNIX® 8.3 should be out by the time the product gets to the market.) Users can pull down a menu and click on the foods they want to cook.

"Having made the wise decision of specifying the software first in the design phase, all that remains is to pick an adequate hardware platform for the implementation phase. An Intel 80386 with 8MB of memory, a 30MB hard disk, and a VGA monitor should be sufficient. If you select a multitasking, object-oriented language that supports multiple inheritance and has a built-in GUI, writing the program will be a snap. (Imagine the difficulty we would have had if we had foolishly allowed a hardware-first design strategy to lock us into a four-bit microcontroller!)."

The king had the computer scientist thrown in the moat, and they all lived happily ever after.

Although it is believed that this story was originally written to parody "modern" software engineering practices, this cautionary tale can also be seen as being quite germane to the OSI approach to network management.

Glossary

abstract syntax: a description of a data type that's independent of machine-oriented structures and restrictions.

Abstract Syntax Notation One: the OSI language for describing abstract syntax.

access mode: (SNMPv1) the level of authorization implied by an SNMP community.

access policy: (SNMPv2) the operations allowed when one party asks another party to perform an operation on the objects in a context.

ACK: the *acknowledgement* bit in a TCP segment.

active open: the sequence of events occurring when an application-entity directs TCP to establish a connection.

address class: a method used to determine the boundary between the network and host portions of an IP address.

address-mask: a 32–bit quantity indicating which bits in an IP address refer to the network portion.

address resolution: a means for mapping network-layer addresses onto media-specific addresses.

Address Resolution Protocol: the protocol in the Internet suite of protocols used to map IP addresses onto Ethernet (and other media) addresses.

administrative model: a scheme for defining authentication and authorization policies.

Advanced Research Projects Agency: see *Defense Advanced Research Projects Agency.*

agent: see *network management agent.*

American National Standards Institute: the US national standardization body. ANSI is a member of ISO.

ANSI: see *American National Standards Institute.*

API: see *Application Programmer's Interface.*

application services: the services collectively offered by the upper four layers of the OSI model.

Applications Programmer's Interface: a set of calling conventions defining how a service is invoked through a software package.

ARP: see *Address Resolution Protocol.*

ARPA: see *Defense Advanced Research Projects Agency.*

ASN.1: see *Abstract Syntax Notation One.*

authentication: the process whereby a message is associated with a particular originating entity.

authentication entity: (SNMPv1) that portion of an SNMP agent responsible for verifying that an SNMP entity is a member of the community to which it claims to belong. This portion of the agent is also responsible for encoding/decoding SNMP messages according to the authentication algorithm of a given community.

authorization: the process whereby an access policy determines whether an entity is allowed to perform an operation.

awesome get-bulk operator: what more need be said?

Basic Encoding Rules: the OSI language for describing transfer syntax.

BER: see *Basic Encoding Rules.*

broadcast address: a media-specific or IP address referring to all stations on a medium.

broadcasting: the act of sending to the broadcast address.

C: the *C programming language.*

Case Diagram: a pictorial representation of the relationship between counter objects in a MIB group.

CCITT: see *International Telegraph and Telephone Consultative Committee.*

checksum: an arithmetic sum used to verify data integrity.

CL-mode: see *connection-less mode.*

CLNS: *connectionless-mode network service*

CLTS: *connectionless-mode transport service*

CMIP: see *Common Management Information Protocol.* Sometimes confused with the *(overly) Complex Management Information Protocol.* Of course, it doesn't exist.

CMIP over TCP: a mapping of the OSI network management framework to management of networks based on the Internet suite of protocols. Commonly thought of as "an idea whose time has come and gone."

CMIS: see *Common Management Information Service.*

CMISE: see *Common Management Information Service Element.*

CMOT: see *CMIP over TCP.*

CO-mode: see *connection-oriented mode.*

Common Management Information Protocol: the OSI protocol for network management.

Common Management Information Service: the service offered by CMIP.

Common Management Information Service Element: the application service element responsible for exchanging network management information.

community: (SNMPv1) an administrative relationship between SNMP entities.

community name: see *community string.*

community profile: (SNMPv1) that portion of the managed objects on an agent that a member of the community is allowed to manipulate.

community string: (SNMPv1) an opaque string of octets identifying a community.

connection: a logical binding between two or more users of a service.

connection-less mode: a service that has a single phase involving control mechanisms such as addressing in addition to data transfer.

connection-oriented mode: a service that has three distinct phases: *establishment*, in which two or more users are bound to a connection; *data transfer*, in which data is exchanged between the users; and, *release*, in which the binding is terminated.

CONS: *connection-oriented network service*

context: (SNMPv2) a collection of object resources.

COTS: *connection-oriented transport service*

DARPA: see *Defense Advanced Research Projects Agency.*

DARPA Internet: see *Internet.*

data: (imprecise usage) see *user-data.*

data link layer: that portion of an OSI system responsible for transmission, framing, and error control over a single communications link.

datagram: a self-contained unit of data transmitted independently of other datagrams.

default route: when sending an IP datagram, an entry in the routing table which will be used if no other route is appropriate.

Defense Advanced Research Projects Agency: an agency of the US Department of Defense that sponsors high-risk, high-payoff research. The Internet suite of protocols was developed under DARPA auspices. DARPA was previously known as ARPA, the Advanced Research Projects Agency, when the ARPANET was built.

device: a network element of some kind.

direct routing: the process of sending an IP datagram when the destination resides on the same IP network (or IP subnet) as the sender.

DNS: see *Domain Name System.*

DNS-connected: the subset of the Internet community which can exchange electronic mail.

domain: an administrative entity responsible for naming entities.

domain name: an administratively assigned name identifying a domain.

Domain Name System: the application protocol offering naming service in the Internet suite of protocols.

dotted decimal notation: see *dotted quad notation.*

dotted quad notation: a convention for writing IP addresses in textual format, e.g., "`192.103.140.1`".

ECMA: see *European Computer Manufacturers Association.*

EGP: see *Exterior Gateway Protocol.*

end-system: a network device performing functions from all layers of the OSI model. End-systems are commonly thought of as hosting applications.

end-to-end services: the services collectively offered by the lower three layers of the OSI model.

enterprise MIB: a MIB module defined in the enterprise-specific portion of the Internet management space.

ES: see *end-system.*

European Computer Manufacturers Association: a group of computer vendors that has performed substantive pre-standardization work for OSI.

Exterior Gateway Protocol: a (deprecated) reachability protocol used by routers in a two-level internet.

experimental MIB: a MIB module defined in the experimental portion of the Internet management space.

External Data Representation: a transfer syntax defined by Sun Microsystems, Inc.

Federal Research Internet: see *Internet.*

File Transfer Protocol: the application protocol offering file service in the Internet suite of protocols.

FIN: the *finish* bit in a TCP segment.

flow control: the mechanism whereby a receiver informs a sender how much data it is willing to accept.

fragment: an IP datagram containing only a portion of the user-data from a larger IP datagram.

fragmentation: the process of breaking an IP datagram into smaller parts, such that each fragment can be transmitted in whole on a given physical medium.

FTP: see *File Transfer Protocol.*

fully-qualified domain name: a domain name containing the complete path of labels to the root of the naming tree.

gateway: (Internet usage) a router; also, (imprecise usage) an entity responsible for complex mappings, usually at the application-layer.

hardware address: see *media address.*

header: (imprecise usage) see *protocol control information.*

host: (Internet usage) an end-system.

host-identifier: that portion of an IP address identifying a host on the IP network.

host-number: that portion of a subnetted IP address identifying a host-number on the subnet.

IAB: see *Internet Architecture Board.*

IANA: see *Internet Assigned Numbers Authority.*

ICMP: see *Internet Control Message Protocol.*

IEEE: see *Institute of Electrical and Electronics Engineers.*

IESG: see *Internet Engineering Steering Group.*

IETF: see *Internet Engineering Task Force.*

IFIP: see *International Federation for Information Processing.*

indirect routing: the process of sending an IP datagram to a router for (ultimate) forwarding to the destination.

instance: see *object instance.*

instance-identifier: a means of identifying an instance of a particular object type.

Institute of Electrical and Electronics Engineers: a professional organization which, as a part of its services to the community, performs some pre-standardization work for OSI.

interface layer: the layer in the Internet suite of protocols responsible for transmission on a single physical network.

intermediate-system: a network device performing functions from the lower three layers of the OSI model. Intermediate-systems are commonly thought of as routing data for end-systems.

International Federation for Information Processing: a research organization that performs substantive pre-standardization work for OSI. IFIP is noted for having formalized the original MHS (X.400) model.

International Organization for Standardization: the organization that produces many of the world's standards. OSI is only one of many areas standardized by ISO/IEC.

International Standards Organization: there is no such thing. See *International Organization for Standardization.*

International Telephone and Telegraph Consultative Committee: a body comprising the national Postal, Telephone, and Telegraph (PTT) administrations.

internet: (Internet usage) a network in the OSI sense; historically termed a *catenet* — a concatenated set of networks. The Internet is the largest internet in existence.

Internet: a large collection of connected networks, primarily in the United States, running the Internet suite of protocols. Sometimes referred to as the *DARPA Internet, NSF/DARPA Internet*, or the *Federal Research Internet.*

Internet Architecture Board: the technical body overseeing the development of the Internet suite of protocols.

Internet Assigned Numbers Authority: the entity responsible for assigning numbers in the Internet suite of protocols.

Internet Community: anyone, anywhere, who uses the Internet suite of protocols.

Internet Control Message Protocol: a simple reporting protocol for IP.

Internet Drafts: a means of documenting the work in progress of the IETF.

Internet Engineering Steering Group: the group coordinating the activities of the IETF, and which is responsible for standards-setting in the Internet.

Internet Engineering Task Force: a task force of the Internet Architecture Board charged with resolving the short-term needs of the Internet.

internet layer: the layer in the Internet suite of protocols responsible for providing transparency over both the topology of the internet and the transmission media used in each physical network.

Internet Protocol: the network protocol offering a connectionless-mode network service in the Internet suite of protocols.

Internet suite of protocols: a collection of computer-communication protocols originally developed under DARPA sponsorship. The Internet suite of protocols is currently the solution of choice for open networking.

Internet-standard MIB: (SNMPv1) RFC 1213.

Internet-standard Network Management Framework: (SNMPv1) RFCs 1155, 1212, 1213, and 1157.

Internet-standard SMI: (SNMPv1) RFC 1155, 1212.

IP: see *Internet Protocol.*

IP address: a 32–bit quantity used to represent a point of attachment in an internet.

IP-connected: the subset of the Internet community which can exchange IP-based traffic.

IS: either *intermediate-system* or *International Standard,* depending on context. In the latter case, such a document is named as "ISO/IEC number", if it represents work under Joint Technical Committee 1; otherwise, it is named as "ISO number".

ISO Development Environment: a research tool developed to study the upper-layers of OSI. It is an unfortunate historical coincidence that the first three letters of ISODE are "ISO." This isn't an acronym for the International Organization for Standardization, but rather three letters which, when pronounced in English, produce a pleasing sound.

ISO/IEC: see *International Organization for Standardization.*

ISODE: see *ISO Development Environment.*

kernel dive: the process of reading data structures out of the UNIX® kernel to determine the state of its protocol entities.

LAN: see *local area network.*

leaf object: an object type defined for which there are no objects with a subordinate name assigned. In particular, tables and rows are not leaf objects.

lexicographic ordering: a collation scheme.

local area network: any one of a number of technologies providing high-speed, low-latency transfer and being limited in geographic size.

loosely-coupled clock: a notion of time whose value is imprecisely coordinated by two or more entities.

managed device: see *managed node.*

managed node: a device containing a network management agent implementation.

managed object: a unit of management information.

management framework: (SNMPv1) see *Internet-standard Network Management Framework.*

Management Information Base: a collection of objects that can be accessed via a network management protocol.   See *Structure of Management Information.*

management protocol: see *network management protocol.*

management station: see *network management station.*

manager: (imprecise usage) an application residing on a network management station.

maximum transmission unit: the largest amount of user-data (e.g., the largest size of an IP datagram) that can be sent in a single frame on a particular medium.

media address: the address of a physical interface.

media device: a low-level device that doesn't use a protocol at the internet layer as its primary function.

MIB: see *Management Information Base.*

MIB module: a collection of related managed object definitions.

MIB view: a collection of managed objects realized by an agent which is visible to a management application.

MIB-I: the predecessor to MIB-II.

MIB-II: see *Internet-standard MIB.*

MTU: see *maximum transmission unit.*

multi-homed: a host or router with an attachment to more than one IP network.

name: an identity associated with an entity of some kind. In the context of an IP network, a name is a textual identifier.

name server: an entity which maps a name to its associated attributes.

naming authority: an administrative entity having the authority to assign names within a given domain.

National Bureau of Standards: see *National Institute of Standards and Technology*.

National Institute of Standards and Technology: the branch of the U.S. Department of Commerce charged with keeping track of standardization. Previously known as the *National Bureau of Standards*.

NBS: see *National Bureau of Standards*.

network: a collection of subnetworks connected by intermediate-systems and populated by end-systems; also, (Internet usage) a single subnetwork or a related set of subnetworks in the OSI sense.

network byte order: the Internet-standard ordering of the bytes corresponding to numeric values.

network layer: that portion of an OSI system responsible for data transfer across the network, independent of both the media comprising the underlying subnetworks and the topology of those subnetworks.

network management: the technology used to manage an internet.

network management agent: the implementation of a network management protocol which exchanges network management information with a network management station.

network management protocol: the protocol used to convey management information.

network management station: an end-system responsible for managing (a portion of) the network.

network-identifier: that portion of an IP address corresponding to a network in an internet.

NIST: see *National Institute of Standards and Technology*.

NMS: see *network management station*.

NSF: *National Science Foundation*

NSF/DARPA Internet: see *Internet*.

object: see *object type.*

object instance: a particular instance of an object type.

object type: an abstract definition of a managed object.

OSI: see *Open Systems Interconnection.*

Open Systems Interconnection: an international effort to facilitate communications among computers of different manufacture and technology.

partially-qualified domain name: an abbreviation of a domain name omitting ancestors common to both communicating parties.

party: (SNMPv2) a communicating entity.

passive open: the sequence of events occurring when an application-entity informs TCP that it is willing to accept connections.

PDU: see *protocol data unit.*

PE: see *presentation element.*

physical layer: that portion of an OSI system responsible for the electro-mechanical interface to the communications media.

ping: a program used to test IP-level connectivity from one IP address to another.

port number: identifies an application-entity to a transport service in the Internet suite of protocols.

powerful get-next operator: what more need be said?

presentation element: in ISODE, a *C* data structure capable of representing any ASN.1 object in a machine-independent form.

presentation layer: that portion of an OSI system responsible for adding structure to the units of data that are exchanged.

presentation stream: in ISODE, a set of routines providing an abstraction to provide transformations on presentation elements.

protocol control information: (conceptually) the initial part of a protocol data unit used by a protocol machine to communicate information to a peer.

protocol data unit: a data object exchanged by protocol machines, usually containing both protocol control information and user-data.

protocol machine: a finite state machine (FSM) that implements a particular protocol. When a particular input (e.g., user request or network activity) occurs in a particular state, the FSM potentially generates a particular output (e.g., user indication or network activity) and possibly moves to another state.

prototype: (management usage) the object type corresponding to an instance.

proxy agent: an agent which has access to management information which isn't held locally, and must perform a non-local interaction in order to satisfy management requests which reference that information.

proxy relationship: an administrative configuration in which a proxy agent is used to access remotely-held management information.

pseudo-header: a 96–bit quantity used by a transport protocol in the Internet suite to guard against misbehaving implementations of IP.

PTT: a *postal, telephone, and telegraph* authority.

reassembly: the process of recombining fragments, at the final destination, into the original IP datagram.

Request for Comments: the document series describing the Internet suite of protocols and related experiments.

retransmission: the process of repeatedly sending a unit of data while waiting for an acknowledgement.

RFC: see *Request for Comments.*

RFC Editor: the entity responsible for publishing RFCs in the Internet suite of protocols.

RFC-822: The format for electronic mail messages in the Internet community.

router: a level-3 (network layer) relay.

segment: the unit of exchange in TCP.

selector: a portion of an address identifying a particular entity at an address (e.g., a session selector identifies a user of the session service residing at a particular session address).

service primitive: an artifact modeling how a service is requested or accepted by a user.

session layer: that portion of an OSI system responsible for adding control mechanisms to the data exchange.

SGMP: see *Simple Gateway Monitoring Protocol.*

Simple Gateway Monitoring Protocol: the predecessor of the Simple Network Management Protocol.

Simple Mail Transfer Protocol: the application protocol offering message handling service in the Internet suite of protocols.

Simple Management Protocol and Framework: a technical proposal which was used as the basis for SNMPv2.

Simple Network Management Protocol: the application protocol offering network management service in the Internet suite of Protocols.

SMAE: see *System Management Application-Entity.*

SMI: see *Structure of Management Information.*

SMP: see *Simple Management Protocol and Framework.*

SMTP: see *Simple Mail Transfer Protocol.*

SNMP: see *Simple Network Management Protocol.*

SNMP Security: early work which was used as the basis for security enhancements in SNMPv2.

SNPA: *subnetwork point of attachment*

socket: a pairing of an IP address and a port number.

Structure of Management Information: the rules used to define the objects that can be accessed via a network management protocol. See *Management Information Base.*

subnet: (most unfortunate Internet usage) a physical network within an IP network.

subnet-mask: a 32–bit quantity indicating which bits in an IP address identify the physical network.

subnet-number: that portion of an IP host-identifier which identifies a particular physical network within an IP network.

subnetting: the process of using IP subnetting procedures.

subnetwork: a single network connecting several devices on a single (virtual) transmission medium.

subtree family: (SNMPv2) a collection of `OBJECT IDENTIFIER`s which are defined by an `OBJECT IDENTIFIER` value and a bit-mask.

SYN: the synchronize bit in a TCP segment.

system management: the OSI name for network management.

TCP: see *Transmission Control Protocol.*

TCP/IP: see *Internet suite of protocols.*

TELNET: the application protocol offering virtual terminal service in the Internet suite of protocols.

three-way handshake: a process whereby two protocol entities synchronize during connection establishment.

TLV: *tag, length, and value*

traceroute: a program used to determine the route from one IP address to another.

transfer syntax: a description of an instance of a data type that's expressed as a string of bits.

Transmission Control Protocol: the transport protocol offering a connection-oriented transport service in the Internet suite of protocols.

transport layer: that portion of an OSI system responsible for reliability and multiplexing of data transfer across the network (over and above that provided by the network layer) to the level required by the application.

transport-stack: the combination of protocols, at the transport layer and below, used in a given context.

UDP: see *User Datagram Protocol.*

upper-layer protocol number: identifies a transport entity to the IP.

URG: the urgent bit in a TCP segment.

urgent data: user-data delivered in sequence but somehow more interesting to the receiving application-entity.

User Datagram Protocol: the transport protocol offering a connection-less-mode transport service in the Internet suite of protocols.

user-data: conceptually, the part of a protocol data unit used to transparently communicate information between the users of the protocol.

variable: (SNMP usage) a particular instance of a particular object.

variable binding: (SNMP usage) a pairing of an object instance name and associated value.

view: see *MIB view.*

WAN: see *wide area network.*

well-known port: a transport endpoint which is documented by the IANA.

wide area network: any one of a number of technologies providing geographically distant transfer.

wires: (colloquial usage) physical medium.

X.121: the addressing format used by X.25–based networks.

X.25: a connection-oriented network facility (some say that's the problem).

X.409: the predecessor to Abstract Syntax Notation One.

XDR: see *External Data Representation.*

yacc: *yet another compiler compiler*, a UNIX®-based compiler generation tool.

Bibliography

[1] John S. Quarterman. *The Matrix: Computer Networks and Conferencing Systems Worldwide*. Digital Press, 1989. ISBN 1–55558–033–5.

[2] Paul V. Mockapetris. Domain Names — Concepts and Facilities. Request for Comments 1033, USC/Information Sciences Institute, November 1987.

[3] Paul V. Mockapetris. Domain Names — Implementation and Specification. Request for Comments 1034, USC/Information Sciences Institute, November 1987.

[4] Bill Croft and John Gilmore. Bootstrap Protocol (BOOTP). Request for Comments 951, Stanford University, September 1985.

[5] Joyce K. Reynolds. BOOTP vendor information extensions. Request for Comments 1084, USC/Information Sciences Institute, December 1988.

[6] Marshall T. Rose. *The Internet Message: Closing the Book with Electronic Mail*. Prentice Hall Series in Innovative Computing. Prentice-Hall, Englewood Cliffs, New Jersey, 1992. ISBN 0–13–092941–7.

[7] Allan Leinwand and Karen Fang. *Network Management: A Practical Perspective*. Addison-Wesley, 1992. ISBN 0–201–52771–5.

[8] Tony Rutkowski. De Facto versus De Jure: The Arrogance of Standards Organizations. *ConneXions—The Interoperability Report*, 6(10):42–43, October 1992. ISSN 0894-5926.

[9] Vinton G. Cerf and Edward A. Cain. The DoD Internet Architecture Model. *Computer Networks and ISDN Systems*, 7(10):307–318, October 1983.

[10] Jon B. Postel. Transmission Control Protocol. Request for Comments 793, USC/Information Sciences Institute, September 1981. See also MIL-STD 1778.

[11] Jon B. Postel. Internet Protocol. Request for Comments 791, USC/Information Sciences Institute, September 1981. See also MIL-STD 1777.

[12] Jon B. Postel. Simple Mail Transfer Protocol. Request for Comments 821, USC/Information Sciences Institute, August 1982. See also MIL-STD 1781.

[13] Craig Partridge. Mail Routing and the Domain System. Request for Comments 974, Bolt, Beranek, and Newman, Inc., January 1986.

[14] David H. Crocker. Standard for the Format of ARPA Internet Text Messages. Request for Comments 822, University of Delaware, August 1982.

[15] Jon B. Postel. File Transfer Protocol. Request for Comments 959, USC/Information Sciences Institute, October 1985. See also MIL-STD 1780.

[16] Jon B. Postel. TELNET Protocol Specification. Request for Comments 854, USC/Information Sciences Institute, May 1983. See also MIL-STD 1782.

[17] Jeffrey D. Case, Mark S. Fedor, Martin L. Schoffstall, and James R. Davin. A Simple Network Management Protocol. Request for Comments 1157, SNMP Research, May 1990.

[18] Jeffrey D. Case, Keith McCloghrie, Marshall T. Rose, and Steven L. Waldbusser. Introduction to version 2 of the Internet-standard Network Management Framework. Request for Comments 1441, SNMP Research, Inc., April 1993.

[19] Sun Microsystems, Inc., Mountain View, California. *Network File System Protocol Specification*, February 1986. Part Number 800-1324-03.

[20] Robert W. Scheifler and Jim Gettys. The X Window System. *ACM Transactions on Graphics*, 5(2):79–109, April 1986. Special Issue on User Interface Software.

[21] Jon B. Postel. Introduction to the STD Notes. Request for Comments 1311, USC/Information Sciences Institute, March 1992.

[22] Lyman Chapin. The Internet Standards Process. Request for Comments 1310, BBN Communications Corporation, March 1992.

[23] Jon B. Postel (editor). IAB Official Protocol Standards. Request for Comments 1410, USC/Information Sciences Institute, March 1993.

[24] Joyce K. Reynolds and Jon B. Postel. Assigned Numbers. Request for Comments 1060, USC/Information Sciences Institute, March 1990.

[25] Robert T. Braden. Perspective on the Host Requirements RFCs. Request for Comments 1127, USC/Information Sciences Institute, October 1989.

[26] Robert T. Braden. Requirements for Internet Hosts — Application and Support. Request for Comments 1123, USC/Information Sciences Institute, October 1989.

[27] Robert T. Braden. Requirements for Internet Hosts — Communication Layers. Request for Comments 1122, USC/Information Sciences Institute, October 1989.

[28] Robert T. Braden and Jon B. Postel. Requirements for Internet Gateways. Request for Comments 1009, USC/Information Sciences Institute, June 1987.

[29] Andrew S. Tanenbaum. *Computer Networks (2$\underline{\underline{nd}}$ edition)*. Prentice Hall Software Series. Prentice-Hall, Englewood Cliffs, New Jersey, 1988. ISBN 0–13–162959–X.

[30] The Ethernet — A Local Area Network. Digital Equipment Corporation, Intel Corporation, Xerox Corporation, September 1980.

[31] Samuel J. Leffler and Mike J. Karels. Trailer Encapsulations. Request for Comments 893, University of California, Berkeley, April 1984.

[32] David C. Plummer. Ethernet Address Resolution Protocol. Request for Comments 826, Massachusetts Institute of Technology, November 1982.

[33] J.H. Saltzer, D.P. Reed, and D.D. Clark. End-to-End Arguments in System Design. *Transactions on Computer Systems*, 2(4):277–288, November 1984.

[34] David L. Mills. Exterior Gateway Protocol Formal Specification. Request for Comments 904, University of Delaware, April 1984.

[35] Kirk Lougheed and Yakov Rekhter. Border Gateway Protocol. Request for Comments 1105, Cisco Systems, June 1989.

[36] Jeff Mogul and Jon B. Postel. Internet Standard Subnetting Procedure. Request for Comments 950, Stanford University, August 1985.

[37] Jon B. Postel. Internet Control Message Protocol. Request for Comments 792, USC/Information Sciences Institute, September 1981. See also MIL-STD 1777.

[38] Steve Deering. ICMP Router Discovery Messages. Request for Comments 1256, Xerox PARC, September 1991.

[39] Jon B. Postel. User Datagram Protocol. Request for Comments 768, USC/Information Sciences Institute, August 1980.

[40] Van Jacobson. Congestion Avoidance and Control. In *Proceedings, SIGCOMM '88 Workshop*, pages 314–329. ACM Press, August 1988. Stanford, California.

[41] Phil Karn and Craig Partridge. Improving Round-Trip Time Estimates in Reliable Transport Protocols. In *Proceedings, SIGCOMM '87 Workshop*, pages 2–7. ACM SIGCOMM, ACM Press, August 1987. Stowe, Vermont.

[42] David C. M. Wood, Sean S. Coleman, and Michael F. Schwartz. Fremont: A System for Discovering Network Characteristics and Problems. In *Proceedings of the 1993 Winter USENIX Conference*, January 1993.

[43] Jeffrey D. Case, James R. Davin, Mark S. Fedor, and Martin L. Schoffstall. Network Management and the Design of SNMP. *ConneXions— The Interoperability Report*, 3(3):22–26, March 1989. ISSN 0894–5926.

[44] Information Processing — Open Systems Interconnection — Specification of Abstract Syntax Notation One (ASN.1). International Organization for Standardization and International Electrotechnical Committee, 1987. International Standard 8824.

[45] Information Processing — Open Systems Interconnection — Abstract Syntax Notation One (ASN.1) — Addendum 1: Extensions to ASN.1. International Organization for Standardization and International Electrotechnical Committee, 1987. International Standard 8824/AD 1.

[46] Douglas Steedman. *Abstract Syntax Notation One (ASN.1): The Tutorial and Reference*. Technology Appraisals Ltd., 1990. ISBN 1-871802-06-7.

[47] American Standard Code for Information Interchange. American National Standards Institute, 1977. ANSI standard X3.4.

[48] Information Processing Systems — Data Communications — Network Service Definition — Addendum 2: Network Layer Addressing. International Organization for Standardization and International Electrotechnical Committee, June 1988. International Standard 8348/AD 2.

[49] Jeffrey D. Case and Craig Partridge. Case Diagrams: A First Step to Diagrammed Management Information Bases. *Computer Communication Review*, 19(1):13–16, January 1989.

[50] Keith McCloghrie and Marshall T. Rose. Management Information Base for Network Management of TCP/IP-based internets. Request for Comments 1213, Hughes LAN Systems, Inc., March 1991.

[51] Keith McCloghrie and Marshall T. Rose. Management Information Base for Network Management of TCP/IP-based internets. Request for Comments 1156, Hughes LAN Systems, May 1990.

[52] Fred Baker. The IP Forwarding Table MIB. Request for Comments 1345, Advanced Computer Communications, July 1992.

[53] Steven L. Waldbusser. Remote Network Monitoring MIB. Request for Comments 1271, Carnegie-Mellon University, November 1991.

[54] Marshall T. Rose and Keith McCloghrie. Structure and Identification of Management Information for TCP/IP-based internets. Request for Comments 1155, Performance Systems International, Inc., May 1990.

[55] Marshall T. Rose and Keith McCloghrie. Concise MIB Definitions. Request for Comments 1212, Performance Systems International, Inc., March 1991.

[56] Ronald L. Rivest. The MD5 Message-Digest Algorithm. Request for Comments 1321, Massachusetts Institute of Technology, April 1992.

[57] US Federal Information Processing Standards Publication #46–1: Data Encryption Standard, December 1988.

[58] US Federal Information Processing Standards Publication #81: DES Modes of Operation, December 1980.

[59] Frank Kastenholz. SNMP Communications Services. Request for Comments 1270, Clearpoint Research Corporation, October 1991.

[60] Marshall T. Rose, Keith McCloghrie, and James R. Davin. Bulk Table Retrieval with the SNMP. Request for Comments 1187, Performance Systems International, Inc., October 1990.

[61] G. Sidhu, R. Andrews, and A. Oppenheimer. *Inside AppleTalk (2$\underline{\text{nd}}$ edition)*, 1990.

[62] Novell, Inc. *Network System Technical Interface Overview*, June 1989.

[63] Information Processing — Open Systems Interconnection — Specification of Basic Encoding Rules for Abstract Syntax Notation One (AS-N.1). International Organization for Standardization and International Electrotechnical Committee, 1987. International Standard 8825.

[64] Marshall T. Rose. *The Open Book: A Practical Perspective on Open Systems Interconnection.* Prentice Hall Series in Innovative Computing. Prentice-Hall, Englewood Cliffs, New Jersey, 1989. ISBN 0–13–643016–3.

[65] Christian Huitema and Ghislain Chave. Measuring the Performance of an ASN.1 Compiler. In *Proceedings, IFIP TC6/WG6.5 International Conference on Upper Layer Protocols, Architectures and Applications*, pages 105–118. IFIP WG 6.5, North-Holland Publishing Company, May 1992. ISBN 0–444–89766–6.

[66] Samual P. Leffler, Marshall Kirk McKusick, Michael J. Karels, and John S. Quarterman. *The Design and Implementation of the 4.3BSD UNIX Operating System.* Addison-Wesley Publishing Co., Reading, Massachussetts, 1989. ISBN 0–201–06196–1.

[67] John K. Ousterhout. Tcl: An Embeddable Command Language. In *Proceedings, Winter USENIX Conference*, pages 133–146, January 1990. Washington, DC.

[68] John K. Ousterhout. An X11 Toolkit Based on the TCL Language. In *Proceedings, Winter USENIX Conference*, pages 105–115, January 1991. Dallas, TX.

[69] Marshall T. Rose. Network Management is Simple: You just need the "Right" Framework. In *Integrated Network Management, II*, pages 9–25. IFIP WG 6.6, North-Holland, April 1991. ISBN 0–444–89028–9.

[70] Marshall T. Rose (editor). Management Information Base for Network Management of TCP/IP-based internets: MIB-II. Request for Comments 1158, Performance Systems International, Inc., May 1990.

[71] Marshall T. Rose (editor). SNMP over OSI. Request for Comments 1283, Dover Beach Consulting, Inc., December 1991.

Index